The Greatest Ever
chess strategies

Sam Collins

EVERYMAN CHESS

Gloucester Publishers plc   www.everymanchess.com

First published in 2012 by Gloucester Publishers Limited, Northburgh House, 10 Northburgh Street, London EC1V 0AT

British Library Cataloguing-in-Publication Data
A catalogue record for this book is available from the British Library.

ISBN: 978 1 85744 676 0

Distributed in North America by The Globe Pequot Press, P.O Box 480, 246 Goose Lane, Guilford, CT 06437-0480.

All other sales enquiries should be directed to Everyman Chess, Northburgh House, 10 Northburgh Street, London EC1V 0AT
tel: 020 7253 7887 fax: 020 7490 3708
email: info@everymanchess.com; website: www.everymanchess.com

Everyman is the registered trade mark of Random House Inc. and is used in this work under licence from Random House Inc.

Everyman Chess Series
Chief advisor: Byron Jacobs
Commissioning editor: John Emms
Assistant editor: Richard Palliser

Typeset and edited by First Rank Publishing, Brighton.
Cover design by Horatio Monteverde.
Printed and bound in Great Britain by Clays, Bungay, Suffolk.

About the Author

Sam Collins is an International Master with two GM norms, and a former Irish and Japanese Champion. He has represented Ireland at seven Olympiads, winning an individual gold medal at Bled 2002. He has written numerous bestselling books on chess and is a regular columnist for www.chesspublishing.com and *Chess Today*.

Also by the Author
The French Advance
Gambit Busters

Contents

Bibliography

Chess Books

101 Tips to Improve your Chess, Kosten (Batsford, 2003)

200 Open Games, Bronstein (Dover, 1991)

Beating Unusual Defences: 1 e4, Greet (Everyman Chess, 2011)

Capablanca's Best Games, Golombek (Batsford, 1997)

Chess for Zebras, Rowson (Gambit, 2005)

Gambit Busters, Collins (Everyman Chess, 2011)

Garry Kasparov on Modern Chess: Parts 1-3, Kasparov (Everyman Chess, 2007-09)

Grandmaster Repertoire: The Caro-Kann, Schandorff (Quality Chess, 2010)

Great Chess Victories and Defeats, Byrne (Times Books, 1991)

How to Beat the French Defence, Tzermiadianos (Everyman Chess, 2008)

My 60 Memorable Games, Fischer (Batsford, 2009)

My Best Games, Karpov (Edition Olms, 2007)

My Great Predecessors: Volumes 1-5, Kasparov (Everyman Chess, 2003-06)

San Luis 2005, Gershon and Nor (Quality Chess, 2007)

Secrets of Practical Chess (New Enlarged Edition), Nunn (Gambit, 2007)

Starting Out: The Slav and Semi-Slav, Flear (Everyman Chess, 2005)

The Berlin Wall, Cox (Quality Chess, 2008)

The Queen's Gambit Accepted: Third Edition, Sakaev and Semkov (Chess Stars, 2008)

The Seven Deadly Chess Sins, Rowson (Gambit, 2000)

Training for the Tournament Player, Dvoretsky and Yusupov (Batsford, 2003)

Understanding the Grünfeld, Rowson (Gambit, 1999)

Victor Bologan: Selected Games 1985-2004, Bologan (Russell Enterprises, 2007)

Zurich International Chess Tournament, 1953, Bronstein (Dover, 1979)

Other Books

Thinking Fast and Slow, Kahneman (Farrar, Straus and Giroux, 2011)

DVDs

How to Play the Queen's Gambit, Kasparov (ChessBase)

Learn from the Open Games, Collins (ChessBase 2012)

The Queen's Gambit Accepted, Collins (ChessBase 2012)

Scandinavian with 3...♕d6, Tiviakov (ChessBase 2011)

Vladimir Kramnik: My Path to the Top, Kramnik (ChessBase 2004)

Periodicals

British Chess Magazine

ChessBase Magazine

Chess Today

Japan Chess Association Magazine

New in Chess

Websites

Chessbase.com

Chesspublishing.com

Databases

Mega Database 2012

Preface

"The situation has provided a cue; this cue has given the expert access to information stored in memory, and the information provides the answer. Intuition is nothing more and nothing less than recognition."
Herbert Simon

"In the end I don't believe intuition is something you're born with. Aptitude is something you're born with, you may have a certain skill for something, but intuition is something you develop by looking at something over and over again. It's almost, I feel, like a way of...you can't quantify this information very well, but it's there, and something in your head is able to deal with it. So intuition you develop by simply working hard, by looking at chess daily, by looking at different kinds of positions, and every time you see the pieces interact, you get a better sense of how these things interplay. However, here the important thing is the breadth of knowledge that you have. You need to be very good even in areas that you might never use, or at least have some interest in areas that you might never use, because you never know when a mechanism that works in one area will suddenly be applicable in another. So the more broad your knowledge is in chess, the more structures and mechanisms you're familiar with, then the easier it is to deal with unexpected situations."
Vishy Anand

One of the most interesting chess training ideas is that of "positional sketches", advocated by Mark Dvoretsky. He recommends that when you come across a particularly interesting idea, you should make a note of the position and why you found the idea so appealing. This can be recorded on paper or (inevitably) in a database, which will gradually build to form a personal library of standard concepts.

While Dvoretsky's idea has a lot of intuitive appeal to me, it goes without saying that I don't have the discipline to consistently apply it. However, I often find myself thinking about a move and realizing that I am in a vaguely similar situation to one I had seen before. This kind of knowledge (pattern recognition/reasoning by analogy) is of enormous help since it helps us find the right path much more quickly than we would by brute calculation alone.

This book is my attempt to make sense of some of the chess concepts which are floating around in my head. I've presented the material much as it is categorized in my mind, so rather than formally similar situations being grouped together, I've sometimes picked a few examples on "Disruptive tactical moves with the b-pawn" or something similar. These ideas are not of equal importance or equal frequency, but they all have repeatedly cropped up in my own games or games I have seen and, basically, I think familiarity with any of them will make someone a slightly better player. I have tried to avoid covering material which is very well covered elsewhere (for instance, IQP positions, or a lot of the stuff in John Watson's wonderful two-volume series on strategy), and where these have cropped up (like the sections on Outposts or Open Files) I hope to have demonstrated something fresh or counterintuitive.

The final collection is, ultimately, slightly quirky and features rather too many of my own games (not even my best ones) but, to use the classic excuse, these are the games I understand the best and from which I hope to extract some instructive material.

I'd like to thank the Everyman team of John Emms, Byron Jacobs and Richard Palliser for their individual and collective assistance and patience, especially as contractual deadlines became distant memories. It's somewhat discouraging to write a section on a particular idea and then lose to the exact same idea a number of months later, especially when the latter game is played in time to make the final edit, but then again losing by doing something you know you're not supposed to is an unavoidable part of competitive chess.

Sam Collins
Dublin,
August 2012

Introduction

Playing by Analogy

To kick things off I thought I would give an example of the associative machinery in action. What follows is a collection of ideas (mainly from endgame theory) which helped me enormously in playing a game in the World Junior Championship. I was in abysmal form in this event so playing on autopilot was the only way forward.

IDEA 1
With a rook's pawn, you need four files

A very familiar position. The winning method is shown in Collins-Sprenger and I won't reproduce it here. However, you should know that if the black king is cut off from the pawn by four files, the position is winning for White.

I should make a confession here – in my game against Simon Williams from the e2e4 tournament in Dublin in 2012, I horribly misassessed a transposition into this position, and lost. I was, at that point, playing only on the 30-second increment. However, 30 seconds should have been loads of time to deal with the position and in any event, as Alekhine pointed out, time trouble is no excuse for anything.

IDEA 2
Rook, f- and h-pawn vs. rook is drawn

Game 1
S.Gligoric-V.Smyslov
Chigorin Memorial,
Moscow 1947

This is another standard theoretical endgame. I recall a conversation with a leading English GM a few years ago where he indicated that the defence is actually not so straightforward here.

The method is demonstrated by Smyslov in this game (too well analysed elsewhere to be reproduced here: *Dvoretsky's Endgame Manual*, amongst others, has an instructive coverage).

I have only had to defend this material balance once in practice, against Mark Hebden in Hastings 2007/08. That was a particularly favourable version for the defender, and I drew after 101 moves – almost a miniature compared to our next encounter at Dun Laoghaire 2011, where we both blundered in a rook + bishop vs. rook endgame (I'll let you guess who had the bishop) and a draw was agreed in 109 moves.

IDEA 3
Rooks belong
behind passed pawns

Game 2
A.Alekhine-J.Capablanca
World Championship
(Game 34), Buenos Aires 1927

This endgame is, of course, a classic. The fact that such technique was displayed in the deciding game of a world championship against the invincible Capablanca (who was especially invincible in rook and pawn endgames!) adds a lot.

52 ♖d5

When this game is reproduced in endgame books, normally the authors start at move 54, where Alekhine puts his rook in the right place. It's funny that, for the classic game demonstrating where the rook should go, he starts by putting his rook on the wrong square.

52...♖f6

Allowing Alekhine to get back on track.

53 ♖d4 ♖a6 54 ♖a4 ♔f6 55 ♔f3 ♔e5 56 ♔e3 h5 57 ♔d3 ♔d5 58 ♔c3 ♔c5 59 ♖a2!

One of the cleanest demonstrations of an endgame idea I've seen. The benefit of having a rook behind a passed pawn is that the rook can move around whereas its counterpart can't do the same lest the pawn advance. While he's wasting a move, Alekhine covers the f2-weakness.

59...♔b5

59...♔d5 60 ♔b4 doesn't bear much consideration. Pawn moves, also, are worse than useless.

60 ♔b3 ♔c5 61 ♔c3 ♔b5 62 ♔d4 ♖d6+ 63 ♔e5 ♖e6+ 64 ♔f4 ♔a6

Capablanca has managed to execute the only available defensive concept, blockading the passed pawn with his king and transferring the rook to kingside defensive duties. However, it's not good enough.

65 ♔g5!

The breakthrough, after which the win should be a formality.

65...♖e5+ 66 ♔h6 ♖f5 67 f4?!

Perhaps Alekhine was influenced by the pressure of the occasion. Although it doesn't give Black serious drawing chances, White had cleaner options available, as set out in all the endgame manuals.

67...♖c5 68 ♖a3 ♖c7 69 ♔g7 ♖d7 70 f5 gxf5 71 ♔h6 f4 72 gxf4 ♖d5 73 ♔g7 ♖f5 74 ♖a4 ♔b5 75 ♖e4 ♔a6 76 ♔h6 ♖xa5 77 ♖e5 ♖a1 78 ♔xh5 ♖g1 79 ♖g5 ♖h1 80 ♖f5 ♔b6 81 ♖xf7 ♔c6 82 ♖e7 1-0

IDEA 4
The weaker side wants to exchange pawns; the stronger side does not

The idea that the weaker side should trade pawns is a trite one. Pawn exchanges in the endgame have the effect of reducing material, eliminating potential weaknesses, and laying the groundwork for various piece-for-pawn sacrifices in the late endgame.

A standard defensive method for Black in, for instance, a rook and pawn endgame where White has four pawns on the kingside and Black has three, is to set up a formation with pawns on f7, g6 and h5. Then, if White wants to create a passed pawn, he has to trade all the black pawns (g4 will be traded by the h5-pawn, f5 will be traded by the g6-pawn, e6 will be traded by the f7 pawn).

Game 3
A.Yusupov-A.Khalifman
Ubeda 1997

26 a4 ♗b7

Rowson suggests 26...h5!.

27 g4!

Rowson remarks: "I'm not at all surprised that Yusupov gives an unexplained exclamation mark here. This move is a very significant gain for White in such endgames but it's also the type of move which is obvious to some and unappreciated by others. I suspect the best way to look at it is to consider that

the winning strategy in such positions normally involves using the extra space to push Black's pieces onto sub-optimal squares and so the more imposing White's space advantage is, the more difficult Black will find it to place his pieces in such a way so as to prevent infiltration. Moreover, it is unlikely that White will be able to win the game by crudely winning a queenside pawn or queening a passed d-pawn. Indeed, White needs to find a way to overstretch the black defences and this will probably require that White creates a weakness in the black kingside. Believe it or not, one of the ideas of g4 is to make the black h- and f-pawns long-term vulnerabilities, as we see in the game. If Black could simply lift the h-pawns from the board, his defence would be eased considerably, which is why 26...h5 is good."

27...♔e8 28 ♗c4 ♘b8 29 ♔d3 a6 30 ♘c7+ ♔d8 31 ♘d5 ♘d7 32 ♘b4 a5 33 ♗d5 ♗xd5 34 ♘xd5 e6 35 ♘c3 ♔c7 36 ♘b5+ ♔c6 37 ♔c4 ♗f8 38 ♗f4 ♗b4 39 f3 ♗f8 40 d5+ exd5+ 41 exd5+ ♔b7 42 ♘d6+ ♗xd6 43 ♗xd6

As Ernst notes, the threat is 44 g5, gaining a decisive amount of space.

43...g5 44 ♗g3 ♘f6

Yusupov analyses 44...♔a6 45 d6 h6 (or 45...♔b7 46 ♔b5 ♘f6 47 ♗e5 ♘d7 48 ♗d4 winning) 46 ♗f2 ♘e5+ 47 ♔d5 and White breaks through.

45 ♗e5 ♘d7 46 ♗d4 ♔c7 47 ♔b5 f6

Yusupov gives 47...♔d6 48 ♗xb6 ♘xb6 49 ♔xb6 ♔xd5 50 ♔xa5 ♔c5! 51 ♔a6 ♔c6 52 a5 f6 53 ♔a7 ♔c7 54 a6 h6 55 h3! and the black king must release his white counterpart.

48 ♗f2 ♔d6 49 ♗xb6 ♘e5 50 ♗xa5 ♘xf3 51 ♗c3 1-0

IDEA 5
Stick with what you know

> ## Game 4
> ## B.Larsen-E.Torre
> Leningrad Interzonal 1973

78 ♖c7

Larsen naturally holds on to his two pawns. However, in so doing, he rejects a simple theoretical win. After 78 ♔g5 ♖xc5 79 ♔g6 Black could resign since the Lucena position will inevitably arise.

78...♔d8 79 ♖c6 ♔d7 80 ♖d6+ ♔e7 81 f6+??

The real slip, though if I were Larsen I'd blame the decision at move 78. Dvoretsky gives two winning alternatives: 81 ♖e6+ ♔f7 82 c6 ♖f1 83 ♔g5 ♖f2 84 ♖d6, and 81 ♖d5.

81...♔f7 82 c6 ♔g6 83 ♔f3 ♖e1 84 ♔f4 ♖e2 85 ♖d5 ♖c2!

Torre doesn't waste the reprieve he's been given.

Dvoretsky notes that 85...♔xf6 loses: 86 ♖c5 ♖e8 87 ♖f5+ ♔g6 (or 87...♔e7 88 ♖e5+ ♔f7 89 ♖xe8 ♔xe8 90 ♔e5) 88 ♖e5 ♖c8 89 ♖e6+ ♔f7 90 ♔e5 and the rook moves to d7 unimpeded.

86 ♖d6 ♖e2 87 f7+ ♔xf7 88 ♔f5 ♔e7 89 ♖d7+ ♔e8 90 ♔f6 ♖e1 91 ♖d5 ♖c1 92 ♖d6 ♖f1+ 93 ♔e6 ♖e1+ 94 ♔d5 ♖d1+ 95 ♔c5 ♖xd6 96 ♔xd6 ♔d8 ½-½

So, a collection of separate but related ideas, drawn from numerous sources. Let's see how this knowledge can facilitate quick decision making, even when a player is in bad form...

> ## Game 5
> ## S.Collins-W.Sprenger
> World Junior Championship
> Goa 2002
> *Scandinavian Defence*

1 e4 d5 2 exd5 ♕xd5 3 ♘c3 ♕d6

The Scandinavian is a deceptive opening. Around the time of this game I still wasn't paying much attention to it, assuming that I could get a better position playing 'on sight'. By the time of my game with Sprenger a key omen had already occurred, namely G.Kasparov-V.Anand, Game 14, World Championship 1995 (1-0 in 45) where Anand obtained an excellent position out of the opening before losing through a late blunder. Now many respectable GMs include the Scandinavian in their repertoires, either with the traditional 3...♛a5, the relatively passive 3...♛d8 (check the recent games of Gergeley Szabo and Nikola Djukic) or the modern 3...♛d6 as pioneered by Tiviakov, who has amassed a ridiculous score with it.

My own pet theory about this line is that the white knight is misplaced on c3 (it is blocking the c-pawn), which forces White to rely on piece activity without sufficient pawn play. Thus I suspect that 3 ♞f3, in addition to perhaps being less theoretical, is in fact the critical move. This view appears to be shared by English IM Andrew Greet, who devotes his opening chapter in the excellent *Beating Unusual Defences: 1 e4* to precisely this line.

4 d4 ♞f6 5 ♗c4

Trying to get the pieces out as quickly as possible.

5 ♞f3 is more standard and now 5...g6 seems to be the modern fashion, and was played against me by a Scandinavian specialist: 6 ♞b5 ♛b6 7 c4 c6 8 ♞c3 ♗g7 9 ♗e2 0-0 10 0-0 ♖d8 11 a3 ♗f5 12 h3 ♞e4 13 ♗e3 ♞xc3 14 bxc3 c5 15 ♗d3 ♗xd3 16 ♛xd3 ♞c6 17 ♖ab1 ♛a6 and Black had no problems in S.Collins-B.Chatalbashev, European Club Cup, Rogaska Slatina 2011 (½-½ in 62).

5 ♞f3 a6 was played in a light game from an Irish weekender: 6 ♗g5 ♞c6 (Andrew Martin suggests 6...b5) 7 d5 ♞e5 8 ♗e2 ♞xf3+ 9 ♗xf3 ♗f5 10 0-0 h6 11 ♗h4 0-0-0 12 ♛e2 ♛d7 13 ♗g3 g5 14 ♛e3 ♚b8 15 b4! (a straightforward minority attack which is absolutely devastating due to the better placed white pieces and the helpful 'hook' on a6) 15...♗g7 16 b5 g4 17 bxa6 gxf3 18 ♛b6 ♛c8 19 ♞b5 and Black resigned in S.Collins-K.McPhillips, Bunratty 2006.

5...a6

Tiviakov appears to prefer 5...c6 in this position, which is authoritative enough for me.

6 ♞ge2 b5 7 ♗f4 ♛b6 8 ♗b3

I remember being happy here. After all, my minor pieces have all developed and (with the possible exception of the knight on e2) to pretty threatening squares.

8...g6?

Too ambitious. Previous praxis (such as it was) in this variation focussed on more containing play with 8...♗b7 or 8...e6. Now I have a square on d5.

9 0-0 ♗g7 10 a4!

A very standard theme, too standard for inclusion in this book. Undermining a pawn on b5 with a4 is known from a range of openings, especially those like the Queen's Gambit Accepted.

10...♗b7

10...b4 11 ♘d5 ♘xd5 12 ♗xd5 c6 13 a5! gives Black no time to play the crucial consolidating move ...a5. Like in the game, the pawn on b4 is cut off from its colleagues, and the black pieces are in no position to support it.

10...bxa4 would be a horrible structural concession, compounded by the fact that after 11 ♘xa4 the black queen struggles to find a decent square.

11 axb5?!

11 ♕d3! would have been more precise. Taking on a4 is always bad for Black, and trying to retain material equality with 11...b4? fails to 12 a5! ♕a7 (only move) 13 ♕c4 with a fork on b4 and f7.

11...axb5 12 ♖xa8 ♗xa8 13 ♕d3 b4 14 ♕b5+

14 ♘a4 was still enough for an edge.

14...♘bd7?

Highly co-operative. 14...♘c6! was the move: 15 ♕xb6 cxb6 and Black has covered the c5-square while preparing play down the c-file to target the white pawn on c2 (see the comment to White's third move).

15 ♕xb6 ♘xb6 16 ♘b5

Now White wins a pawn, though a lot of work remains to be done.

16...♘fd5

16...♘bd5 17 ♘xc7+ ♘xc7 18 ♗xc7 0-0 was more accurate. Black remains a pawn down for basically nothing, though White still needs to demonstrate how he can safely advance on the queenside.

17 ♘xc7+ ♔d7

17...♘xc7 18 ♗xc7 hits the knight on b6, and after 18...♘d5 19 ♗e5 White gains time to seize the a-file.

18 ♘xd5?

A really awful move. Even without thinking, I should have played 18 ♘xa8 ♖xa8 19 ♗d2, guided by two standard concepts.

The first is the idea of "The Superfluous Piece" (the subject of an article by Mark Dvoretsky, reproduced in *Training for the Tournament Player*), which basically says that black has two knights but only one d5-square, so I should leave him with one poorly placed knight on b6.

The second is the bishop pair, pure and simple. Knights should take bishops when they have the chance. Here, my pawns will be grateful for the long-range support the bishops provide once they start rolling.

18...♗xd5 19 ♗xd5 ♘xd5 20 ♗d2 ♖a8

I've now mishandled this enough to allow Black to equalize.

21 ♖b1

21...e5?!

For years, my assessment of this move was that it was wrong because it allowed me to advance my c-pawn and get into the subsequent rook and pawn endgame. However, Black has very serious drawing chances there. In fact 21...e5 is bad, but for an entirely different reason which I missed both during the game and subsequent analysis.

Black could just hold the position with 21...♔c6 22 g3 ♔b5 and the king comes to c4 – once b3+ is played, the white queenside structure is held completely in check by the b4-pawn.

22 dxe5 ♗xe5

23 c4?

This move, which I thought was mandatory, was in fact a serious error, sharply reducing my winning chances.

23 ♘c1! is a move whose strength is obvious as soon as it's played. The knight is heading to d3, where it hits b4 and defends b2 while gaining time on the bishop on e5. White is just a pawn up, for instance 23...♗g7 24 ♘d3 ♖c8 25 ♖c1 and the white king will come to the centre, while the b4-pawn is weak.

23...bxc3 24 ♘xc3 ♘xc3 25 ♗xc3

25 bxc3 ♖a2 26 ♗e1 looks too passive to be a serious winning attempt.

25...♗xc3 26 bxc3 ♖a3

27 ♖c1

(IDEA 3) True, here I don't have much of a choice...

27...♔d6

27...h5!? would have been consistent with IDEA 4.

28 ♔f1

Otherwise my c-pawn was in trouble.

28...♖a2

28...h5 might still have been pre-ferred, though it allows me to activate my king with 29 ♔e2.

29 g4

IDEA 4!

29...h5?!

Black exchanges pawns, but now he is left with two weak pawns.

29...♔e5 would have been the consistent continuation of Black's idea from move 27. After 30 ♔g2 ♔f4 31 h3 f5 32 gxf5 ♔xf5 Black has serious drawing chances.

30 gxh5 gxh5 31 ♔g2

This is the best position I've had since move 23.

31...♖a5 32 h4 ♖f5 33 ♔g3 ♔c5

Now a simple tactical operation to break Black's defence on the kingside:
34 ♖e1! ♔c4?

Makes it easier. 34...♔d6 35 c4 ♖c5 was more tenacious.
35 ♖e4+ ♔xc3 36 ♖f4 ♖a5 37 ♖xf7 ♔d4 38 ♔f4 ♖a2

39 ♖d7+

39 ♔g5 ♖a8 40 ♔xh5 must be winning, despite the f- and h-pawns (IDEA 2), due to the poor placement of the black king. However, having seen that the game continuation led to a certain theoretical win, I could not justify playing into a position where I would still have to think (IDEA 5).
39...♔c5 40 ♔g5 ♖xf2 41 ♔xh5

Now we have a position with a rook's pawn and the black king cut off by four files (IDEA 1).
41...♖g2 42 ♔h6 ♔c6 43 ♖d4 ♔c5 44 ♖d3 ♖g1 45 h5 ♖h1 46 ♔g6 ♖g1+ 47 ♔h7 ♔c6 48 h6 ♔c7 49 ♔h8 ♔c8 50 h7 ♔c7 51 ♖a3

51 ♖f3 works as well. The rook is going to g8 to free the white king.
51...♔d7 52 ♖a8 ♔e6!

The most tenacious. 52...♔e7 is an easier win. (In my game with Simon Williams from Dublin 2012, I was so despondent around here that I chose this continuation and resigned a couple of moves later. Of course, this indicates an awful lack of fighting spirit and is something I'll have to work on.) 53 ♖g8 ♖h1 54 ♔g7 ♖g1+ 55 ♔h6 ♖h1+ 56 ♔g6 ♖g1+ 57 ♔f5 and the pawn queens.
53 ♖g8 ♖h1 54 ♔g7 ♖g1+ 55 ♔f8 ♖f1+ 56 ♔e8 ♖b1

Again best. White can't queen in view of mate. 56...♖a1 is hopeless as will be seen on White's 58th move.
57 ♖g6+ ♔f5

58 ♖f6+!

This is the key tactical idea underpinning the whole endgame. 58 ♖h6 ♖b8+ draws easily.
58...♔g4

Black should have taken the rook and tested my technique with queen against rook.
59 ♖f8 1-0

Chapter One
Pawns

Symmetry

A lot has been written on the topic of symmetry. I have assembled my thoughts into the comments to the following game, where I also talk about the inherent difficulty of playing for a draw with White. Ironically, I needed a draw with White to make a GM norm against Sune in the same tournament, and failed to achieve it – this game is featured in the section on outposts. I had another chance for a norm, needing a draw with White against Zhang Zhong in the last round, and again lost. Hard lessons, and it remains to be seen whether I've learned anything from them...

Game 6
S.B.Hansen-F.Caruana
Khanty Mansiysk
Olympiad 2010
Slav Defence

From an objective point of view, it must be said that the following game contains relatively little of interest. Sune, who was playing well in the Olympiad (as I found out to my cost) plays well beneath his normal level and loses uncharacteristically. However, I think this game contains some useful clues as to what is going on in symmetrical positions, and is as instructive as the much better known M.Gurevich-N.Short, Manila Interzonal 1990 (0-1 in 42).

1 d4 ♘f6 2 ♘f3 d5 3 c4 c6 4 cxd5 cxd5

The Exchange Slav is considerably more interesting than comparable exchange variations (for instance, 1 e4 e6 2 d4 d5 3 exd5 exd5, as in Gurevich-Short, leaves White without any clear way to make progress, at least as far as I know). It has been regularly essayed by a number of strong players who have used it to play for a win, and with success. The examples which are always cited are Lajos Portisch and Artur Yusupov, though looking through the database I find that their scores with the line were pretty underwhelming (notwithstanding the former's fine win over Petrosian) and they regularly used different lines against the Slav. However, certain modern practitioners are worth mentioning, for instance Croatian GM Igor Miladinovic (sometimes known as "Mr. Tromp" due to his fondness for Julian Hodgson's old patent), who has scored heavily with White after 1 d4 d5 2 c4 c6 3 cxd5, and GMs Marin and Milov.

However, the flipside of the coin is also instructive. Black has rarely had any problem winning against the Exchange Slav. While this may be a function of White playing the Exchange Slav ambitiously, playing for an advantage and overpressing, even where White is peacefully inclined taking on d5 does not guarantee a draw. For instance, in my database, Alexey Dreev has had the position after 1 d4 d5 2 c4 c6 3 ♘f3 ♘f6 4 cxd5 cxd5 5 ♘c3 ♘c6 6 ♗f4 28 times with Black, scoring a re-

markable 68% (+10, =18, –0). And before you dismiss these stats on the basis that these games must be by weaker players playing for a draw, while 10 players were rated below 2500, 8 players were rated over 2600. In short, these are unbelievable stats, comparable to Fischer or Kasparov in the Poisoned Pawn Najdorf (respectively +5, =4, –1 and +3, =6, –0).

5 ♘c3 ♘c6 6 ♗f4 a6

One of the main moves for Black. In part this is due to the popularity of the Chebanenko Slav (1 d4 d5 2 c4 c6 3 ♘f3 ♘f6 4 ♘c3 a6 being one normal move order), where these positions arise if White takes on d5 (taking on d5 is obviously not an option in the normal Slav since Black takes on c4 first; in the Semi-Slav, taking on d5 tends to be innocuous since, after ...exd5, Black reaches a favourable version of the QGD Exchange Variation with White's knight prematurely committed to f3).

The symmetrical 6...♗f5 can still lead to exciting positions, and has a lot of sharp tactical content.

6...e6 is Dreev's favourite and anyone playing this line with either colour is directed to his games for details.

6...♞e4 was played in another seminal "Black successfully playing for a win in a decisive round of an Interzonal against a boring variation" (as in Gurevich-Short), namely L.Portisch-V.Kramnik, Biel Interzonal 1993 (0-1 in 42).

7 ♖c1 ♞h5 8 ♗d2 ♞f6 9 ♗f4 ♞h5 10 ♗d2 e6

A move with a certain psychological impact. Caruana was only 105 points higher rated than Hansen at the time of this game. It is debatable exactly what the worth of the white pieces is in rating terms – I know one GM who is of the view that having the white pieces is worth 150 points. I think GM Ivan Sokolov is also meant to have said that if he is playing Black against a 2450 who wants a draw, he won't be able to win (this would suggest closer to a 200-point disparity). White is meant to score approximately 55% generally which, when compared to FIDE rating

tables, signifies a much smaller difference of 36 points.

But the real impact seems to be something more basic. GM Gawain Jones once wrote that a GM should play for a win with White against any player in the world. While we know countless examples where this hasn't happened, the view has at least intuitive appeal. Caruana's 10th move is the chess equivalent of a slap on the wrist, deciding to play on when the draw was there for the asking.

11 e3 ♞f6 12 ♗d3 ♗d6 13 e4

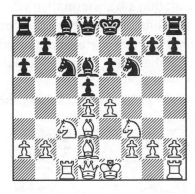

Hansen is an active player and, as such, is basically unsuited to waiting around passively, especially with White. His decision to push e4 is certainly justifiable, but now Black can point to having a little something to hope for, namely a superior structure in the endgame.

13...dxe4 14 ♞xe4 ♗e7 15 ♞xf6+ ♗xf6 16 ♗c3 0-0 17 0-0 ♞e7 18 ♞e5 ♞d5 19 ♗e4 a5 20 ♕f3 b6 21 ♗d2

21 ♗xd5 ♕xd5 22 ♕xd5 exd5 is absolutely equal.

21...♗b7 22 ♖fe1 g6 23 a3 ♗g7 24 ♕b3 ♖b8 25 ♕f3 ♕e7

26 ♘c6

Initiating a transformation which is not in White's favour. The knight on e5 was a dominant piece, and had White kept it there his chances would not have been worse.

26...♗xc6 27 ♖xc6 ♕d7 28 ♗xd5 exd5

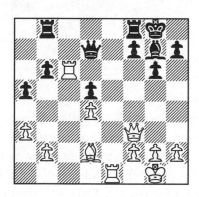

Now Black has the small but clear advantage of the better bishop. White's position is likely tenable but is still unpleasant, especially in view of the psychological shadow boxing which preceded it.

29 ♖c2?!

29 ♖c3 would have prevented 29...♗xd4 (at least as a winning try) in view of 30 ♖d3 ♗xb2 31 ♖b1 when White is active enough to win back his material. However, 29...♖fe8 would have kept a pleasant position.

29...♗xd4 30 ♗h6

There are various alternatives for both sides over the next few moves, but White seems to fall short of establishing full compensation for the pawn.

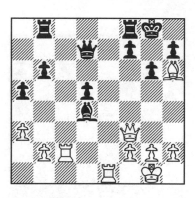

30...♖fe8 31 ♖d1 ♗h8 32 g3 d4 33 ♖c6 ♖e6 34 ♖c4

This retreat certainly doesn't help matters, allowing Black to organize his position with tempo.

34...♖be8 35 ♔g2 ♖f6

35...♗e5!, cutting out ♗f4, was even stronger.

36 ♗f4 ♖f5

36...g5! was stronger, though I understand Caruana's desire to avoid the complications of 37 ♖dxd4.

37 ♕c6 ♕xc6+ 38 ♖xc6 g5 39 ♗c7 ♖e2 40 ♖f1 ♖c5

40...d3 is better.

41 ♖xc5 bxc5 42 ♖c1

White is not in time for 42 ♗xa5 in view of 42...d3.

42...a4 43 ♖xc5 ♗f6

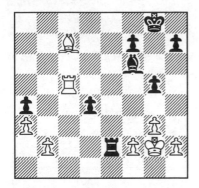

Caruana's technique has not been the best (I can't imagine there was any significant time pressure around here, given the placid course of the game) and Sune has almost equalized.

44 ♖d5 h6

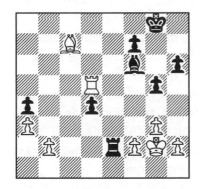

45 g4?

Going into the rook endgame a pawn down proves to be a bad call for White.

45 ♖d6 ♗g7 (or 45...♔g7 46 ♗b6) 46 ♗b6 holds the balance.

45...♖xb2 46 ♗e5

Keeping this bishop on might have retained better drawing chances, though this would have been hard to play since it admits that White's 45th was misguided.

46...♗xe5 47 ♖xe5 d3

Black has a clear advantage. The d-pawn is too dangerous.

48 ♖e4 d2 49 ♖d4 ♔g7 50 ♖d6 ♔f8 51 ♔f3 ♔e7 52 ♖d4 ♖a2 53 ♔e3 ♖xa3+ 54 ♔xd2 ♖f3 0-1

Black wins further material on the kingside, since 55 ♔e2 ♖f4! wins.

Open Files

The basics of open files were comprehensively explained by Nimzowitsch in *My System*. Rooks like open files because they provide avenues to the 7th and 8th ranks, on which serious damage can occur.

My coverage of open files here will be limited to a couple of discrete concepts (after a light game with an opening trap, of course).

The first involves partial movement on an open file (or a rank or diagonal for that matter), which can be easy to overlook and, correspondingly, highly effective.

The second will look at the idea of physically blocking an open file with a piece – I've included both the original Karpovian masterpiece and the modern counterexample, which illustrates that all concepts must be thoroughly checked for appropriateness before being deployed in new contexts.

The appeal of putting a major piece on an open file is easy to understand, since it will control squares deep in the heart of the opponent's position. In the case of the e-file, this will include e8 (e1), which is where the king sits before he castles.

Demonstrations of use of the open e-file come in various hues of sophistication. In Shiyomi-Collins (Game 65), we will see an example where the open e-file was a huge problem to White after a queen exchange. Even in the endgame, with an exposed king on e1, the time gained by bringing a rook into play, with check or with a threat against the king, can be of decisive importance, especially when a player is struggling with a development disadvantage.

The following example is definitely on the lighter end, consisting of an opening trap I used to get a free day at an otherwise disastrous tournament for me. The following notes are based on my contribution to *British Chess Magazine*.

Game 7
S.Collins-T.Spanton
Hastings Masters 2009/10
Ruy Lopez

1 e4 e5 2 ♘f3 ♘c6 3 ♗b5 ♘f6 4 0-0 ♘xe4

5 ♖e1

Definitely not the most theoretically crucial continuation, but one which is not entirely without venom. Luke McShane used the same move to beat Peter Heine Nielsen in 20 moves in Hastings 2002/03. Luke has recently preferred the black side of this line, scoring a rather creditable 2½/3 (the draw was against Anand, in case you were wondering).

5 d4 will be dealt with in the section on Time (Chapter 4).

5...♘d6 6 ♘xe5

6 ♗a4!? is another direction.

6...♘xe5

6...♗e7 is more popular, immediately blocking the dangerous e-file. Exchanges on c6 favour Black.

7 ♖xe5+ ♗e7 8 ♘c3

Black should now castle.

8...♘xb5?! 9 ♘d5

My shell-shocked opponent now went straight down the main line of the trap.

9...0-0??

9...♔f8 10 ♘xe7 d6 is only slightly better for White.

10 ♘xe7+ ♔h8 11 ♕h5

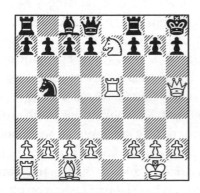

Threatening ♕xh7+.

11...g6

The nicest line I calculated was 11...h6 12 d3 d6 13 ♗xh6 g6 14 ♗xf8+ gxh5 15 ♖xh5 mate.

12 ♕h6 ♖e8 13 ♖h5 1-0

Game 8
W.Unzicker-R.Fischer
Varna Olympiad 1962
Sicilian Defence

1 e4 c5 2 ♘f3 d6 3 d4 cxd4 4 ♘xd4 ♘f6 5 ♘c3 a6 6 ♗e2 e5 7 ♘b3

7...♗e6

This classical approach, based on keeping the pawn on e5 and meeting f4-f5 with ....♗c4, looks artificial and was rejected when it was realized how dangerous White's initiative could be after a quick f4 and g4.

I have nothing to say about the position after 7...♗e7, except to plug 8 0-0 0-0 9 a4 ♗e6 10 f4 exf4 11 ♗xf4 ♘c6 12 ♔h1 d5 13 e5 ♘d7 14 ♘xd5 ♘dxe5 15 ♘xe7+ ♕xe7 16 ♘d4 ♖ad8 17 ♘xc6 ♘xc6 18 ♕e1 ♕b4 19 ♗d3 ♕xe1 20 ♖axe1 ♘b4 21 ♗e4 ♗d5 22 ♗xd5 ♖xd5 with an equal ending in R.Zelcic-S.Collins, Saint Vincent 2005 (0-1 in 40).

8 0-0 ♘bd7 9 f4 ♕c7 10 f5 ♗c4 11 a4

The entire opening from move 7 on has, of course, been deeply developed in different directions in the 50 years since this game. See Kasparov's *My Great Predecessors* series (in particular the sections on Karpov, Fischer and Geller) for comprehensive, authoritative, intimidating coverage.

11...♗e7 12 ♗e3 0-0 13 a5 b5 14 axb6 ♘xb6

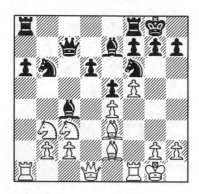

Black's queenside counterplay is, by now, quite real, and no strong players have essayed this line with White for a couple of decades.

15 ♗xb6?!

By round 16 of Curacao, Geller had found the antidote: 15 ♔h1 ♖fc8 16 ♗xb6 ♕xb6 17 ♗xc4 ♖xc4 18 ♕e2 ♖b4 19 ♖a2 was E.Geller-R.Fischer, Curacao 1962 (½-½ in 45) and now Zuckermann gives the sanguine 19...h6 20 ♖fa1 ♗f8 21 ♖xa6 ♖xa6 22 ♖xa6 ♕b7 23 ♘a5 ♕c7 24 ♘b3 ♕b7 with an equal position. However, in the Alekhine Memorial, 1971, Karpov improved with 21 ♖a4! and went on to win against Bronstein.

15...♕xb6+ 16 ♔h1 ♗b5!

A nice anticipation of the idea on

move 19. This concept of allowing certain exchanges, but only when one's structure is consequently improved, is one which featured in a huge number of Capablanca's wins against inferior opposition (i.e. basically everyone).

17 ♗xb5 axb5 18 ♘d5 ♘xd5 19 ♕xd5

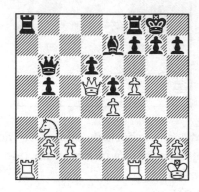

19...♖a4!

My initial impression of this position (when I first read *My 60 Memorable Games* and was sporting a healthy 1200 rating) was that Black needed this shot to survive. Again, this is symptomatic of a classical chess education which places primacy on outposts. In fact, Black could have exchanged on a1, or played his rook to c8, with quite adequate play since White has a number of pawn weaknesses (e4, c2, b2), a weak king, and a badly misplaced knight on b3. The bad bishop on e7 defends a good pawn on d6 (as Suba taught us), and could find more active employment on g5 or b6 (via d8). I deal with this in more detail in the section on Outposts.

20 c3 ♕a6

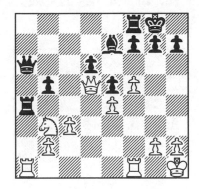

21 h3?

Fischer's game from round 4 of Curacao continued 21 ♖ad1 ♖c8 22 ♘c1 b4 23 ♘d3 bxc3 24 bxc3 and now 24...♖a5 (Kmoch notes that 24...♖xc3 was possible, since the sharp attempt 25 ♘xe5 dxe5 26 ♕xe5 – 26 ♕d8+ ♗f8 – 26...♗b4 27 ♕xc3 ♕xf1+! leaves Black a piece ahead) 25 ♕b3 ♖a3 26 ♕b1 ♖axc3 27 ♘b4 ♕a7 28 ♘d5 ♖3c6 29 ♕b3 with a position where the knight is genuinely strong enough to compensate for the pawn deficit in M.Tal-R.Fischer, Curacao 1962 (½-½ in 58). Another way of looking at the position is that the queening chances of Black's extra pawn (on d6) are close to zero.

Kasparov notes: "Of course, White had to give up dreams of an advantage long ago, but also his problems should not be exaggerated. Forty years later Hübner nevertheless found a constructive plan – 21 g3! leaving the h3-square for the king and intending to meet ...♗g5 with h4, while if 21...♕a8 22 ♕xa8 ♖fxa8, then 23 ♔g2 and 24.♔f3 with a probable draw."

21...♖c8 22 ♖fe1 h6 23 ♔h2 ♗g5 24 g3?

Fischer's suggested 24 ♖ad1 is better, but Black remains on top. The battle for the a-file has been conclusively decided in his favour.

24...♕a7 25 ♔g2

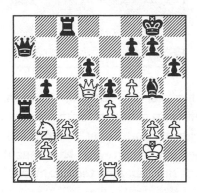

25...♖a2!

The ultimate goal of most operations on an open file – penetration to the 7th rank.

26 ♔f1? ♖xc3! 0-1

Game 9
V.Kovacevic-Y.Seirawan
Wijk aan Zee 1980
Pirc Defence

1 e4 d6 2 d4 ♘f6 3 ♘c3 g6 4 ♗e2 ♗g7 5 g4 c6 6 g5 ♘fd7 7 h4 b5 8 h5 ♖g8 9 hxg6 hxg6 10 ♘f3 b4 11 ♘b1 a5 12 a4 c5 13 d5 ♘b6 14 c4

This game is a beautiful example of Seirawan's quite unique strategic talent. As Joe Gallagher put it, Yasser tends to live on his own, fairly advanced, positional planet.

Just looking at the position, as White you would be looking forward to exploiting your "play" down the h-file, especially when you have spent so much time opening the file. In fact...

14...♔d7!!

Completely refuting White's strategy.

15 ♘bd2 ♖h8 16 ♖g1

Now Black has the open file. His advantage is still within manageable limits, but from a psychological point of view it's hard to play at full strength on encountering such a striking idea.

16...♔c7 17 ♖b1 ♖h3 18 b3 ♕h8 19 ♘f1

19 ♗f1, ejecting the rook, was stronger.

19...♘8d7 20 ♗f4 ♘e5 21 ♘xe5 ♗xe5 22 ♗xe5 ♕xe5

The position has clarified very much in Black's favour. His queen and rook dominate.

23 f3 ♗d7 24 ♕c2 ♕d4 25 ♖g2 ♖h1 26 ♖f2 ♕h8

The mundane 26...♗h3 was better.

27 f4

27 ♕d2 intending ♕e3 set up a tougher defence.

27...♕h4 28 ♖d1 f6 29 gxf6 exf6 30 e5

It's hardly surprising that a strategy of opening the e- and f-files doesn't help White.

30...fxe5 31 fxe5 ♖f8 32 exd6+ ♔b7 33 ♗d3 ♖e8+ 0-1

> *Game 10*
> **A.Karpov-W.Unzicker**
> Nice Olympiad 1974
> *Ruy Lopez*

This is a game everyone has seen. I'm including it here by way of explanation for the next game.

1 e4 e5 2 ♘f3 ♘c6 3 ♗b5 a6 4 ♗a4 ♘f6 5 0-0 ♗e7 6 ♖e1 b5 7 ♗b3 d6 8 c3 0-0 9 h3 ♘a5 10 ♗c2 c5 11 d4 ♕c7 12 ♘bd2 ♘c6 13 d5 ♘d8 14 a4 ♖b8

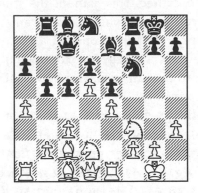

15 axb5

A strong case can be made for 15 b4. This is a theoretical position and so won't be examined in depth here, but Black often chooses 15...c4 when 16 axb5 axb5 leads to a slightly more favourable version of the game from White's perspective.

15...axb5 16 b4 ♘b7 17 ♘f1 ♗d7 18 ♗e3 ♖a8 19 ♕d2 ♖fc8 20 ♗d3 g6 21 ♘g3 ♗f8 22 ♖a2 c4 23 ♗b1 ♕d8

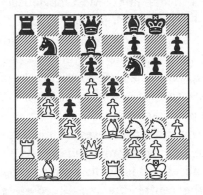

This position is typical of the Rubenstein Ruy Lopez. The blocked centre encourages play on the wings. In many cases, White tries to break through on the kingside while Black uses the a-file to generate counterplay.

Here, however, Karpov finds an incredible idea, keeping all the rooks on the board while stifling Black's queenside counterplay.

24 ♗a7!! ♘e8 25 ♗c2 ♘c7 26 ♖ea1 ♕e7 27 ♗b1

Karpov has a crushing positional bind and, unsurprisingly, smoothly converts.

27...♗e8 28 ♘e2 ♘d8 29 ♘h2 ♗g7 30 f4 f6 31 f5 g5 32 ♗c2 ♗f7 33 ♘g3 ♘b7 34 ♗d1 h6 35 ♘h5 ♕e8 36 ♕d1 ♘d8 37 ♖a3 ♔f8 38 ♖1a2 ♔g8 39 ♘g4 ♔f8 40 ♘e3 ♔g8 41 ♗xf7+ ♘xf7 42 ♕h5 ♘d8 43 ♕g6 ♔f8 44 ♘h5 1-0

A trade on g6 would clear the f5-square for a white knight and create a monster passed pawn on g6, so Unzicker drew the curtain here.

Game 11
S.Halkias-I.Sokolov
Bled Olympiad 2002
Slav Defence

---

1 d4 d5 2 c4 c6 3 cxd5 cxd5 4 ♘c3 ♘f6 5 ♗f4 ♘c6 6 e3 a6 7 ♗d3 ♗g4 8 f3 ♗h5 9 ♘ge2 e6 10 0-0 ♗e7 11 ♖c1 0-0 12 ♗g3 ♖c8 13 ♘f4 ♗g6 14 ♘a4 ♘d7 15 ♗xg6 hxg6 16 ♘d3 ♘b4 17 ♘xb4 ♗xb4 18 a3 ♗e7 19 ♕d2 ♖c4 20 b4 ♕a8 21 ♘b2 ♖xc1 22 ♖xc1 ♖c8

This is a typical, and fairly level, Exchange Slav.

23 ♗c7

Clearly informed by Karpov's example, Halkias wants to build up on the c-file (for instance, with ♖c3 and ♕c2) before moving his bishop. However, the position is much more dynamic here:

23...a5! 24 ♘d3

24 ♗xa5 b6 is the point.

24...axb4 25 axb4 ♕a4 26 h3 ♕b5 27 ♔f2 ♖a8 28 ♕c3 ♖c8 29 ♕a3 ♘f6 30 ♔e2?

Flear gives 30 ♖c3 as equal.

30...♗xb4!

Pointing out the downside of putting the bishop on c7.

31 ♕xb4 ♕xb4 32 ♘xb4 ♘e8 33 ♖a1 ♖xc7 34 ♖a8 ♔f8

White has some drawing chances, but clearly his adventure on the c-file has backfired. This game is the strategic cousin of Kovacevic-Seirawan – in both games White opened a file and based his strategy on controlling it, only to find an unpleasant reversal on that very line.

35 ♖b8 g5 36 e4 dxe4 37 fxe4 ♖c4 38 ♖xb7 ♖xd4 39 ♔f3 ♖c4 40 e5 ♘c7 41 ♖b6 ♖f4+ 42 ♔g3 g6 43 ♘d3 ♖d4 44 ♖b3 ♔g7 45 ♔f3 ♘d5 46 ♔f2 g4 47 hxg4 ♖xg4 48 ♔f3 ♖d4 49 g3 ♘e7 50 ♖a3 ♘c6 51 ♔e3 ♖d5 52 ♔e4 g5 53 ♖c3 ♘xe5 54 ♘xe5 f5+ 55 ♔f3 ♖xe5 56 ♖c8 ♖a5 57 ♖c6 ♔f6 58 ♖b6 ♖a2 59 ♔e3 g4 0-1

The e6-Pawn

I'd like to mention a relatively little-discussed theme, namely the value of a black pawn on e6 against a white bishop on the a2-g8 diagonal.

This value is implicit in a lot of modern openings. Most obviously, in the Fischer Attack in the Najdorf (1 e4 c5 2 ♘f3 d6 3 d4 cxd4 4 ♘xd4 ♘f6 5 ♘c3 a6 6 ♗c4), even players who prefer setups with ...e5 are compelled to play 6...e6 to put some granite on the bishop's diagonal.

The difficulty arises, in my experience, in the early middlegame. As Black equalizes and feels the need to expand in the centre, the move ...e6-e5 is a natural means of making progress.

However, it needs to be carefully considered whether this move liberates White's light-squared bishop.

Game 12
J.Sorensen-S.Collins
European Club Cup
Kallithea 2008
Alekhine Defence

---

1 e4 ♘f6 2 ♘c3 d5 3 exd5 ♘xd5 4 ♗c4 ♘b6 5 ♗b3 ♘c6 6 ♕f3 e6 7 ♘ge2 ♗e7 8 d3 0-0 9 a3

White has chosen an inoffensive variation against the Alekhine, and Black has a choice of ways to achieve a comfortable game.

9...e5?

A strategic blunder. I thought I was increasing my space in the centre and liberating my light-squared bishop. In broad terms, these are both true. However, the real problem with the move is that the b3-bishop is transformed from a problem piece into the best piece on the board.

My preferred method today would be 9...♘a5! 10 ♗a2 c5, gaining space and preparing the manoeuvre of the knight from a5 to d4, with very comfortable play. In fact, White needs to play carefully to avoid an inferior position, precisely because the bishop is at risk of being buried on a2. My bishop, in the meantime, can come out via c6. **10 ♕h5 ♘d4**

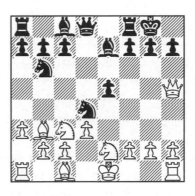

11 ♘xd4 ♕xd4??

And now a tactical blunder.

Despite my 9th move, I still had a route to an acceptable position – 11...exd4 was correct. After 12 ♘e4 Black does best to bite the bullet and offer a trade: 12...♗e6! 13 ♗xe6 fxe6. White has a better structure and a good knight on e4, but Black should be able to hold the balance.

12 ♗e3 ♕g4 13 ♕xe5 ♕xg2 14 0-0-0 ♗f6 15 ♕xc7

With an extra pawn and a better position, White won easily.

15...♗f5 16 ♖hg1 ♕f3 17 ♖g3 ♕c6 18 ♕xc6 bxc6 19 ♘e4 ♗h4 20 ♖gg1 ♗g6 21 ♗g5 ♗xg5+ 22 ♖xg5 ♖fe8 23 f3 a5 24 a4

♘d7 25 ♔d2 ♔f8 26 ♘c5 ♘f6 27 ♖e1 ♖xe1 28 ♔xe1 ♖e8+ 29 ♘e4 ♘d5 30 ♗xd5 cxd5 31 ♖xd5 f5 32 ♖xa5 fxe4 33 fxe4 ♖b8 34 b3 ♔e7 35 ♔d2 ♖f8 36 ♖a7+ ♔d6 37 ♔e3 ♖f1 38 b4 ♖h1 39 c4 ♖xh2 40 c5+ ♔e5 41 c6 ♗h5 42 d4+ ♔d6 43 d5 g5 44 ♖xh7 ♖e2+ 45 ♔d3 ♖xe4 46 ♖d7+ ♔e5 47 c7 ♗e2+ 48 ♔d2 ♗a6 49 b5 ♗b7 50 a5 ♖d4+ 51 ♔e3 ♖xd5 52 a6 ♗c8 53 ♖xd5+ ♔xd5 54 a7 1-0

> ## Game 13
> ## S.Collins-N.Miezis
> Arctic Chess Challenge
> Tromsø 2010
> *Sicilian Defence*

1 e4 c5 2 c3 d5 3 exd5 ♕xd5 4 d4 e6 5 ♘f3 ♘f6 6 a3 ♗e7 7 ♗e3 ♘g4 8 ♘bd2 ♘c6 9 ♗c4 ♕d8 10 0-0 cxd4 11 cxd4 0-0 12 ♖c1 ♘xe3 13 fxe3 ♕b6 14 b4

I like White's position, but this might be a necessary self-delusion for a c3-Sicilian player. Black has the two bishops, though for the moment he's pretty passive.

14...e5?

Played quickly, but this move shocked me. Again, White's light-squared bishop becomes the best piece on the board, especially since its pressure on f7 combines with the rook on f1.

14...♗d7 seems sounder to me, though Black remains passive.

15 ♕b3

Now f7 collapses.

15...exd4 16 ♗xf7+ ♔h8 17 ♘c4 ♕d8 18 b5 ♘a5 19 ♘xa5 ♕xa5

19...dxe3 doesn't work since after 20 ♘c4 e2 21 ♖fe1 ♖xf7 22 ♘ce5 White wins the exchange which, coupled with his superior activity, ought to confer a decisive advantage.

20 exd4 ♕xa3

Restoring material equality, but now Black's position is completely disorganized.

21 ♘e5 g6

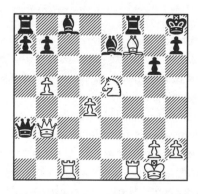

22 g4?!

Directed against ...♗f5, but it should have been obvious that this weakens my king and doesn't advance my plans.

22 ♖c7 is the move one would play in a blitz game. Black's position collapses.

22...♛d6

Also not the best defence, though Black remains worse after any continuation.

23 ♕e3

23 ♕c3! is sharper, setting up play on the long diagonal. If a black bishop appears on f6, an exchange sacrifice becomes very promising for White.

23...♔g7 24 ♗a2

Continuing a series of sub-optimal moves.

24...♗e6 25 ♘xg6 hxg6 26 ♗xe6 ♗g5 27 ♕xg5 ♕xd4+ 28 ♔g2 ♕e4+ 29 ♔g3 ♕xe6

Black has completely equalized and, of more practical concern, I had almost no time in which to play the next 10 moves. In such circumstances, despite my disappointment at not winning the game, I was happy to find a way to swap everything off.

30 ♖c7+ ♔g8 31 ♖xf8+ ♖xf8 32 ♕e7 ♕f7 33 ♕xf7+ ♖xf7 34 ♖xf7 ♔xf7 35 h4

a5 36 bxa6 bxa6 37 ♔f3 a5 38 ♔e3 ♔f6 39 ♔d3 ♔e5 40 ♔c3 ♔f4 41 h5 gxh5 42 gxh5 ♔g5 43 ♔b3 ♔xh5 44 ♔a4 ♔g5 45 ♔xa5 ½-½

Mobile Pawn Centre

Positions with mobile pawn centres arise in a wide range of openings and tend to be highly dynamic. Here I've chosen to concentrate on one classical position, and one classical player, to explore some of the mechanics of play in such positions. These can be briefly summarized as follows:

1) For the side with the mobile centre, activating this centre is critical. Material sacrifices can be used to this end.

2) For the side playing against the mobile centre, blockading the centre tends to lead to an easy game.

Game 14
S.Gligoric-A.Matanovic
Bled 1961
Nimzo-Indian Defence

1 d4 ♘f6 2 c4 e6 3 ♘c3 ♗b4 4 e3 c5 5 ♗d3 0-0 6 ♘f3 d5 7 0-0 ♘c6 8 a3 ♗xc3 9 bxc3 dxc4 10 ♗xc4 ♕c7

This position, like so many others, was explained by David Bronstein in his book on the 1953 Candidates Tournament in Zurich: "Today, this position has been studied as thoroughly as were the Muzio and Evans Gambits a century ago. What are the basic features of this position, and how does the evaluation of those features give rise to the further plans for both sides?

The placement of White's pieces radiates a great deal of potential energy, which ought to be converted into kinetic – White must set his centre pawns in motion, activating both his rooks and his deeply-buried dark-square bishop. The most logical plan would seem to be the advance of the e-pawn, first to e4, and then to e5, to drive Black's knight away from f6 and lay the groundwork for a kingside attack. Black in turn must either prevent the e-pawn's advance or counterattack the white pawn centre, which will lose some of its solidity the moment the pawn advances from e3 to e4."

Given that this position constitutes such a pitched battle between White's potentially mobile centre pawns and Black's attempt to restrain them, I thought it would be worth spending some time looking at the typical plans governing play in this position. This can be done through the lens of Gli-

goric's games with White, since he attempted to prove an advantage in this position with the help of several moves, and against the best defenders of the Nimzo at the time.

11 &d3

Some alternatives:

a) 11 a4 came in for robust criticism in Bronstein's tournament book:

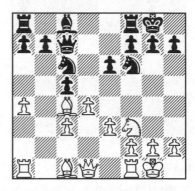

"Of all the possible continuations that have been used here, this one may well be the least logical: it resolves only one problem, the development of the queen's bishop – and to a poor square, at that. The pawn at c5 will find defenders easily enough, and the bishop will find itself out of the action. That outflung pawn at a4 will not be a jewel in White's position either." 11...b6 12 &a3 &b7 13 ♕e2 (Hans Mueller gives 13 dxc5 bxc5 14 &xc5? ♖fd8 15 ♕c2 – 15 &d3 &a6 – 15...♘a5, winning for Black) 13...♘a5 14 &a2 ♕c6 15 &b1 ♖fe8 (Mueller gives 15...♕xa4? 16 dxc5 bxc5 17 &xc5 ♕xa1 18 &xh7+ ♘xh7 19 ♖xa1 ♘b3 20 &xf8 ♘xa1 21 &xg7 and White wins) 16 &c2 ♖ac8 17 ♖ac1 c4

(Gligoric notes that 17...e5 leads to an advantage for White: 18 dxe5 ♖xe5 19 e4 ♖e7 – 19...♘xe4? loses to 20 ♘xe5 ♘xc3 21 ♗xh7+ ♔h8 22 ♘xf7+) 20 ♘d2 ♖d8 21 ♖cd1 ♕c8 22 c4) 18 ♖ce1 ♘h5! 19 ♖d1 g6 20 e4 ♘f4 21 ♕e3 ♘d3! 22 ♘d2 (22 ♗xd3 cxd3 23 ♖xd3 ♕xa4) 22...f5 23 f3 f4 24 ♕e2 e5 and, having blockaded the position, Black should not have gone on to lose in S.Gligoric-N.Rossolimo, Venice 1949.

b) 11 ♗b2 e5 12 h3 was S.Gligoric-A.Stenborg, Dublin 1957, and now the simplest was 12...♗f5 followed by ...♖ad8 with an easy game.

c) 11 ♗b5 was tried on a number of occasions by Gligoric, and netted him 2/2 in the Munich Olympiad 1958. 11...b6 12 ♖e1 ♗b7 13 e4 and White has achieved his central advance, though Black's queenside mobilization should enable him to put pressure on the white central pawns.

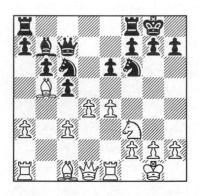

Neither of Gligoric's Olympiad opponents managed to demonstrate this:

c1) 13...♘e7 14 ♗d3 ♘g6 15 ♗g5 ♖ac8 16 ♕d2 cxd4 17 cxd4 ♕c3 18 ♕e2 h6 19 ♗d2 ♕c7 20 g3 ♖fd8 21 a4 ♕d7 22 a5 with the two bishops and the better structure in S.Gligoric-F.Anderson, Munich 1958 (1-0 in 42).

c2) 13...h6 14 ♗d3 ♖fd8 15 ♗b2 ♘e7 16 ♘e5 ♘c6 17 ♘xc6 ♗xc6 18 ♖e3 c4 19 ♗c2 e5 20 ♕e2 b5 21 ♖f1 ♖e8 22 ♗c1 ♕d6 23 ♖d1 ♖ad8 24 d5 ♗d7 25 ♖g3 ♔h8 26 ♖f1 ♘h7 27 ♕h5 f6 28 f4 with a substantial kingside initiative in S.Gligoric-W.Unzicker, Munich 1958 (1-0 in 54).

d) 11 ♗a2 is a normal prophylactic move, getting the bishop out of the queen's sights on the c-file. 11...e5 and now:

d1) 12 ♕c2 ♗g4 13 dxe5 ♘xe5 14 ♘e1!? ♖fd8 15 f3 ♗e6 16 c4 a6 17 f4 ♘c6 18 ♘f3 ♕e7 19 ♗b2 ♗g4 20 ♖ae1 ♘e4 with unclear play in S.Gligoric-V.Zaltsman, Lone Pine 1980 (1-0 in 69), albeit play where the white bishop on b2 looks more threatening than anything in Black's position.

d2) 12 d5 e4 13 dxc6 exf3 14 ♕xf3 ♗g4 15 ♕g3 ♕xc6 looks roughly level.

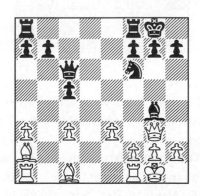

Gligoric tested this in a couple of

games: against D.Mitrovic in Nis 1998 (0-1 in 54) and against L.Ljubojevic in Donji Milanovac 1979 (½-½ in 21).

e) 11 ♗e2 has similar aims to 11 ♗a2 but puts the bishop on a less active diagonal, with the intention of neutralizing an eventual ...♗g4. S.Gligoric-L.Ljubojevic, Bugojno 1982, continued 11...♖d8 12 c4 e5 13 d5 e4 14 ♘d2 ♘e5 15 f4 exf3 16 gxf3 ♕e7 17 a4 ♘d3 18 ♗xd3 ♕xe3+ 19 ♔h1 ♕xd3 20 ♘e4 ♕xd1 21 ♘xf6+ gxf6 22 ♖xd1 h5 with a draw in 48 moves.

11...e5 12 ♕c2 ♖e8

The alternatives 12...♖d8, 12...♕e7 and 12...♗g4 were also tested against Gligoric, but we will focus on the text move.

13 ♘xe5 ♘xe5 14 dxe5 ♕xe5 15 f3

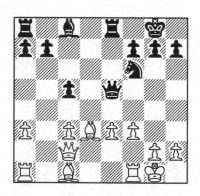

15...♗d7

Black is faced with a fundamental question as to where this bishop belongs.

The fianchetto with 15...b6 was tried in S.Gligoric-P.Clarke, Hastings 1956. After 16 ♖e1 ♗b7 17 e4 Black found a nice method of undermining

the white kingside structure: 17...h5!? 18 ♗e3 h4 19 ♗f1 ♖ad8 20 a4 ♖e6 with good counterplay.

15...♗e6 16 ♖e1 ♖ad8 17 ♖b1 ♕d5 (Black can also play for the b3-outpost with 17...c4 18 ♗f1 ♘d7 19 e4 ♘c5 20 ♗e3 ♘b3 as in S.Gligoric-M.Euwe, Leipzig 1960 (1-0 in 68)) and Black is impressively centralized. After 18 ♗b5 ♗f5 19 e4 ♘xe4 20 ♗xe8 ♘d6 21 ♕e2 ♗xb1 22 ♕e7 ♖a8 23 ♗xf7+ ♕xf7 24 ♕xd6 ♖e8 25 ♖xe8+ ♕xe8 26 ♕d5+ ♔f8 27 ♕xc5+ ♕e7 28 ♕f2 the complications had petered out to an extra pawn for White, but the opposite-coloured bishops meant that after 28...♕d6! 29 ♕e3 ♕b6 30 ♔f2 ♕xe3+ 31 ♔xe3 ♗f5 a draw was agreed in S.Gligoric-F.Olafsson, Bad Lauterberg 1977.

16 a4

The more restrained 16 ♖b1 ♗c6 17 c4 ♖ad8 18 ♖e1 led to similar play in S.Gligoric-B.Larsen, Moscow 1956: 18...h5! 19 ♗f1 h4 20 e4 ♘h5 with good counterplay on the dark squares (½-½ in 36).

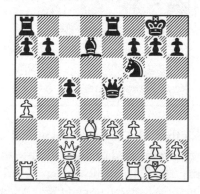

16...♖ac8

Black plays directly for ...c4 to bring his queen to the queenside.

16...♖ad8 looks sensible.

16...♗c6 featured in no fewer than three of Gligoric's games from the Portoroz Interzonal in 1958:

a) 17 ♖e1 ♖ad8 18 e4 h5 19 ♗e3 h4 20 h3 ♘h5 21 ♖ad1 ♘f4 22 ♗f1 b6 23 ♖xd8 ♖xd8 24 ♖d1 ♖xd1 25 ♕xd1 ♘e6 and a draw was agreed in round 2: S.Gligoric-Y.Averbakh.

b) 17 ♖e1 h5 18 e4 ♘d5 19 ♗d2 ♘f4 20 ♗f1 h4 21 ♗e3 ♖ad8 22 ♖ad1 b6 23 h3 with equality in round 12: S.Gligoric-L.Pachman (1-0 in 42).

c) 17 e4 ♖ad8 18 ♗c4 b6 19 ♗d2 ♖d7 20 ♗e3 h5 21 ♖ae1 h4 22 ♗c1 ♕h5 23 h3 ♕g6 24 ♖d1 ♖ed8 with counterplay was the round 14 encounter S.Gligoric-M.Filip (½-½ in 41).

17 ♖e1 c4 18 ♗f1 ♕a5 19 e4 ♖e6 20 ♗e3 ♖a6 21 ♕b2 b6 22 ♗d4

22...♗xa4

Winning an a-pawn while Rome burns. This is highly reminiscent of other classic Nimzo-Indian games, most notably M.Botvinnik-J.R.Capablanca, AVRO 1938. This is Black's normal strategy and accordingly can't be condemned on the basis of one or two games. However, in this instance it seems manifestly ridiculous – whatever about the queen on a5, how did the rook end up on a6?

23 e5!

23 ♗xf6 gxf6 is a Pyrrhic victory for White – the "weakened" black kingside in fact does a good job of restraining the white central majority. In addition, I can't imagine that giving up the magnificent bishop on d4 even crossed Gligoric's mind. Pushing the e-pawn through is a much more effective method of cracking open the kingside.

23...♘e8 24 e6 f6

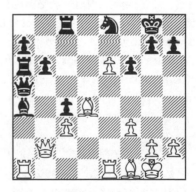

Black desperately tries to keep the e-file and long diagonal closed, but at the price of allowing a huge pawn on e6. White clearly has overwhelming compensation and manages to develop his initiative.

25 ♗e2 b5 26 ♗d1 ♕c7 27 ♗c2 ♕e7 28 ♗e4 ♔h8 29 ♕f2 g6 30 f4 ♘d6 31 f5 g5

32 ♗c2 ♘e8 33 ♕f3 ♖d8 34 ♕h5 ♔g8 35 h4 gxh4 36 ♖e4 ♘g7 37 ♖g4 ♖ad6 38 ♗xa4 ♖xd4 39 cxd4 bxa4 40 ♖xa4 ♔h8 41 ♕f7 ♕xf7 42 exf7 ♘xf5 43 ♖xa7 ♖f8 44 ♖f4 ♘g3 45 ♔f2 c3 46 ♖c7 f5 47 ♖xh4 ♘e4+ 48 ♔e3 ♘f6 49 ♔d3 ♔g7 50 ♖c5 ♔g6 51 ♖f4 c2 52 ♔xc2 ♘g4 53 ♔d3 ♖xf7 54 ♖cxf5 ♖xf5 55 ♖xg4+ ♔f6 56 ♖e4 h5 57 ♖e2 h4 58 ♔c4 ♖a5 59 d5 ♔f7 60 d6 ♖a8 61 ♔d5 ♖a3 62 d7 ♖d3+ 63 ♔c6 ♖c3+ 64 ♔b7 ♖b3+ 65 ♔c8 ♖c3+ 66 ♔d8 1-0

Queenside Space Advantage

In a large number of openings (especially those arising from the Queen's Gambit complex) White secures a huge queenside space advantage. The resulting positions tend to be highly dynamic, and are often informed by White sacrificing a piece for mobile, advanced, connected passed pawns on the queenside, or Black successfully counterattacking on the queenside or in the centre.

Game 15
L.Portisch-T.Petrosian
Candidates Quarter Final
Palma de Mallorca 1974
Queen's Gambit Declined

I found this following example in Robert Byrne's compilation of his New York Times columns, *Great Chess Victories and Defeats*.

Petrosian decided to adopt, with

Black, a system in which Portisch himself was a renowned specialist. When Botvinnik was asked about his thoughts on this approach following his match with Bronstein (where the latter used several patented Botvinnik systems, including the Stonewall Dutch) he said that, in general, he liked playing against these lines since he knew them well. It would seem from this game that Portisch would agree!
1 d4 d5 2 c4 e6 3 ♘c3 ♗e7 4 ♘f3 ♘f6 5 ♗g5 0-0 6 e3 ♘bd7 7 ♖c1 a6

The text is a slight twist on the normal Orthodox lines beginning with 7...c6. Black obtains options of taking on c4 and playing b5, when he might play ...c5 in one go. Such play is very familiar from the Meran Semi Slav.
8 c5

White's most ambitious and principled response, gaining space on the queenside and cutting across the idea indicated in the previous note. Portisch had used this system repeatedly in his playoff with Polugaevsky in Portoroz 1973.

Different systems were explored in those games, for instance 8 a3 c6 9 ♗d3 h6 10 ♗h4 dxc4 11 ♗xc4 b5 12 ♗a2 c5 13 0-0 ♗b7 14 dxc5 ♘xc5 15 ♘d4 ♖c8 16 f3 ♕b6 17 b4 ♘cd7 18 ♗f2 ♗d6 19 e4 ♕c7 20 g3 ♕b8 21 ♕e2 ♘e5 and Black had a healthy Meran setup, going on to win an interesting game in 73 moves (playoff game 1).

Game 3 of the Portoroz playoff saw 8 cxd5 exd5 9 ♗d3 c6 10 ♕c2 ♖e8 11 0-0 with a normal Carlsbad setup which was agreed drawn in 27 moves.

8...c6 9 ♗d3 b6

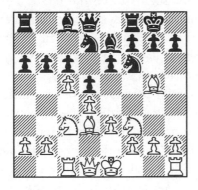

10 cxb6

There seems to be no reason to refrain from 10 b4, but Portisch goes his own way.

10...c5

V.Hort-L.Portisch, Madrid 1973, continued 10...♕xb6 11 0-0! ♕xb2 12 ♘a4 ♕b7 and now the tournament bulletin suggests 13 ♕c2!? ♗a3 14 ♖b1 ♕c7 15 ♗f4 ♗d6 16 ♘b6 with an edge for White.

11 0-0 c4

Exchanging pawns on d4 would leave White with a stable advantage – a white pawn on d4 is not weak since it is covered from frontal attack by the black pawn on d5 (which, incidentally, restricts Black's light-squared bishop).

12 ♗c2 ♘xb6 13 ♘e5 ♗b7 14 f4

14...♖b8?

The bulletin suggests 14...♘fd7! 15 ♕h5 g6!? (15...f5 is better for White) when playing for an attack with 16 ♘xg6?! just appears to lead to a draw in view of 16...hxg6 17 ♗xg6 fxg6 18 ♕xg6+ ♔h8 19 ♖f3 ♗xg5 20 ♖h3+ ♗h4 and White should take the perpetual check.

15 f5

Now White has a risk-free attack on the kingside, which he conducts superbly.

15...♘bd7 16 ♗f4 ♖c8 17 ♕f3 exf5 18 ♗xf5 ♘xe5 19 dxe5 ♘e4 20 ♘xe4

There was nothing wrong with taking on c8 either. However, Portisch was understandably reluctant to allow Petrosian his favourite exchange sacrifice!

20...dxe4 21 ♕h3

Now everything comes with tempo.

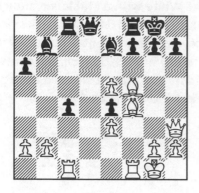

21...g6 22 ♖cd1 ♕b6 23 ♖d7! ♖ce8 24 e6! gxf5

24...f6 is no help: 25 ♗xg6 hxg6 26 ♕h6 wins.

25 ♖xe7

The bulletin gives 25 ♕g3+! ♔h8 26 ♗h6 ♖g8 27 exf7 ♕xh6 28 ♖xe7, winning.

25...♖xe7 26 ♕g3+ ♔h8 27 ♗h6 fxe6

Or 27...♖g8 28 ♕e5+ f6 29 ♕xf6+ ♖eg7 30 ♖d1 and White wins.

28 ♗xf8 ♖d7 29 ♗h6

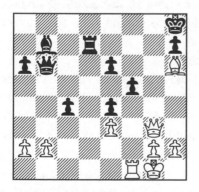

29...♕a5

The bulletin notes that even against the more tenacious 29...♕c5!? there is no defence on the dark-squares: 30 ♗f4

♖d5 (or 30...h6 31 ♕g6 ♕d5 32 ♗e5+) 31 ♗g5 ♕f8 32 ♕c7.

30 ♕b8+ ♔d8 31 ♕e5+ ♔g8 32 ♕xe6+ ♖f7 33 ♖xf5 1-0

Game 16
E.Tomashevsky-A.Riazantsev
Russian Championship
Moscow 2008
Queen's Gambit Declined

1 c4 e6 2 ♘c3 d5 3 d4 ♗e7 4 ♘f3 ♘f6 5 ♗f4 0-0 6 e3 ♘bd7

This seems to be the modern preference of top players. Black often ends up in positions with an Isolated Queen's Pawn, but with very good equalizing chances.

6...c5 is perhaps the most principled method of exploiting the bishop's absence from g5, but it routinely leads to extremely sharp positions with opposite-side castling, which look and feel more like a Sicilian than the quiet, equalizing QGD Black was hoping for.

7 c5

This was Steinitz' old plan, as explained by Kasparov in his wonderful QGD DVD. After waiting moves like 7 a3 (or 8 h3, or 8 ♕c2, both of which have been played against me), Black goes for an IQP with 7...c5 8 cxd5 ♘xd5 9 ♘xd5 exd5 10 dxc5 ♘xc5 with excellent equalizing chances. A couple of authoritative recent games continued 11 ♗e2 ♗f6 12 ♗e5 ♗xe5 13 ♘xe5 ♖e8 (or 13...♕d6 14 ♘f3 ♗d7 15 0-0 ♗a4 16

♕d4 ♖ac8 17 ♕b4 b6 18 ♖ac1 ♗d7 19 ♖fd1 ♗a4 20 ♖e1 ♗d7 21 ♕h4 h6 22 ♘d4 a5 23 ♖ed1 ♖fe8 24 ♕g3 ♕f6 25 ♕f3 ♕e5 26 ♕g3 ♕f6 27 ♕f3 ♕e5 28 ♕g3 ½-½, T.Radjabov-V.Topalov, Wijk aan Zee 2012) 14 ♘f3 ♕b6 15 ♖c1 ♘e6 16 ♕d2 ♖d8 17 ♘d4 ♗d7 18 ♘xe6 ♗xe6 19 ♕d4 ♕xd4 20 exd4 ♔f8 21 ♔d2 ♖dc8 22 ♖c5 ♔e7 23 ♖hc1 b6 24 ♖xc8 ♖xc8 25 ♖xc8 ♗xc8 and a draw was agreed shortly in V.Kramnik-L.Aronian, London 2011 (½-½ in 32).

7...c6 8 h3

A waiting move, trying to save a tempo on the light-squared bishop, which frequently gets exchanged on a6.

Let's follow the game T.Nyback-M.Carlsen, Dresden Olympiad 2008:

8 ♗d3 b6 9 b4 a5 10 a3 ♗a6 11 0-0 ♕c8 12 ♕c2 ♗xd3 13 ♕xd3

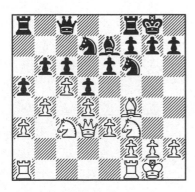

Black's thematic plan here is ...♕b7, ...♖fc8, ...♗d8-c7. Other games to have reached this position have seen Black start right away with 13...♕b7. Looking at the difference between those games (where, incidentally, White also scores well) and Magnus' plan, we can see that in the main line Black contests the e5-square with two pieces (a knight on d7 and a bishop on c7). The strategic defect of Magnus' plan is that his bishop is left ineffective on e7. That said, it takes remarkable play from Nyback to demonstrate the downside:

13...♘h5 14 ♗e5 ♕b7 15 ♖fc1 ♖fc8 16 h3 ♘xe5 17 ♘xe5 b5 18 ♖cb1 ♕c7 19 a4!

A great idea involving a piece sacrifice.

19...axb4 20 axb5

No exclam this time, since no other idea makes sense at this point.

20...bxc3 21 ♘xc6

White will have two pawns for the piece (after capturing on c3), and they're fantastic – connected, supported, passed, advanced, and controlling vital squares, in particular the c6-outpost. The black minor pieces cannot gain any purchase against the rock-solid white structure.

21...♘f6 22 ♕xc3 ♗f8 23 ♖xa8 ♖xa8 24 ♖a1!

White has no objection to trading all the major pieces, since the b5- and c5-pawns, supported by the knight, cannot be blockaded.

24...♘e4 25 ♕b2 ♖e8 (25...♕b7 26 ♖xa8 ♕xa8 27 b6! ends the game) 26 ♘e5!

White needs to stop looking at his powerful knight and push his pawns. The a5-square is tempting, controlling both the b7- and c6-squares (from which Black might attempt a blockade), but on e5 the knight doesn't obstruct the a1-rook. In particular, ideas of b6 and ♖a7, targeting f7, enter the position.

26...♘xc5 27 b6 ♕b7 28 ♕b5 (28 ♖a7 also kills) 28...♖a8 29 ♖xa8 ♕xa8 30 dxc5 ♕a1+ 31 ♔h2 ♕xe5+

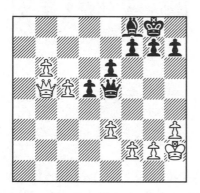

I've no doubt the Olympiad spectators thought that White had blundered. He hadn't.

32 g3 d4 33 b7 ♕f5 (if 33...♕b8, 34 exd4 wins) 34 ♕b2 dxe3 35 fxe3 ♕xc5 36 b8♕ ♕xe3 37 ♕c7 h6 38 ♕bc2 ♕d4 39 ♕7c4 and 1-0 in T.Nyback-M.Carlsen, Dresden Olympiad 2008.

Returning to our main game:

8...b6 9 b4 a5 10 a3 ♗a6

The latest wrinkle of which I'm aware here is 10...h6 11 ♗h2 ♗a6 12 ♗xa6 ♖xa6 13 0-0 ♕c8 14 ♕c2 ♕b7 15 ♖fc1 axb4 16 axb4 ♖fa8 17 ♖ab1 ♖a3 18 ♘d2 ♗d8 19 ♘b3 bxc5 20 bxc5 ♗c7 21 ♗xc7 ♕xc7 22 f4 ♖b8 23 ♘d2 ♖xb1 24 ♕xb1 ♕a5 25 ♕b2 ♕a6 and a draw was agreed in B.Gelfand-M.Adams, Rogaska Slatina 2011. I saw a bit of this game live, and Black always looked very comfortable.

11 ♗xa6 ♖xa6 12 b5 cxb5 13 c6 ♕c8 14 c7 b4

I've covered my game against Nick Pert from the 4NCL 2009/10 (1-0 in 25) in a previous Everyman volume. That game went 14...♗xa3?! and proceeded quickly downhill.

15 ♘b5

15...a4

A sharp and topical variation.

15...bxa3 16 0-0 has led to good results for White: 16...♖a8 17 ♕c2 ♘e4 18 ♕c6 h6 19 ♖fc1 ♗b4 20 ♖c2 ♔h7 21 ♘e1 ♘df6? 22 f3 ♘d2 23 ♖xd2 ♗xd2

24 ♕c2+ winning material in J.Gustaf-sson-J.Oms Pallise, Andorra 2002; or 16...a4 17 ♕c2 ♘e4 18 ♖fc1 h6 19 ♗h2 g6 20 ♘e1 ♖a8 21 f3 ♕a6 22 ♖ab1 ♘ef6 23 ♗d6 and, again, the c7-pawn looks more powerful than the black queenside passers, L.Schandorff-V.Iordachescu, Bled Olympiad 2002.

16 ♖c1

The capture on b4 has also been tested but immediately supporting the c-pawn looks like the most consistent. If Black takes on a3, similar positions to the note to Black's 15th will arise.

16...♘e4

The most active. 16...♘e8 looks too naive: there is no way the c7-pawn will fall. 17 ♕c2 b3 18 ♕c6 ♘c5 19 ♘e5 ♘f6 20 0-0 and White was dominant in I.Farago-S.Cigan, Austrian League 2007 (1-0 in 40).

17 ♘d2 ♘df6

Black's main alternative is the more radical 17...♘c3!? 18 ♘xc3 bxc3 19 ♖xc3 b5, with interesting play.

18 f3 ♖a5

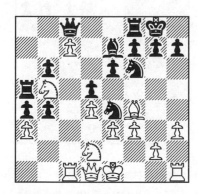

19 ♘xe4!

"Very important moment for the result of the fight. Tomashevsky sees the importance of changing all knights, as then the difference in impact of dark-squared bishops can become visible." (Ftacnik)

Ftacnik gives 19 fxe4? ♖xb5 20 ♗g5 b3! (20...dxe4 21 ♗xf6 gxf6 22 ♘xe4 b3 is clearly better for Black) 21 e5 and now not 21...b2?? 22 ♖c2, R.Leitao-G.Milos, Sao Paulo 2004 (1-0 in 30), but 21...♗xa3! winning: 22 ♖a1 ♘e4 23 ♘xe4 ♗b4+ 24 ♘d2 a3; 22 exf6 ♗xc1 23 ♕xc1 b2; and 22 ♗xf6 gxf6 23 exf6 ♔h8.

19...♘xe4 20 fxe4 ♖xb5 21 ♕xa4 ♖a5 22 ♕c6

Black has the option to take various pawns, but the c7-pawn is the most significant factor in the position.

22...bxa3

22...dxe4 23 a4 f5 24 0-0 leaves Black without counterplay.

23 exd5 ♖xd5

Ftacnik gives 23...exd5 24 0-0 a2 25 ♕xb6 ♖a6 26 ♕b3 ♕e6 27 ♖a1 with a clear advantage for White.

24 ♕xb6 ♕d7 25 0-0 ♖c8

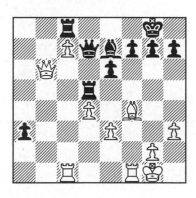

Amazingly, this had all been seen before.

26 ♖c6!

Ftacnik: "White is improving on the Bundesliga game, which saw black's win after the less precise play by white. Now black pieces are failing to cope with enemy's activity, since the pawn on c7 is very restrictive."

26 ♕a6 ♖b5 27 ♖b1 ♖b2 28 ♖xb2 axb2 29 ♕b7 ♗a3 30 ♖d1 g5 31 ♗g3 ♔g7 and, while I think I'd still take White, the b2-pawn is a significant factor in the position. Black eventually won in Z.Gyimesi-R.Vaganian, German League 2006 (0-1 in 78).

26...h6

Ftacnik notes that the attempt to push ...e5, to break the communication between the f4-bishop and the c7-pawn, runs into 26...♗f6 27 ♖fc1 e5 (or 27...♖xd4 28 ♕a6 ♖b4 29 ♕xa3 with a clear advantage) 28 dxe5 ♖d1+ 29 ♖xd1 ♕xd1+ 30 ♔h2 ♗e7 31 ♖d6! ♗xd6 32 exd6 ♕a4 33 ♕b7 ♕d7 34 ♕a6 and White wins.

27 ♖fc1 ♔h7 28 ♕a6 ♖f5

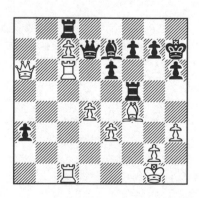

Allowing White's next, but it's difficult to suggest an alternative.

29 ♗d6!

Simply going after the a3-pawn.

29...♗h4

Or 29...♗xd6 30 ♖xd6 ♕e8 31 ♕xc8 ♕xc8 32 ♖d8, winning.

30 ♕xa3 ♗f2+ 31 ♔h1 ♖d5 32 ♗f4 f5 33 ♕c3

Now White simply transfers his rook to b8. Black's kingside counterplay is too slow.

33...♗h4 34 ♖b6 ♗g5 35 ♗e5 ♗d8 36 ♖b8 1-0

Game 17
L.Aronian-S.Volkov
Russian Team Championship
Sochi 2005
Slav Defence

1 d4 d5 2 c4 c6 3 ♘f3 ♘f6 4 ♘c3 a6 5 e3 b5 6 c5

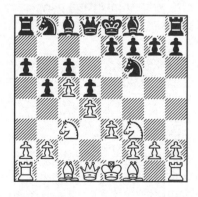

6 b3 was the main line for a long time, but Aronian's move is more critical.

After 6 b3, White's structure remains perfect and solid, but it leaves Black with a number of ideas, in particular the key plan of exchanging twice on c4, and (after ...e6) of the freeing advance ...c5. By playing c5 himself, White cuts across these ideas. However, by taking the pressure off the d5-pawn he makes it easier to break with ...e5 (which becomes even more attractive if a weak white pawn would be left on c5).

6...g6

Personally I prefer the immediate 6...♘bd7 when Black will break with ...e5 on the next move if White opts for 7 ♗d3, while 7 b4 a5 leaves Black with his full share of chances on the queenside.

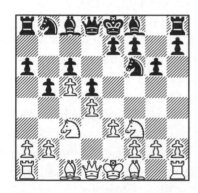

7 ♗d3

Aronian has tested a more dynamic concept with 7 ♕b3 a5 8 ♘e5 ♗g7 9 ♘xb5!? (a remarkable decision; we'll wait until White's 11th move to see what he's after) 9...cxb5 10 ♗xb5+ ♔f8 (interposing with anything loses material) 11 0-0.

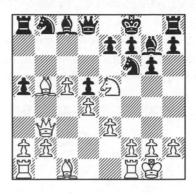

So what does White have for the piece? First, and most obviously, two pawns. Moreover, they're good pawns – the c5-pawn is supported, far-advanced and passed; the other pawn is healthy, although it will take a lot of work to get to b5. Second, the black king has been displaced. There is no question, at least in the short term, of an immediate attack a la Andersson or Morphy. However, it will cost Black a lot of time to mobilize his kingside pieces to create kingside counterplay or contest the queenside.

Looking at this as against Nyback-Carlsen, I think of this game as one where both sides have more to do – White needs to mobilize his queenside pawns, Black needs to mobilize his kingside pieces, and it is basically a race as to who succeeds. This position seems playable for both sides, as illustrated by its current topicality.

a) 11...h5 is an interesting attempt, aiming to bring the king to h7. E.Podolchenko-A.Rustemov, Minsk 2008, continued 12 f3 ♗e6 13 ♗d2 ♔g8

14 ♖fc1 ♔h7 15 c6 ♘a6 16 ♕a4 ♘c7 17 ♗e2 ♘fe8 18 ♗xa5 ♘d6 19 b3 and White, having won a third pawn, went on to win the game in 39 moves.

b) 11...♗a6 12 a4 and now:

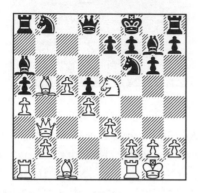

b1) 12...♘e4? is not a good move, though Popov can certainly be forgiven for such play in the early days of this line. The knight invites White's central play with f3 and e4 which we have already seen in the note to Black's 11th. 13 ♘d3 ♗b7 14 f3 and White went on to win after several adventures in L.Aronian-V.Popov, Moscow 2005 (1-0 in 36).

b2) 12...♗c8! 13 f3 ♗e6! is the manoeuvre which has rehabilitated the line, and would make a good exercise in a book on prophylactic thinking. White can't play e4 because of the discovered attack on the queen. Black has won both games played in this line, namely A.Rustemov-K.Sakaev, Sochi 2005, and S.Martinovic-R.Szuhanek, Banja Junakovic 2010, though I wouldn't say the debate is closed.

7...♗g7 8 b4

8...♗g4

8...a5 is more popular and seems more logical. White is not in time to support his b-pawn with a3 and has to take on a5.

9 ♗b2 ♘bd7

9...a5 is pointless in view of 10 a3.

10 ♘e2!

Directed against the...e5-break.

10...♕c7 11 a4 0-0 12 ♖a2

F.Vallejo Pons-A.Shirov, Monte Carlo 2005, continued 12 ♖a3 ♖fb8 13 ♕a1 ♗xf3 14 gxf3 ♕c8 15 ♗c3 ♘e8 16 f4 ♘df6 17 ♘g3 e6 18 ♔e2 ♘c7 19 ♗d2 ♕d8 20 ♕g1 ♔f8 21 ♕g2 bxa4 22 ♖xa4 ♖a7 23 ♖ha1 ♖ba8 24 ♖1a2 ♘d7 25 ♕f3 ♕h4 and now the recorded score of the blindfold/rapid game continues 26 ♕g4 ♕xg4+. Hmmm.

12...♖a7 13 h3 ♗xf3 14 gxf3 ♖fa8

14...e5? doesn't work: 15 axb5 cxb5 16 ♕a1 with a clear advantage.

15 f4

Now White has put the brakes on the ...e5-break and must stand better. Interestingly, *Rybka* (at least my version) assesses this as equal, which must show too little respect to White's bishop pair and queenside prospects.

15...e6 16 0-0 ♘e8 17 ♕c2 ♕b7 18 ♖fa1 ♗f6 19 ♕b3 ♗d8 20 ♕a3 ♘c7 21 ♗c3 bxa4

Passive play would have been met by ♘c1-b3 and, if allowed, to a5.

22 ♕xa4 ♘b5 23 ♗d2 ♗c7 24 ♔h1 ♘f6 25 ♕c2 ♘h5

26 ♘g1!

Starting a beautiful regrouping – look at the position after White's 32nd.

26...♕c8 27 ♕d1 ♗b8 28 ♕g4 f5 29 ♕g2 ♖g7 30 ♘f3 ♖aa7 31 ♖g1 ♘f6 32 ♘e5 ♘e4 33 ♗e1 ♘f6 34 ♖a1 ♕e8

Now Aronian uses his h-pawn as a battering ram.

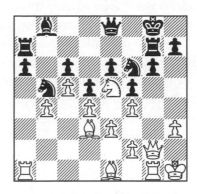

35 h4 ♔h8 36 ♕h3 ♗c7 37 ♖g2 ♗d8 38 ♗e2 ♔g8 39 h5 ♘xh5 40 ♗xh5 gxh5 41 ♖xg7+ ♖xg7 42 ♖xa6

Breaking through on the queenside – a fantastic example of the principle of two weaknesses.

42...♗f6 43 ♘xc6 h6 44 ♖b6 ♔h7 45 ♖xb5 ♕xc6 46 ♖a5 ♕e8 47 b5 h4 48 f3 ♕h5 49 ♖a1 ♕e8 50 ♖a5 ♗d8 51 b6 ♗f6 52 ♗f2 ♗d8 53 ♖a1 ♗f6 54 ♖g1 ♖b7 55 e4 dxe4 56 fxe4 ♕a8 57 d5 ♖g7 58 ♕f3 ♖xg1+ 59 ♗xg1 exd5 60 ♕h5 fxe4 61 ♕f7+ 1-0

A remarkable achievement by Aronian, winning so convincingly against a very strong GM and a6-Slav specialist.

After a white win following c5, it's time for a counter-example:

Game 18
B.Kelly-O.De la Riva Aguado
Calvia Olympiad 2004
Slav Defence

This game was very highly memorable for me, because it occurred at a round in the Calvia Olympiad where Brian Kelly and I were playing on adjacent boards for Ireland and both needed wins to complete our norms (IM for me, GM for him). As it happens, we both lost, though I went on to complete my IM title later in the event.

To compound the norm situation, I think Brian's opponent completed his GM title during the Olympiad, with this game playing a central role.

1 d4 d5 2 c4 c6 3 ♘c3 ♘f6 4 e3 a6 5 ♘f3 b5 6 b3 ♗g4 7 h3 ♗xf3 8 gxf3

A strategically ambitious variation. If White can prevent both ...e5 and ...c5 he'll have a lasting advantage.

8...♘bd7

Threatening ...e5.

9 f4 e6

Now the "threat" is to take twice on c4 and break with ...c5 (d5 would not work in response in view of ...♘b6).

10 c5

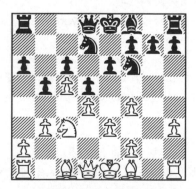

Hence White sets up the big bind. It should be obvious that Black needs to do something quickly, since if White

consolidates we will get into the patterns of Aronian-Volkov.

10...♘e4

This move fits the bill nicely. Black sacrifices his e4-outpost, but gets the d5-square in return. He can consolidate his control of the light squares with ...f5.

11 ♘xe4 dxe4

12 ♗d2?

The start of a plan which is too slow.

12 ♗g2 f5 13 f3 is the correct approach. The pawn can't be held on e4 which means the light-squared bishop will be a significant factor (incidentally, the check on h4 is nothing). However, these considerations are only enough to level the chances. J.Gustafsson-Ni Hua, Reggio Emilia 2008, continued 13...exf3 14 ♗xf3 ♖c8 15 ♕e2 ♘f6 16 ♗d2 ♕d7 17 ♖g1 ♔f7 18 0-0-0 g6 19 ♔c2 ♗e7 and a draw was agreed.

12...f5 13 ♖g1 g6 14 ♕c2 ♗e7 15 0-0-0 ♗h4 16 ♖g2

A really poor square for the rook, in particular because the square is needed for the bishop to make the f3-

break effective.

16...♘f6 17 ♗e2 a5 18 f3

This doesn't really work since there's no pressure on e4. Brian's attempt to get rid of this pawn thus gifts Black several tempi and leads to a tactically critical situation for White.

18...a4 19 fxe4 ♘xe4 20 ♗f3?!

It's funny how one forms views around individual games. My initial comments here read "A remarkably bad move from a player I rate very highly. It should be pretty obvious that allowing the a-file to open is a strategic disaster from White's viewpoint; it quickly turns into a tactical debacle also."

However, this is just completely wrong! In fact, White's blunder only comes at move 22. I would still prefer 20 b4 though, keeping Black's queen-side play bottled up. This looks equal.

20...axb3 21 axb3 ♕d5

22 ♗e1??

22 ♔b2 was one of the moves which would have held the position, though after 22...♗f6 and kingside castling Black must be for choice.

22...♗xe1 23 ♗xe4 ♕xe4 0-1

24 ♕xe4 fxe4 25 ♖xe1 ♖a1+ 26 ♔d2 ♖a2+ is an unfortunate finish.

Game 19
D.Pavasovic-G.Erdene
Khanty Mansiysk
Olympiad 2010
Caro-Kann Defence

This game shows some of the tactical ways in which a queenside space advantage can play out.

1 e4 c6 2 d4 d5 3 exd5 cxd5 4 c4 ♘f6 5 ♘c3 ♘c6 6 ♗g5 e6 7 c5 ♗e7 8 ♗b5 0-0 9 ♘f3 ♘e4 10 ♗xe7 ♘xe7 11 ♖c1 b6

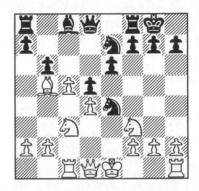

12 c6

I once played 12 ♗d3 here, a move which must have some value as it was also Jakovenko's choice: 12...bxc5 (the most popular response, which is not to say the best; 12...f5 was the choice of a leading Caro-Kann specialist: 13 b4 a5 14 ♘a4 axb4 15 ♘xb6 ♖xa2 16 0-0 ♗a6 17 ♗xa6 ♖xa6 18 ♘e5 and a draw was agreed in D.Jakovenko-I.Khenkin, Sochi

2007) 13 ♘xe4 dxe4 14 ♗xe4 ♖b8 (14...♕a5+ has also been tested in a number of games) 15 ♖xc5, and now my opponent erred with 15...♘d5?! (15...♖xb2 16 0-0 h6 17 ♕a1 ♖b6 was agreed drawn in B.Ivkov-B.Lalic, Yugoslavia 2000) 16 b3 ♗a6 17 ♗d3 ♗xd3 (17...♗b7 18 ♕d2 ♕d6 19 ♘e5 is a slight advantage for White) 18 ♕xd3 with a clear advantage for White, and I went on to win in S.Collins-M.Kantorik, Teplice 2011 (1-0 in 48).

12...♕d6 13 0-0

13 ♕a4 a6 14 0-0 ♗d7 15 cxd7 axb5 16 ♕xb5 ♘xc3 17 ♖xc3 ♖xa2 18 ♘e5 f6 19 ♘c6 ♕xd7 20 ♘xe7+ ♕xe7 21 ♕xb6 ♖a7 22 ♖c6 ♖b7 23 ♖xe6 ♖xb6 24 ♖xe7 ♖xb2 25 ♖d7 ♖d2 26 ♖xd5 ♖b8 27 ♖e1 ♖bb2 28 ♖d7 h5 29 ♖f1 and a draw was agreed in A.Naiditsch-P.Leko Dortmund 2009.

13...a6 14 ♗d3

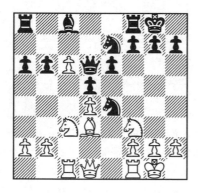

14...♘f6?

A horribly unprincipled move which unsurprisingly meets a cute tactical refutation.

Black should immediately eliminate the advanced pawn with 14...♘xc6. While White has some initiative in the arising positions, it tends to fizzle out: 15 ♘xe4 dxe4 16 ♗xe4 ♗b7 17 ♘e5 (17 d5 exd5 18 ♕xd5 ♕xd5 19 ♗xd5 ♖ac8 20 ♖fd1 h6 21 h4 ♖fd8 22 ♔h2 ♔f8 23 ♔g3 ♔e7 24 b4 ♗a8 25 a3 was marginally better for White in A.Naiditsch-F.Berkes, Hungarian League 2009 (1-0 in 81)) 17...♖ac8 18 ♕d3 ♖fd8 19 ♗xc6 ♗xc6 20 ♕xa6 ♕d5 21 ♘xc6 ♖xc6 is a position where White has no advantage, despite his extra pawn:

a) 22 ♖c3 ♖cd6 23 ♖d1 and White offered a draw since there was no way to make progress in D.Pavasovic-R.Ruck, Sibenik 2009.

b) 22 h3 g6 23 a4 ♖xc1 24 ♖xc1 ♕xd4 25 ♖c8 ♖xc8 26 ♕xc8+ ♔g7 27 ♕c2 e5 28 ♔f1 h5 29 g3 h4 30 gxh4 ♕xh4 was agreed drawn in A.Zhigalko-F.Berkes, Dresden Olympiad 2008.

c) Finally, 22 g3 ♖xc1 23 ♖xc1 ♕xd4 24 ♖c8 ♕d1+ 25 ♔g2 ♕d5+ 26 ♔g1 ♕d1+ with perpetual check as in the game D.Jakovenko-K.Asrian, Heraklio 2007.

15 ♘e5 ♘xc6

In Z.Lanka-B.Bente, Hamburg 2009, Black tried to dodge what was coming with 15...♖a7, but unsurprisingly he was not organized enough to win the c6-pawn given the key squares this pawn controlled on the black queenside. 16 ♕b3 ♕b8 17 ♗b1 b5 18 a4 b4 19 a5 ♖c7 20 ♘a4 ♘e4 21 ♘b6 and White won in 32 moves.

16 ♘xc6 ♕xc6

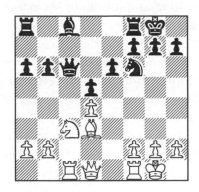

17 ♘e4! dxe4

The best move, but also desperation.

17...♕e8 18 ♘xf6+ gxf6 permits the immediate and typical tactical conclusion 19 ♗xh7+! since the rook is ready to swing to the kingside via c3, after which it will offer the white queen decisive support.

18 ♖xc6 exd3

Two pieces for a queen, against a GM... probably time to resign.

19 ♖xb6 ♘d5 20 ♖d6 ♖b8 21 ♕d2 h6 22 ♖c1 a5 23 b3 ♗b7 24 f3 ♖a8 25 ♕xd3 ♖fb8 26 ♕b5 h5 27 ♖d7 ♗a6 28 ♕xa5 ♗b5 29 ♖a7 ♖xa7 30 ♕xa7 ♖d8 31 ♕b7 1-0

The c6!? Novelty

I can't really think of a heading for this section, which shows a concept which struck me as entirely fresh. I suppose in its effect it is similar to the well-known line 1 d4 ♘f6 2 c4 g6 3 ♘f3 ♗g7 4 g3 d5 5 ♗g2 dxc4 6 ♘a3 c3, but Morozevich's idea is somehow so much better!

1 d4 ♘f6 2 c4 e6 3 ♘c3 ♗b4 4 ♕c2 0-0 5 ♘f3 c5 6 dxc5 ♘a6 7 c6!!

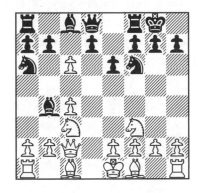

This move divided the commentators.

Krasenkow noted: "This move looks so senseless... However, if you want to avoid thoroughly investigated theoretical lines, you must look for paradoxical decisions."

However, in *Chess Today*, Alex Baburin was more sympathetic: "A novelty on move 7 in a well-known position! Let's try to figure out its idea. First, White is not losing a tempo, as Black will play ...♘c5 at some stage anyway. The idea of 7 c6!? is to change the pawn formation and to worsen the prospects of the c8-bishop. Objectively it should not be too dangerous for Black, but the surprise value in this game must have been great!"

I just find it remarkable that this move was never played before, with players automatically opting for some alternative like 7 a3. Of course, now 7 c6 is perhaps the main move in this position! 85 games are in my database, and this number is increasing weekly.

7...dxc6

7...bxc6 was extensively tested in the blitz tournament during the event, and has since become very much the "main line".

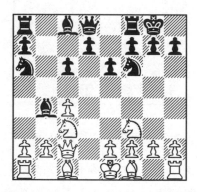

It could be that capturing with the b-pawn is objectively superior – in any event, it is more principled to capture towards the centre. This position has been discussed in a large number of games between 2650+ players, but let's stick with a recent example from the inventor of the line: 8 e3 ♘c5 9 ♗d2 a5 10 a3 ♗xc3 11 ♗xc3 ♘ce4 12 ♗xf6 ♘xf6 13 c5 a4 14 0-0-0 ♖a5 15 ♔b1 ♕e7 16 ♖c1 ♗a6 17 ♗xa6 ♖xa6 18 ♖hd1 with unclear play in A.Morozevich-E.Alekseev, Saratov 2011 (1-0 in 60).

Once Nimzo-Indian players had

some time to think about Morozevich's remarkable move, they discovered that 7...d5!? also has some appeal.

Taking on b7 would leave Black with an intimidating lead in development which can increase with tempo after ...♖c8, so more sensible is 8 a3 ♗xc3+ 9 ♕xc3 ♘e4 10 ♕c2 bxc6 11 e3 ♕a5+ 12 ♗d2 ♘xd2 13 ♘xd2 c5 14 ♗d3 h6 15 0-0 ♗b7 with reasonable play for Black in A.Morozevich-V.Ivanchuk, Leon 2009 (½-½ in 51).

8 a3 ♗xc3+ 9 ♕xc3

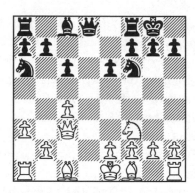

9...♘c5

Krasenkow gives 9...♘e4?! 10 ♕e5 ♘ac5 11 b4 f6 12 ♕f4 ♘c3 13 ♗d2 ♘5e4 14 ♗xc3 ♘xc3 15 ♕e3 ♘a4 16 ♕b3 ♘b6 17 c5 ♘d5 18 e4 with a clear plus for White.

10 ♗e3 ♘ce4?

This is a mistake, but White already had a nice game. Krasenkow suggests 10...♕e7; Baburin suggests 10...♘fe4.

11 ♕e5!

The vulnerability of the e4-knight forces further concessions.

11...b5 12 g4!

Morozevich continues with energy and precision.

12...c5

12...h6 13 h4 merely helps White open lines on the kingside.

13 g5 ♕a5+ 14 b4 cxb4 15 gxf6

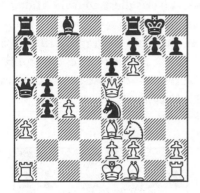

White is winning, despite Ponomariov's dour resistance.

15...♗b7 16 ♗d2 ♖fc8 17 ♗xb4 ♕b6 18 c5 ♕d8 19 ♖g1 g6 20 ♖d1 ♕xf6 21 c6 ♗xc6 22 ♖g4 ♕xe5 23 ♘xe5 f5 24 ♘xc6 ♖xc6 25 ♗g2 a5 26 ♗xe4 fxe4 27 ♗d2 ♖c4 28 ♖g5 ♖a4 29 ♖xb5 ♖xa3 30 ♖b7 a4 31 ♗f4 ♖b3 32 ♖xb3 axb3 33 ♖b1 e3 34 ♗xe3 ♖b8 35 ♔d2 ♖b4 36 f3 e5 37 ♗f2 1-0

The b4 Advance

This section is a miscellany of b4-advances from White. While the g4-advance is very well documented in Watson's books, I have noticed that b4 can often serve similar purposes of disrupting Black's queenside. I have not covered the standard examples of normal pawn play on the queenside (for instance, b4 as part of the minority

attack in the QGD Exchange Variation has been played in literally thousands of games), but rather focussed on examples with more tactical content.

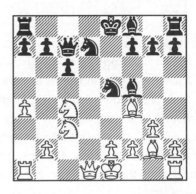

> **Game 21**
> **J.R.Capablanca-M.Euwe**
> Amsterdam 1931
> *Slav Defence*

1 d4 ♘f6 2 ♘f3 d5 3 c4 c6 4 ♘c3 dxc4 5 a4 ♗f5 6 ♘e5 ♘bd7 7 ♘xc4 ♕c7 8 g3 e5 9 dxe5 ♘xe5 10 ♗f4 ♘fd7 11 ♗g2

This line used to be hot theory before being overtaken by more sedate tries such as 7...♘b6 8 ♘e5 a5 (a speciality of Ivan Sokolov), or the game-killing 6...e6 7 f3 c5 8 e4 ♗g6 9 ♗e3 cxd4 10 ♕xd4 ♕xd4 11 ♗xd4 ♘fd7 (a wall fortified by Vladimir Kramnik).

Black plays dynamically, achieving the ...e5-break and obtaining active central positions for his pieces. This line was one of several completely redefined by Alexander Morozevich, both with the modern 11...g5!? and the more classical 11...f6. The utility of the latter move, providing some pawn support for the knight on e5, is clearly demonstrated by the current game.

11...♗e6 12 ♘xe5 ♘xe5 13 0-0 ♕a5

This seems to be an ideal square for the queen, holding the e5-knight without allowing a pin on the h2-b8 diagonal, and seemingly restraining White's ambitions of a queenside minority attack with b4-b5. However, these multiple functions indicate the problem, namely that the queen can be rapidly overloaded.

14 ♘e4 ♖d8 15 ♕c2 ♗e7

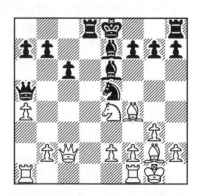

16 b4!!

Perhaps this isn't such a difficult move, however I remember being quite struck by it on first reading Golombek's enthusiastic *Capablanca's Best Games*. The pawn moves, unprotected, on to a doubly attacked square, but horribly upsets Black's piece co-ordination.

16...♗xb4

16...♕c7 is a hard move to play, and also does not seem to solve Black's problems. After 17 ♕c3 f6 18 ♘g5! ♗g4 19 ♖ad1 White is much better.

17 ♕b2 f6

18 ♖fb1??

A very poor move, after which White is not threatening to take on b4 in view of check on the back rank.

18 ♗xe5 fxe5 19 ♖ab1 was straightforward and very strong: 19...♖d4 20 ♘g5 ♗f5 21 ♕b3 ♕c7 22 e3 and Black cannot stabilize the position, while 19...♗e7 20 ♕xb7 gives White a structural advantage with a continuing initiative.

18...0-0 19 ♗xe5 fxe5 20 ♘g5 ♗c3?

20...♗f7 was indicated, after which White has nothing special, though he still has some compensation, for instance 21 ♖d1 ♗c3 22 ♕c2 ♗g6 23 ♕b3+ ♔h8 24 ♖xd8 ♖xd8 25 ♖b1 with enough for the pawn.

21 ♕c2 ♗f5 22 ♗e4

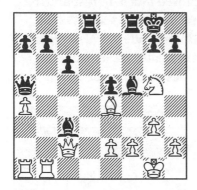

22...g6?

Euwe collapses. The computer suggests the paradoxical 22...♔h8!? 23 ♗xf5 e4 24 ♘e6 ♕xf5 25 ♕xc3 ♕xe6 26 ♖xb7 ♖d7, which gives Black some drawing chances in the major-piece endgame.

22...♗xa1 was also more tenacious: 23 ♗xf5 ♔h8 24 ♘e6 e4 25 ♗xh7 ♔xh7 26 ♕xe4+ ♔g8 27 ♘xf8 ♖xf8 28 ♖xa1 ♕f5 with some drawing chances.

23 ♕a2+ ♔g7 24 ♖xb7+ ♖d7 25 ♖ab1 ♕a6 26 ♕b3

26 ♖xd7+ ♗xd7 27 ♕a3 was sharper.

26...♖xb7 27 ♕xb7+ ♕xb7 28 ♖xb7+ ♔g8 29 ♗xc6 ♖d8 30 ♖xa7

The advance 30 e4! was also strong, but Capablanca's solution is fully sufficient.

30...♖d6 31 ♗e4 ♗d7 32 h4 ♗d4 33 ♖a8+ ♔g7 34 e3 ♗c3 35 ♗f3 1-0

Game 22
R.Dautov-J.Waitzkin
Bad Wiessee 1997
Queen's Gambit Accepted

1 d4 d5 2 c4 dxc4 3 ♘f3 ♘f6 4 e3 e6 5 ♗xc4 a6 6 ♗b3 c5 7 0-0 ♘c6 8 ♘c3 ♗e7 9 ♕e2 cxd4 10 ♖d1 d3 11 ♖xd3 ♕c7 12 e4 0-0 13 e5 ♘d7 14 ♗f4 ♘c5 15 ♖e3 ♘xb3 16 axb3 ♗d7 17 ♖d1 ♖ad8 18 ♘g5 h6 19 ♘ge4 ♘xe5 20 ♖e1 ♕a5

So far, the game has been a typical QGA-gone-wrong for Black. White pushed his pawn to e5, creating a king-side space advantage and serious threats on that flank, and the former US prodigy responded by taking this pawn at the cost of a pin on the h2-b8 diagonal. Having seen the previous example, the winning solution just pops into your head:

21 b4!! ♗xb4 22 ♘f6+ gxf6 23 ♗xe5

White has a completely winning attack.

23...♗xc3 24 ♖g3+ ♔h8 25 ♕e3 ♗d2 26 ♗xf6+ ♔h7 27 ♖g7+ ♔h8 28 ♕g3 1-0

Game 23
A.Baburin-S.Collins
Galway Masters 2005
Slav Defence

This is a tidy game from Alex, completely crushing me in a pretty standard Slav.

1 d4 d5 2 c4 c6 3 ♘f3 ♘f6 4 e3

A line which has gone from being considered completely innocuous to being one of White's main attempts at breaking the rock-solid Slav. Black still has very comfortable development, but White will gain the two bishops in most lines, which at least gives him something to look forward to.

4...♗f5 5 ♘c3 e6 6 ♘h4 ♗g6 7 ♘xg6 hxg6 8 ♕b3 ♕c7 9 g3 ♘bd7 10 ♗g2

10...♗d6

Most serious guys seem to prefer putting the bishop on e7 and castling kingside, keeping the position closed. I do an amazingly good job over the next five moves of making the g2-bishop (which has no opponent) the best piece

on the board.

11 0-0 dxc4 12 ♕xc4 e5 13 dxe5 ♘xe5 14 ♕e2 ♘eg4

Doubtless I was looking forward to giving up a piece on g3 or f2, but reality proved much more mundane.

15 e4! 0-0-0 16 h3 ♗c5 17 ♗f4

Unfortunately, Alex noticed my threat against his g3-pawn.

17...♘e5 18 ♖ac1 ♔b8 19 b4!

There was nothing wrong with the immediate 19 ♘d5 but Alex's move is even more incisive.

19...♗xb4 20 ♘d5

Ripping open the long diagonal which, in combination with the half-open b-file, will create a real problem for Black on b7.

20...♘xd5 21 exd5 ♗d6 22 dxc6 b6

22...♘d3 was another try, but after 23 ♗xd6 ♖xd6 24 ♖b1 b6, the precise 25 a4! leaves Black unable to stabilize the queenside.

23 ♖fd1 f6 24 a4

24 ♗e3 followed by ♕a6 was perhaps more direct, but Alex's play is beautifully thematic and fully ade-

quate to bring home the full point.
24...♗a3 25 ♖b1 g5 26 ♗xe5 fxe5

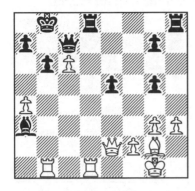

And now a suitable end, given Black's total failure to contain the g2-bishop.
27 ♖d7! ♖xd7 28 cxd7

I really should have had the grace to resign here, but instead played on until the writing was truly on the wall.
28...♖f8 29 ♖d1 ♗c5 30 ♕e4 1-0

Using the Rook's Pawn

Rook's pawns are among the most important pawns to master. One of the attractions of pushing a rook's pawn up the board is that it doesn't tend to create many weaknesses – by definition a rook's pawn cannot leave an outpost by itself (for instance, an a-pawn controls squares on the b-file, all of which are covered by the c-pawn; by contrast, moving a b-pawn leaves outposts on the a-file). Even the outposts that might be created tend to be less significant since they are located away from the centre.

Moving a rook's pawn is a natural response to a fianchetto setup (e.g. meeting ...g6 with h2-h4-h5). However, even in the absence of a fianchetto, moving a rook's pawn can have the effect of developing a rook from its starting square. If the file opens, the rook is perfectly placed. If it doesn't, the rook is still active, and might be brought into the game via a rook lift (e.g. when White pushes his pawn to a5, the rook may develop via a3 or a4 and swing to the right).

Two games on this topic, by those giants of strategy, Kasparov... and Collins. If you need more material, Larsen tended to push his rook's pawns at every opportunity.

1 e4 c5 2 ♘f3 d6 3 d4 cxd4 4 ♘xd4 ♘f6 5 ♘c3 a6 6 ♗e3 ♘g4

This was Kasparov's patent (of course, he was no slouch after 6...e5 and 6...e6 either, with both colours), preventing White from setting up an English Attack with f3, ♕d2, 0-0-0, g4 and so on. White can start with 6 f3 instead to try and prevent the knight hop, but then Black has some other options based around ...♕b6.
7 ♗g5 h6 8 ♗h4 g5 9 ♗g3 ♗g7

Black has established an aggressive formation on the kingside (normally the preserve of White in the English Attack) and his bishop is well established on the long diagonal, but at some cost of weakening key squares and giving White a lever with h4.

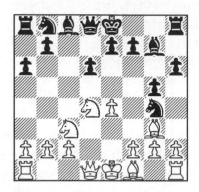

10 ♗e2

10 ♕d2 and 10 h3 are alternatives, but this is pure opening theory so we won't examine these moves. In all lines, interesting, unbalanced play results.

10...h5 11 ♗xg4 ♗xg4

Kasparov experimented with 11...hxg4 against the same opponent in Wijk aan Zee 1999. 12 0-0 e6 13 ♕d2 ♘d7! 14 ♗xd6 ♘e5 showed his concept. Shirov was forced to sacrifice a piece (certainly a concept he is comfortable with in any event!) with 15 ♘cb5 axb5 16 ♘xb5 f6 17 ♖fd1 ♔f7 18 ♕e2 ♗d7 19 ♗xe5 fxe5 20 ♘d6+ ♔g6 with good compensation for White, though Shirov stumbled and lost a technical game in 49 moves.

12 f3 ♗d7 13 0-0 ♘c6 14 ♗f2 e6 15 ♘ce2 ♘e5 16 b3

Now Kasparov sees a chance to increase his kingside space advantage. As

so often in his games, an ambitious strategic plan is accomplished with the help of some elegant tactics.

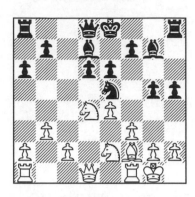

16...g4 17 f4 h4! 18 ♗e3

18 fxe5 dxe5 regains the piece, though there is some merit to White playing this way since the position opens, which gives him opportunities against the black king. Of course, if this attack is repelled, the black bishops will prove highly effective.

18...h3!

The knight is still immune.

19 g3 ♘c6

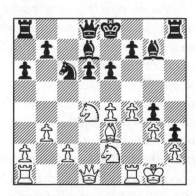

Kasparov's perspective on this position is striking: "The future importance of the long diagonal (a8-h1) is not yet clear, but from my experience I can guarantee that the white king is potentially in a much worse position than his black colleague. Any further opening of the long diagonal or the appearance of the queen on the second rank will create a deadly threat on g2. In fact, the pawn on h3 can be seen as a material advantage for Black, because it is so important that you could value it as a whole piece. It not only helps the queen to create mating threats, but in most endgames, this pawn will also guarantee Black a winning edge because of the threats that Black can create against the h2-pawn, when the black h-pawn is very close to the promotion square."

20 ♕d3 0-0 21 ♖ad1 f5 22 c4 ♕a5

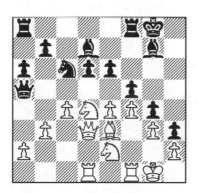

23 ♘c3

Kasparov and Rowson analyse 23 ♕d2 as being much better, though Black seems at least equal. In the game White was unable to deal with all the threats.

23...♖ae8 24 ♖fe1 e5 25 ♘xc6 ♗xc6 26

b4 ♕a3 27 b5 exf4 28 ♗xf4 axb5 29 cxb5 ♕c5+ 30 ♗e3 ♕xc3 31 bxc6 ♕xc6 32 ♕xd6 ♕xe4 33 ♕d5+ ♕xd5 34 ♖xd5 ♗c3 35 ♖e2 ♖e4 36 ♔f2 ♖fe8 37 ♖d3 ♗f6 38 ♖ed2

38...♖xe3! 0-1

A thematic finish. After 39 ♖xe3 ♖xe3 40 ♔xe3 ♗g5+ 41 ♔d3 ♗xd2 42 ♔xd2 the h-pawn shows its worth after 42...f4!.

Game 25
S.Collins-D.Volpinari
Turin Olympiad 2006
Sicilian Defence

1 e4 c5 2 ♘f3 e6 3 c3 d5 4 exd5 ♕xd5 5 d4 ♘f6 6 ♗e3 cxd4 7 cxd4 ♗b4+ 8 ♘c3 0-0 9 ♗d3 b6 10 0-0 ♗xc3 11 bxc3 ♗a6 12 ♗xa6 ♘xa6

Quite an interesting system for Black, and one which was the driving force behind the nuanced move order 6 a3!? which found favour for a while. Black, statically speaking, has a slightly healthier pawn structure and has exchanged two sets of minor pieces, but this comes at the cost of a spatial disadvantage and a slight passivity in his position.

13 ♕a4 ♕b7 14 c4 ♖fc8 15 ♖fc1 ♘b8 16 ♕b5!

White needs to get the a-pawn running.

16...♘bd7 17 a4 ♕c6 18 ♕b3 ♖ab8 19 ♗f4 ♖a8 20 h3 h6 21 a5!

Demonstrating that the structural imbalance is not necessarily in Black's favour. Black is now at hazard of being left with a weakness on the queenside which can counterbalance the requirement for protection of the c- and d-pawns (which, for the moment, look more like strengths).

21...♘e4 22 ♕e3 ♘ef6 23 ♕b3 ♘e4 24 ♕b2

White retains the tension, since it is unfavourable for Black to take on a5.

24...♘ef6 25 ♖a3!

One of the big benefits of a space advantage is that it makes it easy to manoeuvre one's pieces. This rook manoeuvre allows doubling (or more) on the a-file, but the rook can also play on any other central or queenside file, or swing to the kingside.

25...♘e4 26 ♕e2 ♘ef6 27 ♘e5 ♘xe5 28 ♗xe5 ♕e4 29 ♖e3 ♕g6 30 ♖g3 ♕f5 31 ♖e1 ♘e8 32 a6!

I was very happy with this move, all the more so because my teammate GM Alex Baburin seemed surprised/impressed by it. Rather than playing against a weakness on b6, which would give Black counterplay on the queenside files, I fix the weakness on a7.

32...♖c6 33 ♖f3 ♕g6 34 ♕a2 ♖ac8 35 d5

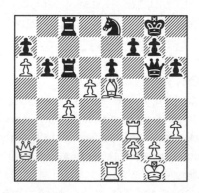

Both players were in time trouble around here.

35...exd5

35...♖xc4 had to be played (see Kasparov-Karpov, World Championship 1984, Game 6, for a similar example). 36 d6 ♖e4 37 ♖xe4 ♕xe4 38 ♖e3 ♕c6 39 ♖c3 ♕d7 40 ♖xc8 ♕xc8 41 ♕a4 ♘f6 42 ♗xf6 gxf6 43 g3! reaches a queen and pawn endgame which looks very promising for White, but at least I have some chances to go wrong, and the variation to get here is not trivial to find.

36 cxd5 ♖c2 37 ♕a4

With a classic, strategically winning position. The d-pawn is enormously powerful and the e8-knight is dominated. The pawn on a6 makes things even worse for Black.

37...♖2c4 38 ♕d7 f6 39 ♗f4 ♔h7 40 ♖g3 ♕h5 41 ♖xe8 1-0

Outposts

I'm somewhat reluctant to deal with outposts since they have been so well covered elsewhere. However, I decided to include a coverage based on two factors.

First, in the older material on outposts, there is a definite overestimation of the importance of an outpost (think white knight on d5 vs. black bishop on e7 in a Najdorf), without an adequate consideration of the other factors which tend to feature in such positions.

Second, I lost a crucial game in the Olympiad by not fully and intuitively

understanding the importance of an outpost on e5. This example (showing materialism and forcing thinking) is highly annoying for me and indicates an area of my game which needs work.

The coverage here will start with a few over-analysed examples by Fischer and Geller, before going on to the lesser-known "corrective" examples which show that outposts don't win games on their own. However, the importance of fully understanding outposts and their value was brought home to me in my game with Hansen at the Olympiad and this game, unfortunately, is also included.

Game 26
R.Fischer-O.Gadia
Mar del Plata 1960
Sicilian Defence

1 e4 c5 2 ♘f3 d6 3 d4 cxd4 4 ♘xd4 ♘f6 5 ♘c3 a6 6 ♗c4 e6 7 ♗b3 b5 8 0-0 ♗b7 9 f4 ♘c6 10 ♘xc6 ♗xc6 11 f5 e5 12 ♕d3 ♗e7 13 ♗g5 ♕b6+ 14 ♔h1 0-0

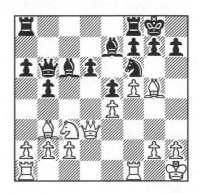

I first learned about outposts from Bobby Fischer's games in the 6 &c4 Najdorf. The weakness of Black's d5-square after ...e5 is something which Fischer's crystal-clear, accurate play revealed with ruthless precision.

This position is so embedded in my mind, and probably that of most experienced players, that it's worth remembering that Black's position looks like a completely typical Najdorf formation and, but for a couple of specific characteristics, Black would have an acceptable game.

In terms of control of the d5-square, Black can only rely on his knights and his light-squared bishop (clearly, the queen and rooks can also attack the square in theory but are too valuable to realistically threaten a minor piece there). All other things being equal, trading like for like, White will not be able to exploit the square because his knights and light-squared bishop will be traded for their black counterparts.

The major imbalancing factor available to White is his dark-squared bishop. If he trades this for a black knight, suddenly he has a piece which can control d5 (a knight) against a piece which can't (a bishop). Normally Black can avoid the nightmare scenario of a knight on d5 against a dark-squared bishop, but in this example he has no counterplay and no method of retaining a piece which can contest the d5-square.

15 &xf6!

Getting rid of the defender.

15...&xf6 16 &d5!

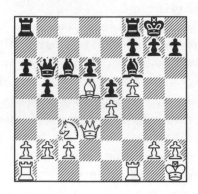

Getting the classic 'good knight vs. bad dark-square bishop', a position which is probably winning.

16...&ac8 17 &xc6 &xc6

Gadia makes it easy, presumably for instructive purposes. 17...Wxc6 would at least force White to spend a move defending c2 before hopping with his knight.

18 &ad1 &fc8 19 &d5 Wd8 20 c3 &e7

21 &a1!

More beautiful play, putting the rook behind the a-pawn to support an opening of the queenside.

21...f6?

None of Gadia's moves are great, but his final two are the worst.

22 a4 ℤb8?? 23 ♘xe7+ 1-0

1 e4 c5 2 ♘f3 d6 3 d4 cxd4 4 ♘xd4 ♘f6 5 ♘c3 a6 6 ♗e2 e5 7 ♘b3 ♗e6 8 0-0 ♘bd7 9 f4 ♕c7 10 f5 ♗c4 11 a4 ℤc8 12 ♗e3 ♗e7 13 a5

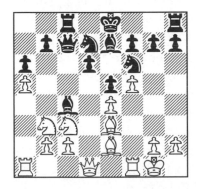

13...h5?

The inventor of the opening in this game was also an eternal optimist. Here he makes an attacking gesture on the kingside which crucially compromises his position, not because of any weakening per se, but rather because it costs a crucial tempo which allows White to stabilize the position.

14 ♗xc4 ♕xc4 15 ℤa4 ♕c7

15...♕c6 doesn't really annoy White,

who can continue with his plan of improving his position. It also makes it next to impossible for Black to achieve the ...b5 break.

16 h3 h4 17 ℤf2 b5 18 axb6 ♘xb6 19 ♗xb6

19 ℤxa6 ♘c4 gives Black excellent counterplay.

19...♕xb6 20 ♕e2 ℤa8 21 ♔h2 0-0 22 ℤf1 ℤa7 23 ℤfa1 ℤfa8

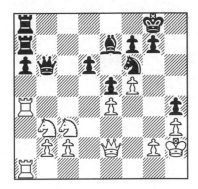

24 ℤ1a2

Bringing the rook from f2 to a2 is clearly the way to free the b3-knight. White has the time for this because he absolutely dominates. Bronstein suggested 24 ♕d3 with the aim of ♘a5 when ...♕xb2 would lose to ℤb1, but Geller notes that this method of playing allows the black queen to penetrate to f2, something he was keen to avoid.

24...♗d8 25 ♘a5 ℤc8 26 ♘c4 ♕c6 27 ♘e3

It's all like clockwork but, to emphasize the theme of this section, normally Black has sufficient counterplay in the Najdorf to prevent White accomplishing such a smooth squeeze.

27...a5 28 ♖c4 ♕a6 29 b3 ♗b6 30 ♖xc8+ ♕xc8 31 ♘ed5 ♘xd5 32 ♘xd5

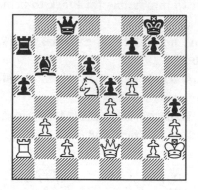

Black is strategically lost, though Geller's conversion is as smooth as any you will see from such a position.

32...♕c5 33 ♖a1 ♕f2 34 ♕xf2 ♗xf2 35 ♖f1 ♗d4

35...♗g3+ 36 ♔g1 leaves the bishop stuck on g3, while the white king can easily enter the game via f1 and e2 once the rook moves.

36 c3 ♗c5 37 g4 hxg3+ 38 ♔xg3 ♖b7 39 ♖b1 f6 40 ♔f3 ♔f7 41 ♔e2 ♖b8 42 b4 g6

43 ♔d3

43 fxg6+ ♔xg6 44 bxc5 ♖xb1 45 c6 ♖b8 46 c7 ♖h8 47 c8♕ ♖xc8 48 ♘e7+ is

absolutely forcing and absolutely devastating.

43...gxf5 44 exf5 axb4 45 cxb4 ♗d4 46 ♖c1 ♔g7 47 ♖c7+ ♔h6 48 ♔e4 ♔g5 49 ♖h7 ♗f2 50 ♖g7+ ♔h4 51 ♔f3 ♗e1 52 ♔g2 ♖f8 53 b5 ♗a5 54 b6 ♗xb6 55 ♘xb6 ♖b8 56 ♖g4+ ♔h5 57 ♘d5 1-0

Game 28
R.Fischer-R.Cardoso
New York 1957
Sicilian Defence

1 e4 c5 2 ♘f3 d6 3 d4 cxd4 4 ♘xd4 ♘f6 5 ♘c3 a6 6 ♗c4 e6 7 0-0

Of course, if the d5-square were a truly fatal weakness, the Najdorf would be unplayable. We know that there is more going on in these positions than just the central outpost. Ironically, Fischer himself demonstrated a true model of how Black should handle White's attempts to jump to d5, in his favourite system: 7 ♗b3 b5 8 f4 ♗b7 9 f5 e5 10 ♘de2 ♘bd7 11 ♗g5 ♗e7 12 ♘g3 ♖c8 13 0-0

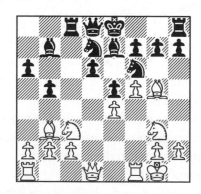

13...h5! (a beautiful disruptive move) 14 h4 b4 15 ♗xf6 ♗xf6 16 ♘d5 ♗xh4 17 ♘xh5 ♕g5 18 f6 g6 19 ♘g7+ ♔d8 20 ♖f3 ♗g3 21 ♕d3 ♗h2+ 22 ♔f1 ♘c5 23 ♖h3 ♖h4 24 ♕f3 ♘xb3 25 axb3 ♖xh3 26 ♕xh3 ♗xd5 27 exd5 ♕xf6+ 28 ♔e1 ♕f4 and White resigned in R.Byrne-R.Fischer, Sousse 1967.

7...♗d7 8 ♗b3 ♘c6 9 ♗e3 ♗e7 10 f4 ♕c7 11 f5 ♘xd4 12 ♗xd4 b5 13 a3 e5 14 ♗e3 ♗c6 15 ♘d5

Here 15 ♗g5 runs into 15...♘xe4. That, in fact, isn't the end of the story, because 16 ♗xe7 ♔xe7 (or 16...♕xe7 17 ♗d5 ♗xd5 18 ♕xd5 ♕a7+ 19 ♔h1 ♘xc3 20 ♕xd6! ♘a4 21 f6! with an attack) 17 ♘d5+ ♗xd5 18 ♕xd5 gives White full compensation on the light squares. However, Fischer's try gives him a risk-free advantage.

15...♘xd5 16 ♗xd5 ♗xd5 17 ♕xd5

This is less clear cut than the classic "good knight vs. bad bishop" scenarios which prevailed in Fischer-Gadia and Geller-Najdorf. Here, the bishop on e3 does not dominate the board the same way the d5-knight did in those games.

However, the square is still chronically weak, and Fischer uses it as a jumping point for both his queen and his king. In addition, this game is a classic example of White's queenside options.

17...♖c8 18 c3 ♕c4 19 ♕b7 ♕c6 20 ♕xc6+ ♖xc6 21 a4!

Opening the a-file.

21...♔d7 22 axb5 axb5 23 ♖a7+ ♖c7 24 ♖fa1

Textbook play from Fischer.

24...♖b8 25 ♔f2 ♖bb7

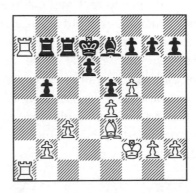

26 ♖xb7!

Another remarkable decision. It seems tempting to keep the passive black rooks on the board and try to do something with the active white ones. However, one rook is enough to control the a-file. Also, as we will see, Fischer isn't worried about a pure bishop endgame. In some respects, this move reminds me of Fischer's 22nd move in Game 7 of his 1971 Candidates Final with Petrosian which, however obvious it looks in retrospect, remains one of the most surprising decisions ever taken in top-flight chess.

26...♖xb7 27 ♔e2 ♗d8

Clearly 27...b4 28 c4 doesn't help matters – another pawn is fixed on a dark square, where it will likely fall to a combined attack from a rook on a4, a king on b3, and a bishop on d2.

28 ♔d3 h6

28...♗b6 is a move Black would very much like to play, trading his passive bishop. His problem is that the rook endgame after 29 ♗xb6 ♖xb6 30 ♖a7+ ♔e8 is completely hopeless. The best metric for judging rook and pawn endgames is not material but activity. Here it can easily be seen that both white pieces are dramatically more active than their black counterparts. White wins as he chooses, most convincingly by creating more kingside opportunities starting with 31 g4!.

29 ♖a8 h5 30 b4 ♗e7

Conceding that ...♗b6 is still unplayable.

31 ♖g8

It is interesting that Fischer rejected 31 ♖h8 h4 32 ♗f2. White wins a pawn, but the rook and pawn endgame after

32...♔c6 33 ♗xh4 ♗xh4 34 ♖xh4 ♖d7 followed by ...d5 gives Black a measure of counterplay. Fischer correctly prefers to keep Cardoso bottled up.

31...♗f6 32 ♖f8

Fischer is still searching for an additional kingside weakness.

32...♔c6 33 c4!

Creating a passed pawn. The backward d6-pawn is unable to advance, leaving White effectively a pawn ahead.

33...♖d7 34 ♖a8 bxc4+ 35 ♔xc4 ♖c7

36 ♖a7!

Finally exchanging rooks and entering a winning bishop endgame. Note that Fischer only played this after his king gained access to c4. Had he done so earlier, matters would not have been nearly so clear since Black could meet c4 with ...♔c6 after which an exchange on b5 would have led to a blockade.

36...♖xa7 37 ♗xa7 ♗d8 38 ♗e3 f6

Here Fischer doesn't have a knight to occupy his favourite square, but the king will do just as well.

39 b5+ ♔d7 40 ♔d5 ♗a5 41 ♗a7 ♗b4

42 ♗b8 ♗c5 43 g3! ♔e7

43...♗b4 44 b6 ♗c5 45 b7 also wins.

44 ♔c6 g6 45 fxg6 f5 46 ♗xd6+ 1-0

> *Game 29*
> **Y.Averbakh-T.Petrosian**
> USSR Championship
> Tbilisi 1959
> *Sicilian Defence*

1 e4 c5 2 ♘f3 d6 3 d4 cxd4 4 ♘xd4 ♘f6 5 ♘c3 a6 6 ♗e2 e5 7 ♘b3 ♗e7 8 0-0 0-0 9 ♗g5 ♗e6

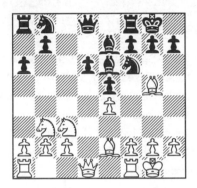

10 ♗xf6

This position is a million miles from Fischer-Gadia. If such a straightforward exchange led to a white advantage, the Najdorf would be unplayable, to say nothing of the Sveshnikov.

10...♗xf6 11 ♘d5 ♘d7 12 ♕d3 ♖c8 13 c3 ♗g5

Note that the knight on d5, while undoubtedly a magnificent piece, doesn't attack anything and, most significantly, shields the backward d6-pawn from a frontal attack.

14 ♖ad1 ♔h8 15 ♗f3 g6!

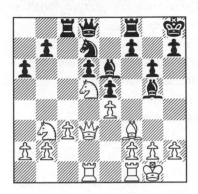

Introducing a key component: *counterplay*. The idea of...f5 needs considerable preparation (and Black's 14th move certainly counts – the king steps off the a2-g8 diagonal and prepares the g8-square for a rook after exf5, ...gxf5), but it is enough to worry White.

16 ♘e3 ♖c6 17 ♖fe1 ♘f6 18 ♕e2 b5

19 ♖a1

Borrowing from Fischer-Gadia? Not really. The a4-advance is not possible at the moment due to the vulnerability of the b3-knight, but just in case, Petrosian shows that Black is master of the queenside:

19...♕b6! 20 ♘d2 a5!

Queenside counterplay with a classic minority attack.

21 ♘df1 ♖fc8 22 a3 b4 23 cxb4 axb4 24 a4 ♕a7 25 ♖ed1 ♖a6 26 ♖d3 b3

26...♗d7 with a view to 27 b3 ♗b5! is a cute tactic.

27 a5 ♖cc6 28 ♕d1 ♕c7

29 ♘d5

Admitting that White's assets on the d-file count for nought. Occupying d5 when a pawn must recapture means there's no more outpost and no more backward d-pawn.

29...♗xd5 30 exd5 ♖c5 31 ♖xb3 ♖axa5 32 ♖xa5 ♖xa5

White now has three pawn islands against two. More specifically, both b2 and d5 are weak. Remarkably, the great endgame expert lasted only eight more moves.

33 ♖c3 ♕b6 34 ♖b3 ♕a7 35 ♖b4 ♔g7 36 h4 ♗h6 37 b3 ♖a2 38 ♕e1

Entering into a fatal pin.

38...♕a5 39 ♕b1 ♖a1 40 ♖b5 ♕c3 0-1

Game 30
R.Ponomariov-A.Graf
European Team
Championship, Plovdiv 2003
Ruy Lopez

1 e4 e5 2 ♘f3 ♘c6 3 ♗b5 a6 4 ♗a4 ♘f6 5 0-0 ♗e7 6 ♖e1 b5 7 ♗b3 d6 8 c3 0-0 9 h3 ♘a5 10 ♗c2 c5 11 d4 ♘d7 12 ♘bd2

White has significant alternatives on move twelve, 12 dxc5 or 12 d5. 12 ♘bd2 is perhaps the main move.

12...exd4 13 cxd4 ♘c6!?

Leading to a pawn structure which is more characteristic of the Modern Benoni.

14 d5

White has also allowed the exchange on d4, but pushing the pawn has to be more critical.

14...♘ce5 15 ♘h2!?

Wedberg suggests this must be critical, since White has a space advantage and should be trying to retain more pieces on the board.

15...g5

A very dynamic approach which,

though it may look wild, is positionally well-founded. Black secures his e5-outpost from attack by f4. Of course, the price for this is a weakening of the kingside in general, and the f5- and h5-squares in particular.

Perhaps influenced by the text game, players have steered away from the kingside push, preferring the more conservative 15...♞g6, with complex play.

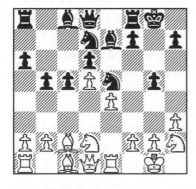

16 ♞df1 ♝f6 17 ♕h5

A very attractive square for the queen, especially given that it can't be harassed.

17...♚h8 18 ♞g3 ♜g8 19 ♞g4 ♜g6

Wedberg suggests that Black should have exchanged on g4 to relieve the cramp. Of course, White could have avoided this option if he wished by going via f1.

20 ♞e3 c4 21 ♜b1 ♞c5 22 b3 ♞cd3 23 ♝xd3 ♞xd3 24 ♜d1 ♞xc1 25 ♜dxc1 c3

Graf has staked his claim to queen-side counterplay, but Ponomariov's next move causes Black some concerns on this side of the board also.

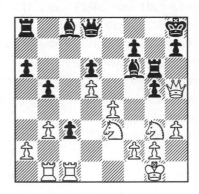

26 b4!

Separating the c3-pawn from its colleagues.

26...♝d7 27 ♜c2 ♕e7 28 ♕f3 ♜e8 29 ♜e1 ♕e5 30 ♞h5!

Aiming at the black kingside and indirectly undermining the support of the c3-pawn. White has a clear advantage and Ponomariov went on to convert smoothly:

30...g4 31 hxg4 ♝d8 32 ♕xf7 ♝xg4 33 ♞f4 ♜gg8 34 ♞xg4 ♕g5 35 ♜xc3 ♜ef8 36 ♞g6+ ♕xg6 37 ♕xg6 ♜xg6 38 ♞e3 1-0

> ### Game 31
> **B.Damljanovic-R.Ponomariov**
> European Team
> Championship, Plovdiv 2003
> *Ruy Lopez*

Same tournament, same opening, next round, reversed colours.

1 e4 e5 2 ♞f3 ♞c6 3 ♝b5 a6 4 ♝a4 ♞f6 5 0-0 ♝e7 6 ♜e1 b5 7 ♝b3 d6 8 c3 0-0 9 h3 ♞a5 10 ♝c2 c5 11 d4 ♞d7 12 ♞bd2

exd4 13 cxd4 ♘c6 14 d5 ♘ce5 15 ♘xe5
♘xe5 16 f4 ♘g6 17 ♘f3 ♗h4

Ponomariov famously lost a rapid game to Alexander Beliavsky who played the sharper 17...f5!? 18 e5 dxe5 19 fxe5 ♗b7 with highly complex and theoretical play.

18 ♘xh4 ♕xh4 19 f5

I once played 19 ♖f1 against Stuart Haslinger, after which 19...♗xh3 led to a draw.

19...♘e5

This is Khalifman's recommendation for White in his famous series of repertoire books. He seems very bullish about White's prospects in view of the bishop pair and space advantage, but I would be wary of supporting such an assessment – Ponomariov's treatment has always looked very convincing to me.

20 ♖f1 ♗d7 21 ♗f4 ♕e7 22 ♕e1 f6 23 ♕g3?

This has to be wrong. If White is to make anything of his position, his g-pawn must be pushed up the board.

23...♖fe8 24 b3 a5

Black's queenside play looks much more convincing than anything White can show on the kingside.

25 ♗d1 ♕d8 26 ♗h5 ♖e7 27 ♔h2 ♗e8 28 ♗xe8 ♕xe8 29 ♖ae1 a4 30 ♖e3 b4 31 ♕h4 ♔h8 32 ♗xe5 ♖xe5!

Of course, taking with either pawn would have been a positional blunder.

33 ♕f4 axb3 34 axb3 ♖a2 35 ♖fe1 ♔g8 36 ♖g3 ♖a7 37 ♖ge3 ♕c8 38 ♖g3 ♕a6 39 ♖ge3 ♕a2 40 ♕f1 ♖a5 41 ♖g3 ♕b2 42 ♕f4 ♖a7 43 ♕f1 ♖e8

44 e5

White is unwilling to suffer any longer and makes a desperate bid for counterplay.

Ponomariov deals with it easily.

44...fxe5 45 f6 e4 46 ♖g5 ♕d2 47 h4 ♖f7 48 ♕b5 ♖ef8 49 fxg7 ♕f4+ 50 g3 ♕f2+ 51 ♔h3 ♖xg7 52 ♖xg7+ ♔xg7 53 ♕d7+ ♖f7 54 ♕g4+ ♔h8 55 ♖a1 ♖f8 0-1

I was the reluctant pupil in a lesson on the outpost, in the following game against Sune Berg Hansen:

Game 32
S.Collins-S.B.Hansen
Khanty Mansiysk
Olympiad 2010
Ruy Lopez

1 e4 e5 2 ♘f3 ♘c6 3 ♗b5 a6 4 ♗a4 ♘f6 5 0-0 ♗e7 6 ♖e1 b5 7 ♗b3 0-0 8 d3 d6 9 c3 ♘a5 10 ♗c2 c5 11 ♘bd2 ♘d7 12 a4 ♘b6 13 axb5 axb5 14 h3 ♗d7 15 ♘f1 ♕c7 16 ♘e3 ♗f6 17 ♗d2 ♘c6 18 ♘g4 ♗e7 19 ♖xa8 ♖xa8 20 ♘g5 ♖f8 21 f4 ♕d8 22 ♘f3 ♗xg4 23 hxg4 exf4 24 ♗xf4 ♕d7 25 g5 ♘d8 26 d4 ♘e6 27 ♗c1 g6 28 ♕e2 ♖a8 29 ♗d3 c4 30 ♗c2 ♕d8

Both players have conducted the game in enterprising fashion so far, and the position would remain dynamically balanced after 31 ♕e3. Instead, I was tempted by a sacrifice, missing Black's elegant response.

31 d5? ♘xg5 32 ♘d4 ♘d7!

32...♕d7 was what I was counting on, when 33 ♘c6 leaves Black's pieces in a tangle. Sune, of course, sees no need for this, and plays his knight to the fresh outpost on e5.

33 ♘xb5 ♕b6+ 34 ♘d4 ♘e5

The combination of a dominating black knight on e5 and the weak white king render White's position strategically lost. I'm sure I could have put up better resistance, but the finish was thematic.

35 ♔h1 ♖a1 36 b4 cxb3 37 ♗xb3 h5 38 ♗d2 ♖xe1+ 39 ♗xe1 ♘g4 40 ♗c2 ♗f6 41 ♘f3 ♕b2 42 ♕d2 ♕a1 43 ♘xg5 ♗xg5 44 ♕d1 ♕a7 45 ♕d4 ♕a6 46 ♕d3 ♕a2 47 ♗d1 ♕a1 48 ♕e2 ♘e3 49 ♗b3 ♕b1 50 ♗a2 ♕xe4 51 ♗d2 ♕h4+ 52 ♔g1 ♘g4 53 ♕e8+ ♔g7 54 ♗xg5 ♕f2+ 0-1

Chapter Two
Bishops

Bad Bishop Trades

An idea which tends to get overlooked when thinking about strategy is the notion of a trade-off. Chess is fundamentally a game of exchanges, both in the traditional sense of pieces taking other pieces, and in the sense of giving something (e.g. time, material) for something else (e.g. initiative, structure etc.).

I have developed an interest in one of these trade-offs in particular. Everyone knows that Black's problem piece in the French Defence is his light-squared bishop. Why, then, are systems where he gets rid of this piece with ...b6 and ...&a6 not more popular? I try to explore this in a few games which I saw live (including one of my own losses). First, however, we will see a light example by Bronstein, which shows that single-mindedly pursuing one idea while ignoring an opponent's threats is rarely good.

Game 33
D.Bronstein-T.Van Scheltinga
Beverwijk 1963
Ruy Lopez

It should be noted that, whatever the trade-offs inherent in spending time to exchange a bad bishop in closed positions, in open positions a significant time investment should rarely be made for such an end. This game is rather light, but perfectly demonstrates the concept. Bronstein states as follows in his wonderful book *200 Open Games*:

"Black's attempt to rid himself of his dark-squared bishop, so as not to have to worry about its future fate should a position arise where pawn chains are interlocked, will be of some interest to those readers who would like to classify variations.

"As many hundreds and thousands

of Ruy Lopez games have shown, White's pawn chains are for the greater part deployed on squares of a different colour to Black's dark-squared bishop, and this powerful piece ends up cramped for space, hemmed in by its own pawns.

"To avoid so bitter a fate, the experienced Dutch master arranged to exchange the dark-squared bishops, being content to spend three tempi on doing it – the normal value of a clear piece in positions of an open type.

"Sometimes it is possible to delay one's development. But this is what happened here: whilst Black was preparing for trench warfare, the game suddenly came alive. Because of the threat of ♗xc4 and d5, winning Black's pawn on c4, Black was forced to liquidate White's d4-pawn; the centre opened up and a gaping hole appeared in Black's position on d6.

"But the square d6 is a black one, and since the black bishop had left the board, there was no one left to defend it.

"A certain amount of responsibility for the course of events lies with White too: I saw that the black bishop would be exchanged, so why then should I block up the centre?"

1 e4 e5 2 ♘f3 ♘c6 3 ♗b5 a6 4 ♗a4 ♘f6 5 0-0 ♗e7 6 ♖e1 b5 7 ♗b3 d6 8 c3 0-0 9 h3 ♘a5 10 ♗c2 c5 11 d4 ♕c7 12 ♘bd2 h6

Black has tried virtually every move in this position, but this one looks rather committal.

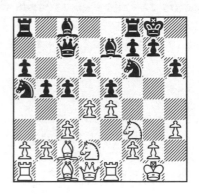

13 ♘f1 ♘c4

13...♖e8 14 ♘g3 ♗f8 15 b3 (½-½, A.Karpatchev-G.Timoshenko, Ismailia 2004) looks more sensible than Van Scheltinga's treatment from moves 13-16 – Black retains options of playing ...g6 in order to keep the white knight out of f5.

14 ♘g3 ♖e8 15 ♘h4 ♘h7 16 ♘hf5

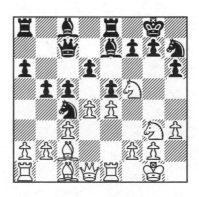

This already looks menacing for Black. He consistently follows his plan of trading dark-square bishops, but allows a central and kingside collapse.

16...♗g5 17 ♗b3 exd4 18 cxd4 cxd4 19 ♗xg5 ♘xg5 20 ♗xc4 bxc4 21 ♕xd4

With a fork on d6 and g7.

21...♗xf5 22 ♘xf5 ♘e6 23 ♕xd6 ♕b7
24 ♕g3 ♖ed8 25 ♘xh6+ ♔h7 26 ♘f5
♕xb2 27 ♕h4+ ♔g8 28 ♘e7+ 1-0

I saw this game live. As often happens when players with a class or two between them meet, it is an ideal demonstration of a difficult strategic concept, namely Black trading his light-squared bishop in the French and living to tell the tale.

1 e4 e6 2 d4 d5 3 ♘d2 ♘f6 4 e5 ♘fd7 5 c3 c5 6 ♗d3 b6

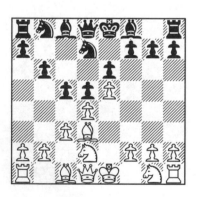

7 ♘e2

Making the case for the arguably more incisive 7 ♘h3 in his remarkably thorough book *How to Beat the French Defence*, Tzermiadianos states "This is the strongest continuation. The knight heads for f4 to exert pressure on the d5- and e6-pawns now that there's no longer a light-squared bishop to protect them. Development via the h3-square is better than e2 because the white queen can jump to g4 at an appropriate moment."

Adams, in the game quoted at move 13, also played 7 ♘e2, but I have a sneaking suspicion this may be because he hasn't had to learn any theory after 3...♘f6, since the resulting positions perfectly suit his style and most top players opt for 3...♗e7 or 3...c5. His score with the Tarrasch as a whole is around 75%, increasing to 85% after 3...♘f6. In short, I have no sympathy for anyone who plays 1...e6 against him, while if you're a fan of 3...♘f6, at least you'll get an afternoon off.

7...♗a6 8 ♗xa6 ♘xa6 9 ♘f4 ♘c7 10 0-0 c4

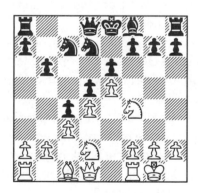

Clearly drawing the battle lines – unlike the majority of lines in the French, there is zero pressure on the white centre. Instead Black stakes his claim on the queenside. This plan really strikes me as ambitious to the point of being dubious, since White's kingside play ought to be more dangerous. However, White must play energetically, since a few inaccurate moves will cede the initiative, as this game demonstrates.

11 ♕g4 b5 12 a4

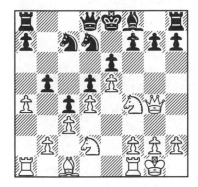

An interesting moment. 12.a4 has been played in all three games to reach this position. We all know that you're not meant to play on the side where you're weaker, so what's going on?

I don't think that White is seriously contending that he is better on the queenside. Rather, he is trying to open the play in order to exploit the fact that it will be difficult for Black to castle. Black's central construction, supported by his queen on d8 and knights on c7 and d7, is hard to break down, so White needs to create tension anywhere he can.

12...bxa4

Creating a target on b2. 12...a6 13 axb5 axb5 14 ♖xa8 ♕xa8 is a different direction, T.Warakomski-S.Birjukov, Mielno 2007 (½-½ in 43).

13 ♖xa4 g6

13...a5 14 h4 ♘b6 15 ♖a1 g6 16 h5 a4 17 ♕h3! g5 (Mueller analyses 17...♖g8 and 17...gxh5, neither of which equalize) 18 ♘e2 ♕d7 19 ♘f3 h6 20 ♘h2 ♗e7 21 f4 and White's kingside advantage means he is clearly better, even if Black castles long, M.Adams-Nguyen Chi Minh, French League 2003 (1-0 in 35).

14 ♘f3

By analogy with the Adams precedent, there seems to be no reason to avoid the immediate 14 h4!?.

14...a5

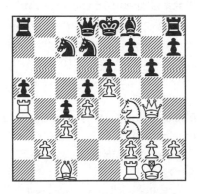

15 ♖e1?!

Peter is starting to drift. The rook is not necessary on e1 – as can be seen in the Adams game, it can find useful employment on f1. Again 15 h4 was the move.

15...♘b6 16 ♖a1 ♕d7 17 h4 h6!

Taking advantage of White's 14th and 15th moves – now h5 will be met by ...g5 when the f4-advance really needs a rook on f1 and the knight off f3.

18 g3 a4 19 ♘g2 ♘b5 20 ♕f4

Peter seems to be aiming for g4 with his knight, but this doesn't look too threatening.

20...a3!

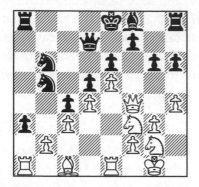

Black is ahead in the race and has a slight advantage. Peter now should have continued aggressively with 21 ♘e3, but instead falls into passivity.

21 ♕d2 ♘a4 22 ♕c2 ♕b7 23 ♘e3 ♔d7 24 ♘g4 ♔c7

Houdini thinks this is equal or a bit better for White, but to my eyes Black clearly has the initiative.

25 ♖e3??

This fails to a surprising shot.

25...h5 26 ♘f6 ♗h6

If the rook moves, b2 collapses after an exchange on c1.

27 ♘g5 ♗xg5 28 hxg5 axb2 29 ♗xb2 ♘xd4!

The other point.

30 cxd4 ♕xb2 31 ♕xb2 ♘xb2 32 ♖ea3 ♖xa3 33 ♖xa3 ♘d3 34 ♔f1 ♖b8 35 ♔e2 ♖b2+ 36 ♔e3 ♘xf2 0-1

> ## Game 35
> ### T.Kett-B.Kelly
> European Team Ch'ship,
> Gothenburg 2005
> *French Defence*

1 e4 e6 2 d4 d5 3 ♘c3 ♗b4 4 e5 ♘e7 5 a3 ♗xc3+ 6 bxc3 b6

A pet line of my teammate Brian Kelly (and, for that matter, Ivkov and Riazantsev). Black plays ambitiously, aiming to deprive White of the advantage of the bishop pair and trade the worst black piece. Strategically, it's hard to fault this idea, but the time it takes to implement gives White some chances to generate an initiative. One less obvious feature of the position is that, without the bishop on c8, it's harder for Black to challenge the white centre with ...f6 since this would weaken the e6-pawn. This means that White's kingside actions are harder to defend against, since the spearhead on e5 makes it difficult for Black to bring pieces across from the queenside for defensive purposes.

7 ♕g4

Quiet play with 7 ♘f3 ♗a6 8 ♗d3 does not seek to take advantage of the main drawback of Black's plan (the time investment) and accordingly can't pose any significant problems. Indeed, in the long run, I prefer Black's game. 8...♗xd3 9 cxd3 c5 10 0-0 ♘d7 11 ♗g5 h6 12 ♗e3 ♘f5 13 g4 ♘h4 14 ♘xh4 ♕xh4 15 f4 ♕h3 16 ♕f3 ♕xf3 17 ♖xf3 h5 18 g5 g6 and Black went on to win the endgame with his superior minor piece in I.Salcedo-B.Kelly, Calvia Olympiad 2004 (0-1 in 31).

7 ♘h3!? is an unconventional development of the knight, but given that it blocks neither the white queen nor the f2-pawn, I think this is an interesting attempt. 7...♘g6 8 ♕h5 ♗a6 9 ♗xa6 ♘xa6 10 0-0 ♕d7 11 f4 0-0-0 12 a4 ♘b8 13 f5 ♘e7 14 fxe6 fxe6 with unclear play in P.Piscopo-B.Kelly, Turin Olympiad 2006 (0-1 in 71).

7...♘g6 8 h4 h5

9 ♕g3

9 ♕d1 is the main line. This is quite a common response in the French, that once the queen on g4 has forced a concession on the kingside (...h5 in this instance) she retreats to guard the queenside. In the meantime, pressure is maintained on the h5-pawn. Certainly, Kelly's experiences here have not been as happy as in other lines, though this probably has something to do with the higher level of opposition which tends to play this queen retreat. Some examples: 9...♗a6 10 ♗xa6 ♘xa6 and now:

a) 11 ♘e2!? ♕d7 (11...♘xh4 seems better: 12 ♘f4 g6 13 g3 ♘f5 14 g4 ♘e7 15 gxh5 ♕d7 followed by play on the queenside) 12 ♘g3 ♕c6 13 ♗d2 ♕a4 14 ♘xh5 ♖h7 15 ♘f4 ♘e7 (15...♘xf4 16 ♗xf4 ♘c5!? gives some compensation) 16 h5 c5 17 ♗e3 ♖c8 18 0-0 cxd4 19 cxd4 ♕xc2 20 ♕g4 with a significant advantage for White in J.Rowson-B.Kelly, British League 1999.

b) 11 ♗g5 ♕d7 12 ♘e2 ♕a4!? (Kelly's improvement over 12...♕c6 13 0-0 ♘e7 14 ♗xe7 ♔xe7 15 ♕d2 g6 16 a4 ♘b8 17 ♖a3 ♘d7 18 ♕g5+ ♔e8 19 ♘f4 with a free attack against the black king in J.Gallagher-B.Kelly, British League 2000 (1-0 in 46)) 13 0-0 ♘e7 14 ♘g3 (A.Ramirez Alvarez-B.Kelly, Bled Olympiad 2002, proceeded 14 ♗xe7 ♔xe7 15 ♘f4 ♖ac8 16 ♕d3 c5 17 ♖ac1 ♘b8 18 ♕g3 ♔f8 19 ♕f3 ♖h6! 20 ♖fd1 ♘c6 and Black's advantage was quickly transformed into a win: 21 ♘xh5 ♕xa3 22 ♖a1 ♕b2 23 ♕g4 ♖g6 24 ♕h3 ♕xc2 25 ♘f4 ♖h6 26 ♘xd5 ♕e4 27 ♘e3 ♖xh4 28 ♕f3 ♕xf3 29 gxf3 cxd4 30 cxd4 ♖xd4 31 ♖dc1 ♖dd8 32 ♘c4 ♘d4 and

White resigned) 14...g6 15 ♕f3 ♖h7 16 ♖ac1 ♖c8 17 ♖fd1 ♘b8 18 ♘f1 ♘bc6 19 ♘e3 ♘a5 with balanced play and an eventual draw in A.Zhigalko-B.Kelly, Rethymnon 2003 (½-½ in 41).

9 ♕f3 looks like an odd move, blocking both the knight and the f2-pawn, but it might be playable: 9...♗a6 10 ♗g5 ♕d7 11 ♗xa6 ♘xa6 12 a4 c5 13 ♘e2 cxd4 14 cxd4 ♘b4, and now instead of the 15 0-0?! of R.Eames-B.Kelly, British Ch., Scarborough 2001 (½-½ in 53), 15 ♕b3 was sufficient for equality.

9 ♕g5?! is completely misguided – in the endgame Black holds all the trumps, while his king is no longer vulnerable to attack: 9...♕xg5 10 hxg5 ♗a6 11 ♗e2 ♗xe2 12 ♘xe2 ♘c6 and Black went on to win a slow, convincing endgame in N.Alfred-B.Kelly, British Ch., Torquay 1998 (0-1 in 49).

9...♗a6 10 ♗xa6

The IM (at that time) and highly dangerous attacking player (at all times) Simon Williams chose 10 ♘e2 against Kelly in the British League, 2004. After 10...♕d7 11 a4 ♘c6 12 ♘f4 ♗xf1 13 ♘xg6 fxg6 14 ♕xg6+ ♕f7 15 ♕xf7+ ♔xf7 16 ♖xf1 ♘a5 17 ♔e2 ♘c4 Black's superior minor piece and pawn structure gave him full compensation for the pawn, though White went on to win in 50 moves.

10...♘xa6 11 ♘e2

Presumably Kelly had an improvement prepared (that, or he was bluffing), since he went into this line again against Stephen Jessel in Dublin 2007.

After 11 ♗g5 ♕d7 12 a4 ♘b8 13 ♘e2 ♘c6 14 0-0 ♘ce7 15 ♕d3 ♖c8 16 a5 ♘c6 17 axb6 cxb6 18 ♖a2 ♖c7 19 ♖fa1 ♘a5 20 ♘c1 ♘e7 21 ♗xe7 ♕xe7 22 g3 0-0 Black's queenside play looked more convincing, and he went on to win in 59 moves.

11...♘b8 12 ♘f4 ♘xf4 13 ♗xf4

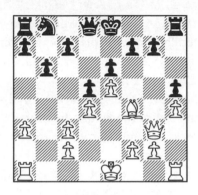

13...♔f8

I wonder if 13...♖h7 is more accurate, retaining the option of castling queenside. The rook looks passive here, but the queen isn't doing a lot on g3 either. This concept is well known from the a6-Slav, viz. 1 d4 d5 2 c4 c6 3 ♘f3 ♘f6 4 ♘c3 a6 5 c5 ♗f5 6 e3 ♘bd7 7 ♕b3 ♖a7!?, when the threat to the b7-pawn is addressed and, if the queen moves away, so does the rook.

From a practical point of view, Brian probably rejected the rook move since 14 ♕d3 ♖h8 15 ♕g3 repeats, which was unappetizing given the rating difference.

14 0-0 ♕d7 15 ♗g5 ♕a4 16 f4 g6 17 f5!

Fine attacking play from the dangerous Welshman.

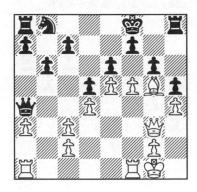

17...gxf5

17...exf5 18 e6 is even worse.

18 ♗f6 ♖h7 19 ♕g5

White has a very simple plan of bringing his rook to g3 and announcing mate on g8. Brian does well to stay in the game, though he needs some help from his opponent.

19...♘c6

19...♘d7 might be the best defence: 20 ♖f3 ♘xf6 21 exf6 f4!, to try and defend the rook with his queen on c2, and stop the white rook getting to g3. Still, Black's position looks unappetizing.

20 ♖f3 f4 21 ♖xf4 ♕xc2 22 ♖af1 ♖e8 23 ♖1f3 ♘e7

24 ♗xe7+

24 ♗g7+! was the way to go. 24...♖xg7 (24...♔g8 25 ♖xf7) 25 ♖xf7+ ♖xf7 26 ♕h6+ ♔g8 27 ♖g3+ ♘g6 28 ♖xg6+ ♕xg6 29 ♕xg6+ and the rooks will not be able to counterbalance the white kingside passers and the exposed black king.

24...♖xe7 25 ♖g3 ♔e8 26 ♖f2 ½-½

Brian buys off the risk by using his 300 rating point advantage to encourage a premature draw offer. 26 ♕g8+ ♔d7 27 ♕a8 would still have been dangerous for Black.

Game 36
S.Collins-B.Ostenstad
European Club Cup,
Rogaska Slatina 2011
French Defence

1 e4 e6 2 d4 d5 3 ♘d2 ♗e7 4 ♘gf3 ♘f6 5 e5 ♘fd7 6 ♗d3 c5 7 c3 b6

Another version of the ...b6 and ...♗a6 idea. Black avoids the sharper lines after 7...♘c6 8 0-0 when he can go after the d4-pawn or launch radical counterplay with 8...g5!?, with interesting play.

8 ♕e2 a5 9 0-0 ♗a6 10 c4 ♘c6 11 cxd5 ♗xd3 12 ♕xd3 ♘b4 13 ♕e4 ♘xd5

As so often in the French, Black has decent long-term prospects at the cost of having to endure a strong white initiative in the middlegame.

14 ♕g4 ♔f8

The only move I considered. Black

needs the g-pawn on g7 to cover the dark squares.

15 ♘e4 cxd4

15...h6 16 ♘c3 ♘xc3 17 bxc3 is slightly better for White.

16 ♗g5

It seemed logical to me to try and exploit the dark squares. However, perhaps the immediate 16 ♘xd4 was stronger: 16...♕c7 (if 16...♘xe5 17 ♘xe6+ fxe6 18 ♕xe6 ♘d3 19 ♕f5+ ♘f6 20 ♘xf6 ♗xf6 21 ♖d1 ♕e8 22 ♕xd3) 17 f4 ♖d8 18 ♕f3 with a slight edge for White.

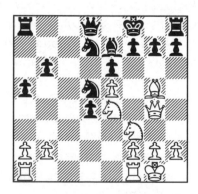

16...♗xg5 17 ♘exg5

17 ♘fxg5? doesn't work: 17...♘xe5

18 ♘xe6+ fxe6 19 ♕xe6 ♘f7.

17...h6

18 ♘e4

I considered the sharper 18 ♘xe6+ fxe6 19 ♘xd4 but thought Black could defend after 19...♘c7 20 ♘xe6+ ♘xe6 21 ♕xe6 ♕e7.

18...♕b8

Black has another typical defensive device: 18...h5!? (gaining space and potential counterplay on the kingside) 19 ♕g3 h4 20 ♕g4 ♕c7, and Black has a slight advantage.

19 ♕g3 g5 20 ♖ad1 ♘f4 21 ♘xd4 ♘xe5

21...♕xe5 seems to peter out to equality: 22 ♕f3 ♘d5 23 ♘c3 ♔g7 24 ♘xd5 ♕xd5 25 ♕xd5 exd5 26 f4 ♘f6 27 ♘f5+ ♔h7 28 fxg5 hxg5 29 ♘e3 ♔g6 30 ♘xd5 ♘xd5 31 ♖xd5 ♖ad8 32 ♖df5 ♖d2.

22 ♖fe1

Aiming at the knight on e5. However, the knight on f4 was also a legitimate target: 22 h4 ♕c7 23 hxg5 hxg5 24 ♘xg5 ♖e8 with an equal position.

22...♕c7 23 h4

Starting a good plan, but one move too late.

23 ♕a3+ ♔g8 (23...♔g7 24 ♘d6 ♕c5 25 ♕xc5 bxc5 26 ♘xe6+ ♘xe6 27 ♖xe5) 24 ♖c1 ♕d8 25 ♖ed1, with equality, looks more sensible.

23...♖d8

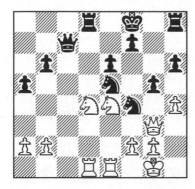

24 hxg5?

Opening lines for the black pieces.

After the game I suggested something like 24 a4 ♕e7 25 ♕c3 ♘d5 26 ♕g3 ♘f4. Berge indicated he probably would have gone for the repetition here since White has some residual compensation.

24...hxg5

25 ♕xg5??

I really can't explain this, although by this stage White is in trouble.

The problem with 25 ♘xg5 is that it loses: 25...♖xd4 26 ♖xd4 ♘e2+ 27 ♖xe2 ♕c1+. 25 ♕a3+ ♔g7 26 ♕g3 ♖xd4 also loses, while Black has a clear advantage after 25 ♘c3 ♖h5.

25...♘h3+

Oh dear.

26 gxh3 ♖g8 27 f4 ♖xd4 28 ♖xd4 ♘f3+ 29 ♔f2 ♘xg5 30 ♘xg5?

30 fxg5 is a bit more tenacious: 30...♕f4+ 31 ♔e2 ♖xg5 and Black wins.

30...♖xg5 31 fxg5 ♕h2+?

I was going to resign after 31...♕c5 32 ♖ed1 (or to e4) 32...e5.

32 ♔e3??

Completing the collapse.

32 ♔f1 would at least keep the game going, which is always of some value in a team tournament.

32...♕g3+ 33 ♔e2 ♕e5+ 0-1

Fresh Pastures

This is a slightly unusual section but, in keeping with the theme of the book, I have attempted to categorize something which is perhaps too pedestrian for mainstream strategic texts. The idea I want to discuss is re-routing a bishop (often White's king's bishop, oddly) to the long diagonal. The idea is often counterintuitive, especially if the bishop is already active and developed.

1 d4 d5 2 c4 dxc4 3 e3 ♘f6 4 ♗xc4 e6 5 ♘f3 c5 6 0-0 a6 7 dxc5 ♗xc5 8 ♕xd8+ ♔xd8

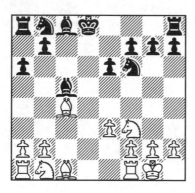

9 ♗e2

The first hint at what will be a masterful handling of this bishop. In particular, since Black's inaccurate play will result in a trade of his light-squared bishop for a knight, it will be particularly important for White to emphasize the power of the bishop without an opponent – if this piece can

start dominating, White will have uncontested control of the light squares.

9...♔e7 10 ♘bd2 ♗d7 11 ♘b3 ♗d6

A new move, but (it seems) not a good one. Both retreats along the a7-g1 diagonal had yielded Black completely satisfactory results in several high-level games.

12 ♘a5!

A bishop on b6 would have prevented this manoeuvre, while a bishop on a7 would not have been hit by the knight once it lands on c4.

12...♖a7 13 ♘c4 ♗b5 14 b3 ♖d8 15 ♗b2

15...♗xc4

Deciding to concede the light-squared bishop.

After the game Carlsen showed that 15...♘c6 16 ♖fd1 ♖aa8 17 ♖xd6 ♖xd6 18 ♘xd6 ♔xd6 19 ♗d1! would still leave him with the bishop pair. Nisipeanu's decision appears reasonable since, remembering that the primary task of the player with the bishop pair is to emphasize the power of the bishop without an opponent, it is immediately obvious that White's bishop on b2 is the best minor piece on the board. In the game, Magnus will have to put in more work to show that his light-squared bishop is as effective. Magnus' comment during the post-game interview is similar: "Now his pieces are uncoordinated and I have the bishop pair, and the bishop on b2 which has no opponent is very strong."

16 ♗xc4 ♘c6 17 ♖fd1 ♖aa8 18 h3

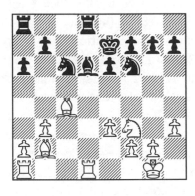

Rogozenko (who both conducted instructive post-game interviews with the winners of the games in Bazna and provided good annotations to the games in MegaBase 2012) makes an instructive comment here: "Black's position is worse than it looks. White's bishop pair together with the lack of any counterplay makes it difficult to defend it especially in a practical game and especially with little time. White's plan is to advance the kingside pawns, gaining more space and trying to create a weakness in Black's pawn formation. Possibly disappointed by the course of the game Nisipeanu fails to put up his usual tough resistance."

18...g6 19 g4 h6

Re-routing the bishop was clearly at the front of Magnus' mind during the game – his post-game variation of 19...h5 20 g5 ♘d7 21 ♗d3 ends with the comment "and the bishop will have a very nice square on e4".

20 ♗f1

The post-game interview is especially instructive at this point, in illustrating the difference in thinking between Rogozenko, a good GM, and Carlsen. It is this exchange which convinces me that this concept of re-routing bishops is not trivial and is easily overlooked, especially where (as here) the bishop already looks active.

Rogozenko: "♗f1, why do you need this move?"

Carlsen: "I dunno. I thought it was useful to have ♗g2 in some lines. Additionally it's not..."

Rogozenko: "At least you hold him from ...♘d5 with a bishop on c4."

Carlsen: "Yeah but I wasn't concerned about that. I thought that when he plays ...♘d5 I will play h4 and g5.

And my bishop wasn't really doing much on c4."

This strikes me as pure genius.

20...♖ac8 21 ♖ac1 ♘d5 22 h4 ♔e8 23 g5 hxg5

The same theme:

Carlsen: "I thought he should play 23...h5. But it's not very nice. Let's say 24 ♗d3 here."

Rogozenko: "So again you're coming to e4."

Carlsen: "Yeah."

Rogozenko: "But maybe I can play 24...♘db4?"

Carlsen: "Yeah but then 25 ♗b1 and a3. And also in some lines I might put the knight on e4. Okay, it's by no means a decisive advantage, it's just a very nice position. And again Black has no targets."

24 hxg5 ♗e7 25 ♔g2 ♘b6 26 ♗d3 ♘b4 27 ♗e4

Carlsen: "I think it's here more or less lost. I'm just penetrating on the h-file."

27...♘xa2 28 ♖xd8+ ♔xd8 29 ♖h1 ♘d5 30 ♘e5 f5 31 ♗xd5 1-0

Game 38
M.Carlsen-N.Short
London Classic 2010
French Defence

1 e4 e6 2 d4 d5 3 ♘d2 dxe4

A variation where the bishop commonly drops back to e2 arises after 3...c5 4 exd5 ♕xd5 5 ♘gf3 cxd4 6 ♗c4 ♕d6 7 0-0 ♘f6 8 ♘b3 ♘c6 9 ♘bxd4 ♘xd4 10 ♕xd4 (instead of the more popular and critical 10 ♘xd4) 10...♕xd4 11 ♘xd4 ♗d7, and now already 12 ♗e2 is possible, for instance 12...♗c5 13 ♘b3 ♗b6 14 a4 a6 15 ♗f3 0-0-0 16 ♖e1 ♔b8 17 a5 ♗a7 18 ♗f4+ and a draw was agreed in V.Nevednichy-V.Akopian, Heraklion 2007.

4 ♘xe4 ♘d7 5 ♘f3 ♗e7 6 ♗c4 ♘gf6 7 ♘xf6+ ♘xf6 8 0-0 0-0 9 ♘e5 c5 10 dxc5 ♕xd1 11 ♖xd1 ♗xc5

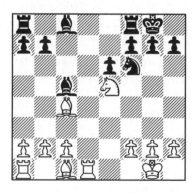

12 ♗e2

Carlsen in the post-game interview: "I think ♗e2 is a nice move, which is actually typical for another line of the French... [see the note to Black's 3rd move]. In that variation it's absolutely harmless, but here at least I have the d-file and better development so it should amount to something."

12...♘e4 13 ♘d3 ♗e7 14 ♗e3

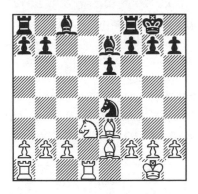

14...h6?

Postny suggests 14...b6, since after 15 a4 ♗b7 16 a5 ♖fc8 Black has more active play on the queenside.

15 a4 a5

15...b6 16 a5 with a clear advantage.

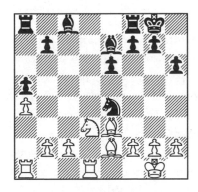

16 g3 ♖d8 17 ♘e5 ♘f6 18 ♘c4 ♖xd1+ 19 ♖xd1 ♘d5 20 ♘b6 ♘xe3

Or 20...♘xb6 21 ♗xb6 with a complete bind.

21 fxe3 ♖b8 22 ♔f2 e5

It is difficult to suggest alternatives.
23 ♖d5 ♗e6 24 ♖xa5 ♖d8

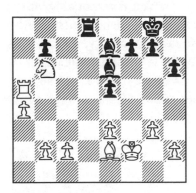

Black looks like he's beginning to generate activity, but in fact it comes to nothing, and White's 3-1 queenside majority decides.

25 ♗d3 ♗f6 26 e4 ♖d4 27 ♖b5 g6 28 a5 ♔g7 29 ♔e2 ♗g4+ 30 ♔f2 ♗e6 31 ♔f3 h5 32 ♘d5 ♗d8 33 b4 ♗c8 34 ♔e2 ♗g4+ 35 ♔e1 f5 36 ♖xb7+ ♔h6 37 ♘e3 ♗f3 38 a6 fxe4 39 ♗e2 ♗g5 40 a7 1-0

One downside of the bishop re-routing is that it involves a reasonably significant investment of time (two tempi at least). If Black can mobilize himself, he can use this time to generate meaningful counterplay:

Game 39
A.Yusupov-V.Kunin
German Championship,
Osterburg 2006
Queen's Gambit Accepted

1 d4 d5 2 ♘f3 ♘f6 3 c4 dxc4 4 e3 ♗g4

I recently recorded a DVD for Chess-Base on this line from Black's point of view. I think it is reasonably interesting to develop the bishop outside the pawn chain rather than play for ...a6, ...b5 and ...♗b7, as is normal in the QGA.

5 ♗xc4 e6 6 h3 ♗h5 7 ♘c3 a6 8 g4 ♗g6 9 ♘e5 ♘bd7 10 ♘xg6 hxg6 11 ♗f1 c6 12 ♗g2 ♗d6!

Indicative of the active approach which Black must use in such positions. John Watson has written definitively and instructively about how the side playing against the bishop pair frequently has to play aggressively to open the position while the opponent is behind in development – this ideological shift (previous generations would have tried to keep such positions closed, only to be strangled by the bishop pair around move 40-50 as the position gradually became more open) is well illustrated by this opening variation.

The plan with 11 ♗f1 was popularized by the game G.Kasparov-T.Petrosian, Tilburg 1981 (0-1 in 42), when after 12...♕c7 13 0-0 ♗e7 (Kunin has also used his active approach in this move order: 13...♘d5 14 f4 ♗e7 15 g5 0-0-0 16 ♕g4 ♘7b6 17 ♕e2 c5 with counterplay in J.Gustafsson-V.Kunin, Osterburg 2006 (0-1 in 67)) 14 f4 ♘b6 15 g5 ♘fd7 16 ♕g4 0-0-0 17 ♖b1 ♚b8 18 b4 Black had a passive game, though he sensationally went on to win in the end.

13 0-0 ♕e7 14 g5 ♘d5 15 ♕g4 ♗c7 16 f4 ♗b6 17 ♗d2 0-0-0 18 ♖ac1 ♚b8 19 a3 f6 20 h4 ♖h7 21 ♖f3 c5

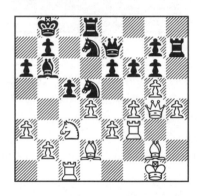

White's pawn chain is under pressure from pawns at two key points (d4 and g5) while h4 is being kept under observation by the black rook on the h-file. Black has excellent counterplay.

22 ♘xd5 exd5 23 f5

Playing on the side where he's weaker, but there were no compelling alternatives for White.

23...♖dh8

23...♕e4!? 24 ♕xe4 (24 ♖f4 ♕d3) 24...dxe4 is also nice for Black, but Kunin opts to keep the queens on for a while.

24 ♖h3?

24 ♗e1 kept the balance.

24...fxg5 25 fxg6 ♖xh4 26 ♖xh4 ♖xh4

Black has extra material and an attack, which persists into the endgame.

27 ♕f5

27 ♕g3+ was more tenacious.

27...cxd4 28 e4 ♕d6

28...d3+ 29 ♔f1 dxe4 would have won on the spot.

29 e5 ♕xe5 30 ♕xe5+ ♘xe5 31 ♗xd5 ♖g4+ 32 ♔h1 ♘xg6

Three extra pawns is too much, and the rest of the game holds no particular interest.

33 ♖e1 ♗c7 34 ♖e8+ ♔a7 35 ♗e1 ♖f4 36 ♗g3 ♖f1+ 37 ♔g2 ♖c1 38 ♗e4 ♘f4+ 39 ♗xf4 gxf4 40 ♖g8 ♖e1 41 ♖xg7 ♖xe4 42 ♖xc7 ♖e2+ 43 ♔f3 ♖xb2 44 ♔xf4 ♖a2 45 ♔e4 ♖xa3 46 ♔xd4 ♖h3 47 ♔c4 ♖h4+ 48 ♔c5 ♖h5+ 49 ♔b4 a5+ 50 ♔a4 ♔a6 51 ♖g7 b5+ 52 ♔a3 ♖h3+ 53 ♔a2 a4 54 ♖g4 ♔a5 55 ♖f4 ♖h2+ 56 ♔a1 ♖e2 57 ♖f3 b4 58 ♖f5+ ♔b6 59 ♖f6+ ♔c5 60 ♖f5+ ♔c4 61 ♔b1 a3 62 ♖f4+ ♔c3 63 ♖f3+ ♔d4 64 ♖h3 ♖e3 65 ♖h8 b3 66 ♖d8+ ♔c5 67 ♖c8+ ♔d6 68 ♖d8+ ♔c7 69 ♖d1 ♖e2 70 ♔a1 ♔c6 71 ♔b1 ♔c5 72 ♔a1 ♔c4 73 ♔b1 ♔c3 74 ♔a1 ♔c2 75 ♖h1 ♔d2 0-1

Opposite-Coloured Bishops

Positions with bishops of opposite colours merit more attention than they have received to date. Dvoretsky has addressed this to some extent in a couple of excellent chapters based around the games of Karpov and Smagin.

I have personally struggled with these positions, as will be indicated by a selection of my own games. As will appear, the addition of rooks dramatically changes the assessment of opposite-colour bishop endgames, and can change a trivial draw into a torturous defensive exercise.

Game 40
S.Collins-Z.Ilincic
Budapest 2007
Petroff Defence

1 e4 e5 2 ♘f3 ♘f6 3 d4 ♘xe4 4 ♗d3 d5 5 ♘xe5 ♘d7 6 ♘c3 ♘xe5 7 dxe5 ♘xc3 8 bxc3 ♗c5 9 ♕h5 h6 10 0-0 ♗e6 11 ♖b1 ♗b6 12 h3 ♕e7 13 a4 0-0-0 14 ♔h2 g6 15 ♕e2 c5 16 ♗a6 bxa6 17 ♕xa6+ ♕b7 18 ♕xb7+ ♔xb7 19 a5 ♔c6 20 axb6 axb6

After some distinctly uninspired opening play by White (I think I was trying to follow some Topalov game after about 30 minutes of preparation, which is normally a recipe for disaster – the disclaimer "don't try this at home" should attend most of the Bulgarian's efforts) we reach an endgame.

While it was obvious that only Black can play for a win, I was reasonably optimistic about my drawing chances – equal material and opposite-coloured bishops seem to increase the possibility of a handshake. My c-pawns aren't pretty but seem to do a reasonable job of holding up Black's central majority.

In fact, this is a horrible misassessment. Black is at the very least clearly better and may be winning in this position.

21 g4

I find it hard to criticize this move, since I have to make some efforts to mobilize my kingside majority. This illustrates one of the main factors which inform assessment of opposite-coloured bishop endgames: *the presence of rooks*. Without rooks, the normal prescription for the defending side is to put pawns on the same colour as one's own bishop so that they are im-

mune from attack (in fact, in this particular structure, I wouldn't really fancy defending the pure opposite colour bishop endgame, but still pawns on dark squares would be the way to proceed for White). With rooks, however, I can't simply concede the light squares since, as in a middlegame, my king would be subject to an attack.

21...h5 22 ♔g3 hxg4 23 hxg4 d4!

A good practical try from Ilincic, who shows good technique throughout this endgame. The merits of the move will be assessed in the next note.

24 ♗g5 ♖d5 25 cxd4 ♖xd4 26 f3 ♖a8

Essentially, Black's only advantage is the comparative mobility of his pawn majority, coupled with superior piece activity. This doesn't sound like an enormous amount, yet I think it is sufficient for a win. White can show nothing against the simple plan of pushing and queening the b-pawn.

27 ♖fd1 ♖xd1 28 ♖xd1 ♗d5!

A great square for the bishop, frustrating my counterplay on the d-file.

29 ♖d3 b5 30 c3 ♖a3 31 ♖e3 ♖b3 32

♔h4 ♗e6 33 ♗f4

33 f4 b4 is the tactical problem with trying to push my majority. After 34 f5 gxf5 35 gxf5 ♗xf5 36 cxb4 ♖xb4+ Black has excellent winning chances. Perhaps I should have tried this anyway since at least a number of pawns get exchanged.

33...♔d5 34 ♗g5 ♔c4

My light-squares couldn't be weaker.

35 ♗e7 ♗d5 36 f4

At last my pawns get moving, but the black majority is at least five moves faster.

36...b4 37 f5 gxf5 38 gxf5 bxc3

38...♖xc3 might be better but the text move is easily good enough.

39 ♖e1 c2 40 ♗g5 ♖b1 41 ♖c1 ♔b3 0-1

Game 41
S.Collins-D.Kosic
Budapest 2007
French Defence

1 e4 e6 2 d4 d5 3 ♘c3 dxe4 4 ♘xe4 ♘d7

5 ♘f3 ♘gf6 6 ♘xf6+ ♘xf6 7 c3 c5 8 ♘e5 a6 9 ♕a4+ ♗d7 10 ♘xd7 ♕xd7 11 ♕xd7+ ♔xd7 12 dxc5 ♗xc5 13 ♗e2 ♖ad8 14 0-0 ♔e7 15 a4 ♖d7 16 b4?? ♗d6 17 ♗a3 ♘d5 18 ♖fc1 ♖c8 19 c4 ♘xb4 20 ♗xb4 ♗xb4 21 ♖d1 ♖xd1+ 22 ♖xd1 ♖c7 23 ♖b1 ♗c5 24 ♗f3 b6 25 ♔f1 ♗d4 26 ♗e2 ♖c6 27 ♖d1 e5 28 ♖b1 g6 29 f3 ♔d6 30 c5+ ♗xc5 31 ♗xa6 ♗d4 32 ♖e1 ♖c3 33 ♗b5

Two rounds after the previous game, I have another awful opposite-coloured bishop endgame to defend with White.

Again, this is an example of following fashion with appalling results. White's 7th and 8th moves were made famous by Kasparov's wonderful win over Ponomariov. Black's 8th move is the critical response, but the main line is to interpose with his knight on d7 on move 9, where White tries to demonstrate the strength of his initiative before Black untangles.

Kosic's 9th move (his usual recipe) is safer but more compliant. It leads to an endgame where Black is solid but, frankly, should never generate winning chances in view of White's two bishops. The way I handled this endgame still embarrasses me somewhat: my 16th move is incredible given that I was around 2400 at the time.

We now have a position where, without rooks, a draw would be agreed with no further discussion. With rooks, White's game is hopeless. It's worth spending a moment thinking about the black e-pawn. Without rooks, the white king could sit on e2 without complaint. With rooks, it would surely be checked away. Accordingly, Black's material advantage gives him one additional attacker (his e-pawn) which should prove decisive.

In the game, I managed to survive, but only with considerable help from my GM opponent.

33...f5! 34 ♖e2 ♔e6 35 ♖a2 ♖c1+ 36 ♔e2 ♔d5 37 ♗e8 ♗c3 38 ♗f7+ ♔d6

38...♔d4 was sensible and strong.

39 ♗g8 ♔e7 40 ♔d3 ♔f8 41 ♗b3 ♗b4 42 ♖c2!

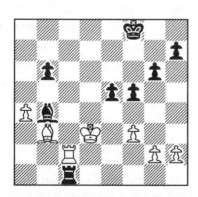

Black has gone astray by letting me

activate my rook, and while some winning chances remain, it's no longer straightforward. Kosic continued playing passively and I levelled the chances.

42...♖d1+ 43 ♔e2 ♖d7

43...♖b1.

44 g4!

44...fxg4

44...♔e7 is a bit better, but I think White should be safe since there are several vulnerable black pawns which could form targets for counterplay.

45 fxg4 ♔e7 46 ♖c4 ♗c5

47 a5

Getting rid of the queenside weakness is another improvement of the white position.

47...♖a7 48 axb6 ♗xb6 49 ♖c6 ♗d4 50 ♔d3 ♖b7 ½-½

I think the game ended in a time scramble some moves later, but the official score stops here. White has real counterplay against h7 and good squares on e4 and d5 for his king, and should (and did) hold.

> ### Game 42
> ### S.Collins-G.Jones
> Kilkenny Masters 2010
> *Ruy Lopez*

1 e4 e5 2 ♘f3 ♘c6 3 ♗b5 f5 4 d3 fxe4 5 dxe4 ♘f6 6 0-0 ♗c5 7 ♕d3 ♘d4

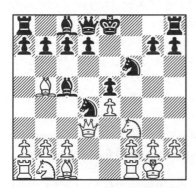

This is a line which Radjabov had used to gain an effortless draw against Svidler in a rapid game. As with many lines of the Schliemann, if Black gets out the opening without any bruises, he can look forward to the middlegame and endgame with confidence drawn from his extra centre pawn and half-open f-file. However, spending time in

the opening weakening his a2-g8 diagonal always increases the risk of not getting a playable position. In this game, Gawain made natural moves but White went material up in an endgame without doing anything special.

8 ♘xd4 ♗xd4 9 ♘d2 a6 10 ♗a4

Svidler chose 10 ♗c4 in the aforementioned game.

10...♕e7 11 ♘f3 ♗b6 12 ♗g5 0-0

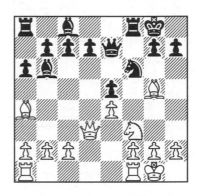

13 ♗xf6 ♕xf6

13...♖xf6 14 ♗b3+ ♔h8 15 ♕d5 is pretty nasty for Black.

My initial notes read "13...gxf6 is positionally horrible but was probably the best of a bad bunch." This was largely based on our post-mortem. However, it was this very move which Radjabov subsequently used against Nisipeanu: 14 ♘h4 d6 15 ♔h1 ♔h8 16 f4 ♗g4 17 c3 ♖ad8 18 ♗b3 c6 19 ♕g3 ♕g7 20 fxe5 fxe5 21 h3 ♗c8 22 ♕xg7+ ♔xg7 23 g4 ♗e3 24 ♘f5+ ♗xf5 25 ♖xf5 ♖xf5 26 gxf5 d5 27 ♖d1 d4 28 cxd4 ♗xd4 29 ♗e6 ♔f6 30 ♔g2 ♖e8 31 b3 ♖e7 and a draw was agreed in L.Nisipeanu-T.Radjabov, Medias 2011.

14 ♕d5+ ♔h8 15 ♕xe5 ♕xe5 16 ♘xe5 ♗d4 17 ♘xd7 ♗xd7

17...♖d8 18 ♖ad1 ♗xb2 (18...♗xd7 19 ♖xd4 with two extra pawns) 19 ♘b6! wins.

18 ♗xd7 ♖ad8 19 ♗g4 ♗xb2 20 ♖ad1 g6 21 g3

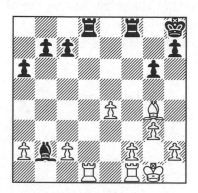

The beginning of a plan which is very hard to stop – White mobilizes his kingside pawns.

21...♖d4 22 ♖xd4 ♗xd4 23 ♔g2 ♖f6

Gawain aims for queenside counterplay.

24 ♗e2!

Forcing Black to go for the a2-pawn.

24...♖c6 25 ♗d3 b5 26 ♖d1 ♖c3

Allowing my next move, but there was nothing better. 26...♗b6, for instance, fails to 27 e5 and the kingside pawns roll through.

27 ♗xb5 ♗xf2 28 ♖d8+ ♔g7 29 ♗d3 ♗b6 30 e5

The e-pawn looks less dangerous without the f-pawn, but in fact I now force the win of both of Black's kingside pawns.

30...♔f7 31 ♖d7+ ♔e6 32 ♖xh7 ♔xe5

33 ♗xg6 a5 34 h4 ♖a3 35 h5 ♔f6 36 ♗d3 ♖xa2 37 h6 ♖a1 38 ♖d7 ♖g1+ 39 ♔h2 ♖e1 40 ♖d8 ♔e7 41 h7 ♔xd8 42 h8♕+ ♔e7 43 ♕g7+ ♔d6 44 ♕f6+ ♖e6 45 ♕d8+ ♔c6 46 ♗e4+ 1-0

Game 43
G.Jones-S.Collins
British League 2011
Scotch Game

This is a game which I wanted to include, but I wasn't sure which section was most suitable. Given the propensity of gambit play in the notes, it could well have sat in the "Material" part, but ultimately I drew because of opposite-coloured bishops so I've decided to discuss it here.

The position arising after Black's 23rd move is one where the traditional drawish properties of opposite-coloured bishops are demonstrated, notwithstanding the presence of rooks.

1 e4 e5 2 ♘f3 ♘c6 3 d4 exd4 4 ♘xd4 ♘f6 5 ♘xc6 bxc6 6 e5 ♘e4!?

Quite an interesting line, used frequently and with success by German GM Christian Gabriel.

7 豐f3 ②g5 8 豐g3

8 豐h5!? ②e6 9 ②d3 g6 10 豐e2 ②g7 11 f4 0-0 12 ②e3 f6 13 f5 gxf5 14 ②xf5 with unclear play in B.Macieja-C.Gabriel, German League 2002 (1-0 in 71).

8...②e6

9 ②c3

Black frequently offers a pawn sacrifice after the main continuation 9 ②d3: 9...d6 10 0-0 g6 11 ②c3 dxe5 12 豐xe5 (12 ②e4 ②d7 13 豐xe5 ②g7 14 豐g3 0-0 15 罩d1 豐e7 16 ②f4 ②xf4 17 豐xf4 ②e6 18 ②xc6 and a draw was agreed in T.Fogarasi-C.Gabriel, Budapest 1996) 12...②g7 13 豐e4 0-0 14 ②e3 (14 豐xc6 罩b8 15 罩d1 ②b7 16 豐c4 ②d4 17 ②f1 豐f6 18 ②e3 c5 19 ②xd4 was another draw, I.Balinov-C.Gabriel, Makarska 1997) 14...罩b8 15 罩ab1 c5 16 豐a4 罩b4 17 豐xa7 ②b7 18 a3 豐h4 19 axb4 ②xg2 20 ☖xg2 and a draw was agreed in P.Svidler-C.Gabriel, Newark 1995.

Another way of going after the pawn with 9 ②d2 d6 10 ②f3 dxe5 11 ②xe5 ②d6 12 豐c3 0-0 13 ②xc6 also leaves Black with compensation: 13...豐e8 14 ②e3 ②c5 15 ②e2 豐xc6 16 ②f3 豐b5 17 ②xa8 was G.Sax-C.Gabriel, German League 1996 (0-1 in 35) and now 17...罩a6! 18 ②f3 ②e5! would have won back the sacrificed material.

9...d6

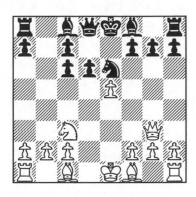

10 ②d3

A very interesting and aggressive approach was used against me by a young Spanish player: 10 ②d2 g6 11 h4!? (11 0-0-0 ②g7 12 exd6 豐xd6 13 豐f3 is slightly better for White) 11...②g7 12 h5 ②xe5 13 f4 ②g7 (13...②d4) 14 hxg6 (or 14 0-0-0 with compensation) 14...hxg6 15 罩xh8+ ②xh8 16 0-0-0 豐f6 17 ②d3 ②c5 18 ②c4. White has real compensation here and I am not sure that I played the right move. I chose 18...②e6 (18...d5 19 ②e3 ②e4 20 豐f3 ②xc3 [20...②f5 21 ②d4 豐h4 22 ②xd5 cxd5 23 ②xd5 0-0-0 24 ②xe4 ②xe4 25 豐xe4 罩xd4 26 罩xd4 ②xd4 27 豐xd4 豐h1+ 28 豐d1 豐xg2 is equal] 21 ②d4 豐h4 22 g3 ②g4 23 豐xc3 ②xd4 24 豐xd4 豐e7 is unclear) 19 豐f3 ☖d7 (19...d5 20

♗e3 ♕e7 21 ♕f2 ♘d7 is slightly better for Black) 20 ♗b5 d5 (20...cxb5 21 ♕xa8 b4 22 ♔b1) 21 ♗e3 cxb5 22 ♗xc5 (22 ♖xd5+ ♗xd5 23 ♕xd5+ ♕d6 24 ♕xa8 ♗xc3 25 bxc3 ♘a4 and Black has a clear advantage) 22...c6 23 ♕e3 (23 ♗d4 ♕xd4 24 ♖xd4 ♗xd4) 23...a5 (23...♗f5! 24 ♗xa7?! ♗g4 25 ♖d3 ♕h4) 24 ♗d4 ♕d8 25 ♗xh8 (25 ♘e4) 25...♕xh8 26 ♘e4 ♔c7 27 ♘c5 ♕f6 28 g3 a4 29 a3 ♗f5 30 ♖e1 d4 31 ♕d2 d3 (31...♔b6 32 ♕b4 with compensation) 32 ♖e5 (32 ♘xd3 ♗xd3 33 ♕xd3 ♖d8 34 ♕e3 ♕d4 is equal) 32...dxc2 33 ♕e3? ♖d8? (33...♖h8 with a clear advantage) 34 ♖e7+?? (White missed a nice draw with 34 ♘d7! and perpetual) 34...♔c8 35 ♖e8 ♕d6 36 ♖xd8+ ♕xd8 37 ♕e1 ♔b8 and White resigned in A.Diaz Herrero-S.Collins, San Sebastian 2011.

10...g6 11 ♘e4 dxe5 12 ♕xe5 ♗g7 13 ♕g3 0-0 14 0-0 ♖b8

In the post mortem Gawain thought Black was even slightly better here. Certainly I was very happy with the results of the opening.

15 ♖b1 f5 16 ♘g5

16...f4

Going for a forcing continuation which seems to lead to a forced draw.

Borrowing an idea from the Svidler-Gabriel game with 16...♖b4!? was also playable, but wholesale liquidation was too tempting with Black against such a dangerous player.

17 ♘xe6 fxg3 18 ♘xd8 gxf2+ 19 ♖xf2 ♗d4

19...♖xd8 should also give Black enough play to hold, but the text is clearer.

20 ♗c4+ ♔g7 21 ♘f7 ♖xf7

The immediate 21...♗xf2+ 22 ♔xf2 comes to the same thing when I take on f7 – from a few moves ago I think I had missed that I can't play 22...♖b4? because of 23 ♗h6+ ♔g8 24 b3 ♖xc4 (24...♖xf7+ 25 ♔g3! and Black has nothing better than taking on c4) 25 bxc4 ♖xf7+ 26 ♔g3 with an opposite-coloured bishop endgame which is very much less comfortable than that obtained in the game – my king and back rank are seriously compromised here.

22 ♗xf7 ♗xf2+ 23 ♔xf2 ♔xf7

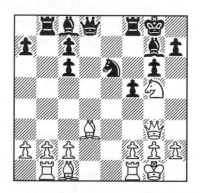

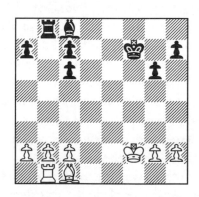

There's nothing in this position, especially if the rooks come off.

24 b3 ♗f5 25 ♖b2 h5 26 ♗f4 ♖d8 27 c4 ♖d7 28 ♖e2 ♖e7

Too obvious to deserve an exclamation mark. Black offers a pawn in order to get the rooks off.

29 ♖d2 ♖d7 30 ♖xd7+ ♗xd7 31 ♔e3 ♗f5 32 ♔d4 ♗b1 33 ♔c3 ♔e6 34 ♗xc7 ♔d7 35 ♗f4 ♔c8 36 g3 ½-½

Game 44
D.Arutinian-S.Collins
Rome 2011
Queen's Gambit Declined

1 d4 d5 2 c4 e6 3 ♘f3 ♘f6 4 ♘c3 ♗e7 5 ♗g5 h6 6 ♗h4 0-0 7 e3 b6 8 ♗e2

This was the second game of a double-round day, which added to the unpleasantness of the defensive task facing me.

In the morning game, where I had also played the black side of a QGD, things had gone rather better: 8 ♗d3 ♗b7 9 0-0 ♘bd7 10 ♕e2 ♘e4 11 ♗g3 c5 12 ♖fd1 cxd4 13 exd4 ♘df6 14 ♘e5 ♘xc3 15 bxc3 ♖c8 with comfortable play for Black. My opponent got creative with 16 c5?, but after 16...bxc5 17 ♖ab1 ♗a8 18 ♗a6 ♖c7 19 ♘g4 ♘e4! Black was clearly better in M.Skliba-S.Collins, Rome 2011 (0-1 in 35).

8...♗b7 9 ♗xf6 ♗xf6 10 cxd5 exd5 11 b4 c6 12 ♕b3 a5 13 b5

Normally they take on a5, with a reasonably comfortable game for Black.

For instance, 13 bxa5 ♖xa5 14 ♖b1 ♘d7 15 0-0 ♗e7 16 a4 ♗d6 17 e4 dxe4 18 ♘xe4 ♗c7 19 ♖fe1 ♘f6 20 ♗d3 c5 21 dxc5 ♘xe4 22 ♗xe4 ♗xe4 23 ♖xe4 ♖xc5 24 g3 ♕f6 25 ♔g2 ♖c3 26 ♕d1 ♕c6 27 ♕e2 ♖c2 28 ♕e3 ♖c3 29 ♕e2 and a draw was agreed in V.Topalov - V.Kramnik, Monte Carlo (blindfold) 1999.

13...c5 14 ♖d1

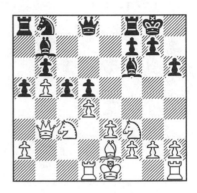

This appears to be a novelty.

14...cxd4?!

One of those ideas which took me about half an hour of muddled thought, but in retrospect is clearly risky. With White having just put his rook on the d-file, I open the d-file for him. I had seen that I could get my knight to c5, which is nice, but doesn't fully compensate for the disparity in piece activity when the position opens up.

It turns out that Black still has a good game after this, and I had a couple of decent ways to proceed at move 16. However, opening the d-file for the White rook is wrong in principle and leads at best to equality, while pushing my c-pawn would have left me with an excellent game.

14...c4, with a slight advantage for Black, was the way to go, especially in response to White's last move. I didn't see how I would follow it up, but some combination of ...♘d7, ...♖e8 and then either ...♕e7 and ...♖ad8 or ...♗e7-d6 and...♘f6 looks pretty sensible.

15 ♘xd4 ♘d7 16 ♗f3

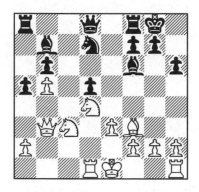

16...♘c5

I played this quite quickly with a sense of relief, though I had seen the transformation which occurs at move 21 and was rather concerned about the resulting position. Not sufficiently concerned, it seems.

Black had a couple of playable alternatives:

a) *Houdini* suggests the elegant 16...a4! 17 ♘xa4 (after 17 ♕b4 ♘e5 18 0-0 ♖c8 Black has good play on the c-file) 17...♘c5 18 ♘xc5 bxc5 19 ♘c6 ♗xc6 20 bxc6 ♕a5+ 21 ♔f1 d4, when Black has the better side of an "opposite-coloured bishop + initiative" posi-

tion. This sacrifice is rather remarkable to me; even though I know that computers are getting stronger (Moore's law and so on), the suggestion by a calculating machine of an elegant pawn sacrifice for a long-term initiative is something surprising. That said, just looking at this position it is apparent that White is not sufficiently mobilized to offer support to his queenside weaknesses, most notably the one on a2.

b) 16...♘e5 17 0-0 ♖e8 18 h3 ♘xf3+ 19 ♘xf3 ♗xc3 20 ♕xc3 ♖c8 21 ♕d3 ♖c4, with active play, also looks reasonable.

17 ♕a3 ♘e4 18 0-0 ♘xc3 19 ♕xc3 ♖c8 20 ♕b3

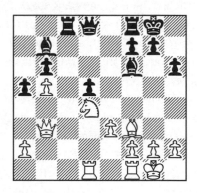

20...♖c4?

This is the real mistake. 20...♕d6 21 ♘c6 ♗xc6 22 bxc6 ♕xc6 23 ♗xd5 ♕c5 is more active. While I'm still wary about such a position, because White has that amazing pawn on e3 which will either blunt my attack on the g1-a7 diagonal or (more likely) support a dominant bishop on d5, this is a better version than the game. Initially the computer thinks the position is equal but gradually the evaluation starts ramping up in White's favour – such a position is strategically very dangerous for Black.

21 ♘c6 ♗xc6 22 bxc6 ♖xc6 23 ♗xd5 ♖d6 24 e4

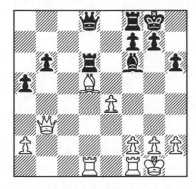

It would be interesting to take a poll of some GMs as to their thoughts on this position. From a practical point of view, I think Black is lost. The bishop on d5 is dominant, completely secure (because of the e4-pawn) and has the effect of preventing major piece exchanges on the d-file. White can try to break through without touching his kingside pawns, followed (if necessary) by pushing the e- and/or f-pawns to open up the black king. It is quite significant that my bishop cannot easily get to c5. My queenside pawns are impossible to mobilize.

In light of this assessment, the rest of the game is given with only light notes.

24...♕c7 25 f4 ♗e7 26 ♖c1 ♕b8 27 ♔h1

♖dd8 28 ♖c6 ♖d6 29 ♖c3 ♖dd8 30 ♖g3 ♕d6 31 ♖d3 ♕b4 32 ♕d1 ♖c8 33 ♖b3 ♕c5 34 ♖g3 ♗h4 35 ♖d3 ♕c2 36 ♕f3 ♕b2 37 ♖b3 ♕d4 38 ♖d3 ♕b2 39 ♕g4 ♖c1 40 ♖dd1 ♖xd1 41 ♖xd1 ♕c2 42 ♕f3 ♗e7 43 ♗b3 ♕b2 44 e5 ♗c5

44...♖d8 45 ♗d5 a4 looks better.

45 ♕e4 ♕f2 46 ♗c4 ♕e3 47 ♕f5 ♕f2 48 h3 ♕g3 49 ♖f1 ♕c3 50 ♗d5 ♕d4 51 ♗b3 ♕c3 52 ♖d1 ♕g3 53 ♗c2 ♕g6

Or 53...g6 54 ♕f6.

54 ♕xg6 fxg6 55 g3

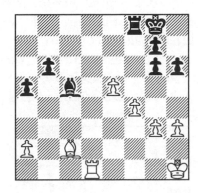

55...g5?

55...♔f7 56 ♖d7+ ♔e6 57 ♖xg7 g5 is a better try: 58 ♗b3+ ♔f5 59 fxg5 hxg5 60 e6 a4 61 ♗c4 ♔f6 62 ♖b7 ♖c8 with good drawing chances. I was short of time here, which is never an excuse, but it ought to be mentioned that defending such positions consumes an ungodly amount of time since you must avoid tactical shots on every move.

56 f5 ♖e8 57 ♖d5 ♔f7 58 ♗a4 ♖e7 59 ♔g2

59 ♗d1 is stronger.

59...♗b4 60 ♔f3 ♖c7 61 ♖d8 ♗c3 62 ♗b3+ ♔e7 63 ♖d6 ♖c5 64 ♖e6+ ♔d7 65

♔e4 b5 66 ♗d5+- ♖c7 67 ♖d6+ ♔e7 68
♗c6 ♔f7 69 ♗d5+ ♔e7 70 ♖b6 b4 71
♖b8 a4 72 ♖g8 b3 73 axb3 a3 74 ♖xg7+
♔d8 75 ♖g8+ ♔d7 76 ♖a8 1-0

Game 45
S.Collins-B.Macieja
Northern California
International 2011/12
Caro-Kann Defence

This was a painful loss for several
reasons, not least because had I won I
would have gained a GM norm.

**1 e4 c6 2 c4 d5 3 exd5 ♘f6 4 ♘c3 cxd5 5
cxd5 ♘xd5 6 ♘f3 ♘xc3 7 bxc3 g6 8 d4
♗g7 9 ♗d3 0-0 10 0-0 ♘c6 11 ♖e1 ♗g4**

12 h3

12 ♗e4 e5! was an important contribution from Magnus: 13 dxe5 (13 d5
keeps the game alive) 13...♕xd1 14
♖xd1 ♗xe5 15 ♖b1 ♗xc3 16 ♖xb7 ♖ad8
17 ♖f1 ♘d4 18 ♗g5 ♖d7 19 ♖xd7 and a
draw was agreed in L.Aronian-
M.Carlsen, FIDE World Ch., Tripoli 2004.
12...♗xf3 13 ♕xf3 ♕a5 14 ♗b2 e5

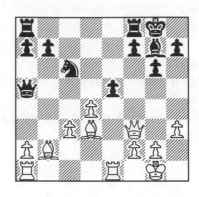

Black has other good options here,
including 14...♖ac8 and 14...e6, but
Macieja's move is fully adequate.

**15 d5 ♘e7 16 d6 ♘c8 17 ♕xb7 ♘xd6 18
♕b4?**

I had calculated (as had my opponent) 18 ♕a6 ♕xa6 19 ♗xa6 ♖fb8 20
♗a3 ♖b6 21 ♗xd6 ♖xd6 22 ♗b7 ♖b8
23 ♖ab1 ♖d2 24 c4 followed by ♗d5
with an easy draw. However, I decided
to "keep more tension" and selected
the alternative.

18...♕d5

Somehow I missed this obvious response, after which Black has an edge.

19 ♖ad1 ♖ab8

Other options like 20 ♕h4 and 20
♕a3 are possible but I haven't found
full equality anywhere.

20 ♗b1 ♖xb4 21 ♖xd5 ♖xb2 22 ♖xd6

Again, a very tough position to assess. Black has a kingside majority, but
if he mobilizes it his king will become
exposed. My passed c-pawn is a real
asset. Overall I think White should be
able to make a draw here, though he
needs to find some good moves.

22...♖fb8 23 ♗e4 ♗f8 24 ♖c6!

Covering c5.

The computer seems to prefer 24 ♖d7 ♗c5 25 ♖f1 but I can't believe that going passive with the rook is the way to go.

24...♖xa2

24...♖d8 25 c4! and my bishop gets to d5.

25 ♗d5 ♖d2 26 c4 ♖b7?

26...♖b6!, with an edge for Black, was a good resource which we both missed, aiming for the optimal f6-square.

27 ♖c8 ♖b6

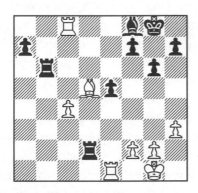

28 f4!

The extra tempo makes the difference. I have now completely equalized.

28...e4 29 ♖xe4 ♔g7 30 ♖c7 ♖f6 31 g3 a5 32 ♔f1?!

In the post-mortem I found 32 ♖e6! instantly. This seems to draw without problems, for instance 32...♖xe6 33 ♗xe6 ♔h8 34 ♗xf7 a4 35 ♗d5 ♗d6 36 ♖c8+ ♔g7 37 c5 ♖xd5 38 cxd6 ♖xd6 39 ♖a8 ♖d4 40 ♔f2 with a draw.

32...a4 33 ♖e2 ♖d3 34 ♔g2?

Again 34 ♖e6! was indicated.

34...a3

I'm not sure if this position can be saved any more.

35 h4 h5 36 ♖c8 ♖a6 37 ♖a8

37 ♖a2 ♖a7 is also grim.

37...♖xa8 38 ♗xa8 ♗c5 39 ♗e4 ♖b3 40 ♗d5

Losing straight away, but there is nothing better.

40...f5! 0-1

...♖b2 follows, so I resigned.

Game 46
S.Collins-R.Nokes
Turin Olympiad 2006
Sicilian Defence

1 e4 c5 2 c3 ♘f6 3 e5 ♘d5 4 d4 cxd4 5 ♘f3 ♘c6 6 cxd4 d6 7 ♗c4 e6 8 0-0 ♗e7 9 ♖e1 0-0 10 exd6 ♕xd6 11 ♘c3 ♘xc3?! 12 bxc3 b6 13 ♘g5!

I was delighted to be able to use this line, in which I'd suffered a painful defeat – my opponent defends better than I did.

13...♗xg5!

13...g6? is a poor line: 14 h4! ♘a5 15 ♗d3 ♗b7 16 ♘xh7 ♕c6 (16...♚xh7 17 ♕h5+ ♚g7 18 ♕h6+ ♚g8 19 ♗xg6 fxg6 20 ♕xg6+ ♚h8 21 ♖xe6 ♕d5 22 ♖xe7 ♕xg2+ 23 ♕xg2 ♗xg2 24 ♚xg2 is hopeless for Black) 17 ♗e4 ♕xc3 18 ♗d2 ♕xd4 19 ♗xb7 ♘xb7 20 ♘xf8 ♗xh4? (taking on f8 would have held White to a clear advantage – now my kingside gets weakened) 21 g3 ♗f6 22 ♘xe6 fxe6 23 ♕f3 ♖f8 24 ♗e3 ♕d5 25 ♕xd5 exd5 26 ♖ad1 ♖d8 27 ♗d4 ♚f7 28 ♖e3 ♘c5 29 ♖a3 ♖d7 30 ♖f3. Of course, I have very little for the exchange here. I went on to lose in C.Landenbergue-S.Collins, Saint Vincent 2005 (1-0 in 61).

14 ♗xg5 ♗b7 15 ♕h5

15 ♕g4 might be more precise.

15...♘e7 16 ♗d3 ♘f5

16...♘g6 is a tighter defence.

17 ♕h3 ♕c6 18 ♖ad1 h6

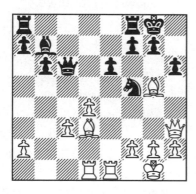

19 ♗xf5!?

Not an obvious transformation, but a good one I think. I now get a huge d-pawn, with no counterplay for Black.

19...exf5 20 d5 ♕d7 21 ♗e7 ♖fe8 22 d6

This advantage must be pretty significant.

22...♖ac8 23 ♕d3 ♖c5 24 f3 ♖ec8 25 ♖c1 ♗d5 26 ♕d2 ♗e6

Fritz thinks this is dead level. To my eyes, White will always have good long-term chances.

This type of situation is basically unique to opposite-coloured bishop positions, and makes them extremely difficult to assess. On the one hand, Black has an absolutely perfect blockade on the light squares, effectively neutralizing my passed d-pawn. However, if I am able to generate an attack on his king (which is quite possible, given that every dark square on the board will be under my control), then this blockade may have to be loosened to enable defenders to reach the kingside. The question of what is the objective assessment is very difficult to answer, and not especially interesting. More significant, in my view, is that Black will have to defend this position for about 200 moves. I can avoid exchanges, play around with various piece setups, and he will never be able to win my d-pawn or trade bishops. This is another important and often overlooked aspect of opposite-coloured bishops – even in positions which should be drawn, the defence can often be extremely tedious.

27 ♖e3 b5 28 f4 ♖c4 29 ♖g3

A good (if obvious) rook lift.

29...♔h7 30 a3 ♖8c5?

A major slip – Black can't let me get to f8.

31 ♗f8 g6 32 ♖h3 h5

The dark squares are now extremely weak.

33 ♕f2 ♖d5 34 ♖f1?

Giving my opponent a chance.

34...♖c8?

34...♕c8, winning a pawn, was critical – Black just has to go for this, since otherwise he is suffering for nothing. 35 ♗e7 ♖xc3 36 ♖xc3 ♕xc3 37 ♕xa7 ♖d2 and suddenly Black is on top.

35 ♗e7 ♖c6 36 ♕g3 f6 37 ♕h4 ♖dxd6 38 ♗xd6 ♖xd6

I thought this was good for me, but in fact Black can hold comfortably.

39 ♖e3 ♔g7??

39...♗d5! 40 ♖fe1 ♗e4 and I have nothing.

40 ♖fe1 a6 41 h3 ♕c8 42 ♕f2 ♗f7 43 ♔h2 ♖d7 44 ♖e7 ♖xe7 45 ♖xe7 ♕xc3 46 ♕a2 ♕c4 47 ♕xc4 bxc4 48 ♖a7 c3 49 ♖c7 c2 50 ♖xc2 ♗d5 51 ♖c7+ ♔h6 52 h4 ♗e4 53 ♖f7 ♗d3 54 g3 ♗c4 55 ♖xf6 ♔g7 56 ♖d6 ♔f7 57 ♔g1 ♗b5 58 ♔f2 1-0

Two Bishops in the Ruy Lopez

Just how much of a material advantage does two bishops vs. bishop + knight/two knights confer?

There are definitely some positions where the bishop pair, in and of itself, is fully sufficient to compensate for a pawn deficit. We'll look at two examples from the Ruy Lopez, both demonstrating very different types of position. Broadly, the ways in which I've seen two bishops make a draw from a pawn down are as follows:

Just sitting

The bishops become more powerful the more the game opens up. Accordingly, it is sometimes difficult for the player a pawn up to make progress without allowing the bishops to dominate the game.

Trading

One of the benefits of having the bishop pair is that you can choose when to give up one of them. This breaks down into a few possibilities:

♙ Trading a bishop for a knight, leaving opposite-coloured bishops;

♙ Trading a bishop for a knight, leaving same-coloured bishops, but extracting some other concession (e.g. damaging the opponent's pawn structure).

Game 47
E.Bacrot-L.Aronian
Kallithea 2008
Ruy Lopez

In his post-game comments to his encounter with Karjakin from the King's Tournament 2011, Radjabov noted that Aronian constantly plays a position a pawn down with the bishop pair in the Ruy Lopez. He does indeed, and is absolutely untouchable in this system.

1 e4 e5 2 ♘f3 ♘c6 3 ♗b5 a6 4 ♗a4 ♘f6 5 0-0 ♗e7 6 ♖e1 b5 7 ♗b3 0-0 8 c3 d5 9 exd5 ♘xd5 10 ♘xe5 ♘xe5 11 ♖xe5 c6

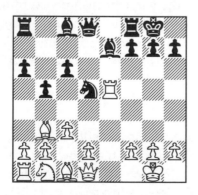

12 d3

A different way to obtain a similar position has been tried in more recent games against Aronian, viz. 12 d4 ♗d6 13 ♖e1 ♕h4 14 g3 ♕h3 15 ♗e3 ♗g4 16 ♕d3 ♖ae8 17 ♘d2 ♕h5 18 ♕f1 ♖e7 19 a4 ♖fe8 20 axb5 axb5 21 ♗xd5 ♕xd5 22 ♕g2 ♕xg2+ 23 ♔xg2, but Black has no problems after 23...h5! as Aronian has demonstrated:

a) 24 ♖a5 h4 25 ♖ea1 hxg3 26 hxg3 ♗e6 27 ♖a8 ♗d5+ 28 ♔f1 ♗xg3 29 ♗g5 f6 30 ♗xf6 ♖e1+ 31 ♖xe1 ♖xa8 32 fxg3 gxf6 33 ♘e4 ♔f7 34 ♘d6+ ♔g6 35 ♖e8 ♖a1+ 36 ♖e1 ♖a8 37 ♖e8 ♖a1+ 38 ♖e1 and a draw was agreed in E.Bacrot-L.Aronian, Nalchik 2009.

b) 24 ♖ec1 f6 25 b3 g5 26 c4 bxc4 27 ♘xc4 ♗c7 28 ♘a5 ♗xa5 29 ♖xa5 ♗d7 30 b4 ♖b8 31 ♖c4 ♔f7 32 ♔f1 ♔g6 33 ♔e2 ♗g4+ 34 ♔d2 with a draw in V.Anand-L.Aronian, Wijk aan Zee 2011.

12...♗d6 13 ♖e1 ♗f5 14 ♕f3 ♕h4 15 g3 ♕h3 16 ♗xd5 cxd5

17 ♕xd5

17 ♗e3 ♗xd3 18 ♕xd5 ♖ad8 19 ♕f3 ♗c4 20 ♘d2 ♗e6 21 ♗d4 and now:

a) Commenting on the position after 21...h6, Rowson writes: "My first impression on seeing this position was that White is better. White is a clear pawn up, his king is not in any particular danger, his d4-bishop is excellent and Black has no particular ideas in the pipeline. I realize that Black's light-squared bishop is strong, and that the two bishops count for something, but is it really worth a whole pawn? Evidently so." 22 a3 ♗b8 23 ♕g2 ♕f5 24 f3 ♖fe8 25 ♘e4 ♗d5 26 ♖e2 ♖e6 27 ♖ae1 and a draw was agreed in R.Kasimdzhanov-M.Adams, Linares 2005.

b) 21...♗b8 22 ♕g2 (22 ♘e4 ♗d5 23 ♗xg7 ♔xg7 24 ♕f6+ ♔g8 25 ♕g5+ ♔h8 26 ♕f6+ ♔g8 with a repetition in E.Bacrot-L.Aronian, Khanty Mansiysk 2005) 22...♕h5 23 f3 ♕g6 24 a3 h5 25 ♖e2 ♖d5 26 ♖ae1 ♖fd8 27 ♘e4 ♗d6 28 ♕f2 ♖f5 29 ♘xd6 and another draw in V.Anand-L.Aronian, Nice (rapid) 2008, this time informed by the opposite-coloured bishops.

17...♖ad8 18 ♕g2 ♕xg2+ 19 ♔xg2 ♗xd3 20 ♗e3

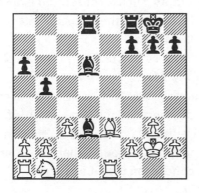

20...♗e4+

20...♖fe8 21 ♘d2 b4 22 ♗b6 ♖xe1 23 ♖xe1 ♖b8 24 ♗a5 bxc3 25 ♗xc3 f6 led to a different type of position in A.Shirov-L.Aronian, Morelia/Linares 2008 (½-½ in 77). White's extra pawn is very healthy and forms part of a dangerous queenside majority, but with the position completely open the black bishops will be highly effective.

21 f3

Bacrot fared no better against Aronian in Dresden 2008: 21 ♔f1 ♗c6 22 ♘d2 f6 23 ♗d4 ♖fe8 24 ♖e2 ♔f7 25 ♖ae1 ♖xe2 26 ♔xe2 ♖e8+ 27 ♔d1 ♖xe1+ 28 ♔xe1 with a draw in 50 moves.

21...♗c6 22 ♘d2 ♖fe8

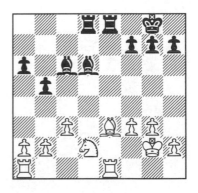

23 ♘b3

23 ♗d4 h5 24 ♔f2 f6 25 ♖xe8+ ♖xe8 26 ♘f1 ♔f7 27 ♘e3 ♖d8 28 a3 ♗c7 29 ♖e1 ♖d7 30 ♘c2 ♗d6 31 ♘e3 ♗f8 32 h3 g6 33 g4 ♗h6 34 gxh5 ♗xe3+ 35 ♖xe3 gxh5 with opposite-coloured bishops and a draw in 41 moves in P.Leko-L.Aronian, Yerevan (rapid) 2008.

23...f6 24 ♗b6 ♖xe1 25 ♖xe1 ♖d7 26

♖d1 ♔f7 27 ♗c5 ♗c7 28 ♖xd7+ ♗xd7 29 ♘d2 h5 30 ♗d4 ♗c6 31 b3 f5 32 ♔f2 g5 33 ♗e3 g4 34 f4 ♔e6 35 ♗d4 ½-½

This game represents the modern reality of the Marshall Attack which, in the most respectable main lines, is a straightforward attempt to draw a pawn-down endgame with the bishop pair.

Game 48
S.Karjakin-T.Radjabov
Kings Tournament,
Medias 2011
Ruy Lopez

1 e4 e5 2 ♘f3 ♘c6 3 ♗b5 f5 4 ♘c3 fxe4 5 ♘xe4 ♘f6

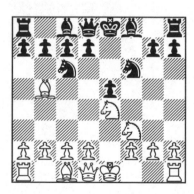

This is Radjabov's patent. The line with 5...d5 6 ♘xe5 dxe4 7 ♘xc6 ♕g5 was tested by Nisipeanu against Carlsen and Karjakin in the same tournament.

6 ♘xf6+ ♕xf6 7 ♕e2 ♗e7 8 ♗xc6 bxc6 9 ♘xe5 ♕e6

This is basically a new move – Kar-

jakin pointed out that the move had been played before (with 10...d6) to which Radjabov pointed out that he doesn't look at such games and "there were probably some games on ICC also"!

9...0-0 was the previous method of handling the position.

10 ♘f3

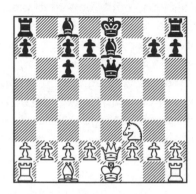

10...♕xe2+

Rogozenko: "Strictly speaking, only this is a new move, but in principle the entire Black's conception is quite remarkable: Black enters an endgame a pawn down in belief that the bishop pair will secure enough compensation for a draw. Such a conception is typical for instance in the Marshall Attack of the Ruy Lopez."

11 ♔xe2 c5 12 ♖e1 ♗b7 13 ♔f1 ♗xf3 14 gxf3 ♖f8

Rogozenko: "This looks like the critical position for the evaluation of the entire line starting with 9...♕e6. In his home preparation Radjabov came to the conclusion that it is a draw."

15 ♔g2

Radjabov suggested that White might try the alternative 15 d4 cxd4 16 ♗g5 ♖f7 17 ♖e4 d5 18 ♖e5 ♖d8 19 ♖ae1 ♖d7 20 b4 h6 21 ♗xe7 ♖fxe7 22 ♖e6! (the pawn endgame is not promising for White: 22 ♖xe7+ ♖xe7 23 ♖xe7+ ♔xe7 24 ♔e2 ♔e6 25 ♔d3 ♔e5 26 b5 g5).

15...♖f5 16 d3 d5 17 f4 ♖f7

Radjabov indicated that Black can also play 17...♔d7 and after 18 ♖e5 ♖af8 19 ♖xf5 ♖xf5 20 ♗d2 g6 wait with ...♗d6 and ...c6. White's only plan is to play his rook to g5, but then taking on f5 would lead to a fortress.

18 ♖e5 0-0-0

19 ♖b1

Radjabov's preparation in this line was remarkably deep. Straight after the game he demonstrated 19 ♗d2 ♗f6 20 ♖e6 ♗xb2 21 ♖b1 ♗d4 22 c3 ♗f6 23 ♖a6 d4 24 c4 ♗e7 25 ♖xa7 ♔d7 with equality.

19...c6 20 ♗d2 ♗d6 21 ♖e6 ♔d7 22 ♖be1 ♖df8 23 ♖1e2 ♖f6

The most precise, exchanging one pair of rooks.

Rogozenko notes that 23...♗xf4? 24 ♗xf4 ♖xf4 fails to 25 ♖e7+.

24 ♖xf6 ♖xf6 25 ♗e3 ♖e6

25...d4 26 ♗d2 ♗xf4 27 ♗xf4 ♖xf4 28 ♖e5 ♔d6 29 ♖e8 appears less clear.

26 ♔f3 d4 27 ♗d2 ♖xe2 28 ♔xe2 ♔e6 29 ♔f3 ♔f5 30 h3 ½-½

Obviously White can make no progress.

Double Bishop Sacrifice

Initially I was planning on making this section into a collection of the best double bishop sacrifices of recent years. Instead, however, I'm going to present one of my own games where I played a double bishop sacrifice, which turned out to be a completely incorrect decision!

It takes an enormous amount of self-discipline to avoid spectacular continuations in favour of good, simple moves, but this is a discipline which must be cultivated if you want to improve your chess.

Game 49
S.Collins-I.Snape
Hastings Premier 2007/08
Sicilian Defence

1 e4 c5 2 c3 ♘f6 3 e5 ♘d5 4 d4 cxd4 5 ♘f3 ♘c6 6 cxd4 d6 7 ♗c4 e6 8 0-0 ♗e7 9 ♖e1 0-0 10 exd6 ♕xd6 11 ♘c3 ♗d7

This is a new move, though it looks quite logical. 11...a6 has been the main choice of most strong GMs with Black in recent games. 11...罝d8 is Rogozenko's recommendation.

For 11...公xc3?! see Collins-Nokes (Game 46).

12 a3

Rybka points out the fascinating 12 g3!?, intending to take advantage of the boxed-in black queen. 12...公b6 (12...罝ac8? 13 奧xd5 exd5 14 奧f4 wins material) 13 奧b3 公a5 (if 13...營b4 then 14 a3 營a5 15 奧f4 with a slight advantage for White) 14 奧f4 營b4 15 奧d2 公xb3 16 axb3 營d6 17 公e4 營c7 18 公e5 with roughly level chances.

12...公xc3 13 bxc3 公a5 14 奧d3 罝ac8 15 公e5

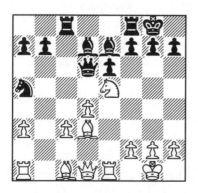

15...公c6

15...罝xc3 16 罝e3! (16 奧d2 allows Black to take a second pawn, with equality: 16...罝xd3 17 公xd3 公c6 18 公e5 營d5) keeps an advantage in all lines. White threatens the standard 奧xh7+, 營h5+ and 罝h3, so Black must give up the exchange: 16...罝fc8 17 奧d2 罝xd3 18 罝xd3 公c6 19 罝c1!! and if 19...公xe5? 20 罝xc8+ 奧xc8 21 奧b4 營c6 22 dxe5 奧xb4 23 axb4 winning.

16 奧f4 公xe5 17 奧xe5 營c6

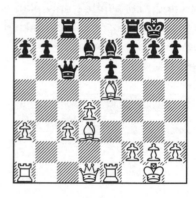

18 奧xh7+??

An example of the "I might regret it if I don't try this beautiful combination" school of chess, which often ends painfully. As it turned out, I had to exert myself to win this game, and had my opponent found the correct defence I would have really struggled to draw.

18 罝e3 f5 19 罝b1 brings both rooks into play in an extremely efficient way, while the threat of 奧b5 prevents Black from taking on a3. White's advantage looks quite serious, viz. 19...a6 (19...b6 20 奧a6 罝cd8 21 營e2!? 奧xa3 22 奧b5

♕c8 23 ♗c4 with more than enough for the pawn) 20 c4 ♗f6 21 ♗e2 ♗xe5 22 ♖xe5 b6 23 ♕b3 ♖b8 24 f4.

18...♔xh7 19 ♕h5+ ♔g8 20 ♗xg7 ♔xg7 21 ♖e3

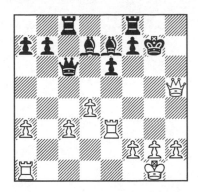

21...e5?

Now the position becomes roughly level.

However, after 21...♖h8 22 ♖g3+ ♗g5 23 ♕xg5+ (23 ♖xg5+ ♔f6) 23...♔f8 White doesn't have enough for the piece, since his initiative is pretty weak, e.g. 24 ♕g7+ ♔e7 25 ♕g5+ ♔e8 26 ♕e5 ♖f8 27 ♖e1 ♕c7 and Black has a material advantage, plus a weakness to exploit on a3.

22 ♖g3+ ♕g6 23 ♕xe5+ ♗f6 24 ♖xg6+

24 ♕d6!?.

24...fxg6 25 ♕a5 a6 26 ♕b4 ♗c6 27 ♖d1

27...♗d5

Black can't get co-ordination by just moving this bishop. 27...♖fe8! was preferable, with the better game.

28 ♕d6 ♗b3?!

Putting the bishop on an exposed square. 28...♖fd8 (activity) or 28...♗f7 (solidity) was preferable.

29 ♖d3 ♖fe8 30 h3 ♖ed8 31 ♕b6 ♗d5 32 ♖g3 ♖d7 33 f4 ♗e4??

33...♗f7 keeps the game alive.

34 ♕e6 ♗c6 35 d5?!

White is still winning after this, but he had a much more incisive continuation: 35 f5! g5 36 h4.

35...♗b5 36 a4 ♖xc3 37 ♖xc3 ♗xc3 38 axb5 ♖f7 39 bxa6 bxa6 40 d6 ♖xf4 41 d7 ♗f6 42 ♕xf6+ ♖xf6 43 d8♕ g5 44 ♔h2 ♔g6 45 ♕d3+ ♔h6 46 ♔g3 a5 47 ♕b5 1-0

Chapter Three

Material

Material Revisited

As I've become a better player, and had more conversations with (and read the annotations of) good grandmasters, I have noticed that my attitude to material has changed over time. Specifically:

1) An increased value is placed on passed pawns, especially far-advanced passed pawns. This has a corollary that one tends to value three pawns more than a piece in most endgames.

2) Less value is placed on the exchange. In particular, exchange sacrifices become a highly ordinary part of the game, roughly equivalent to pawn sacrifices, and used for similar ends (compromising an opponent's pawn structure, gaining the two bishops, gaining the initiative, etc).

In my experience, misassessing material imbalances is one of the most common mistakes made by weak players, and is one of the hardest misjudgements to correct.

Game 50
S.Collins-D.Wheeler
British League 2011
French Defence

I was pretty annoyed at the result of this game and, when looking up my notes, found that I had left it entirely unannotated! It hardly needs to be said that this isn't the best approach to a disappointing game, which must be analysed and understood in order to be of maximum benefit. Still, I'll make up for it now.

Incidentally, I wanted to use this game to demonstrate the "pawns vs. pieces" debate. The various exchange sacrifices which populate the key variations were completely hidden to me during the game.

1 e4 e6 2 d3

For a long time (and perhaps even now) I didn't have a decent repertoire with White against the French. I had written previously (a chapter, then a book!) on the Advance Variation with 2 d4 d5 3 e5, but found it too committal for my tastes. Recently I've been using a couple of sidelines in the Tarrasch (3 ♘d2): the Korchnoi Gambit (which arises in its pure form after 3...♘f6 4 e5 ♘fd7 5 ♗d3 c5 6 c3 ♘c6 7 ♘gf3!?; this can also be used against 3...♗e7 and in some lines after 3...c5) and a sideline where White gets a relatively unpromising position with an isolated queen's pawn (3...♘f6 4 ♗d3 c5 5 c3).

Occasionally, as here, I have opted for the King's Indian Attack.

2...d5 3 ♘d2 ♘f6 4 ♘gf3 b6

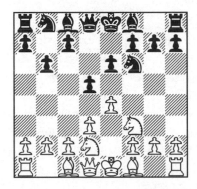

A line about which I knew very little, though it has been played by Dreev a number of times. I managed to notice (despite being a Sunday morning game) that my planned kingside fianchetto would either drop an e-pawn or lead to complications, but wasn't too upset at the prospect of transposing to Tarrasch-type positions where Black had committed to an early ...b6.

5 c3

Probably the best move, and the preference of Bologan who is perhaps the strongest top GM to regularly play the King's Indian Attack (probably since he played it with success in his youth).

5 g3 is the most common move, but White has a negative score after 5...dxe4 6 dxe4 with Black scoring well with, amongst others, 6...♗c5 and 6...♗b7 7 ♕e2 ♗a6, when White has to mess around to get his pieces out.

5...♗b7

This strikes me as rather committal, and not a helpful commitment at that. Given that White intends e5 and d4, the bishop will be misplaced on b7.

5...♗e7, intending to castle and make use of ...b6 with a later ...c5, seems more logical and is the main line here. Of course, if Black plays in mechanical fashion with the standard ...c5, ...b5, ...a5 pawn storm, he might find himself a tempo down on the main lines.

6 e5

Clearly indicated after Black's last move, though some players (including Tal) have attempted to keep the central tension with 6 ♕a4+.

6...♘fd7 7 d4

I think this is nice for White. Black has spent his 'extra' move (caused by the stutter-step of my d-pawn, reaching d4 in two moves) putting his bishop on a bad square. He also, at the moment, has no central pressure, and in so far as I understand the French, it's all about blowing up the white centre as quickly as possible.

7...c5 8 &b5

Playing 8 &d3 is the most natural and most popular, but I wanted to have the option of meeting ...&a6 with a4.

8...❒c6 9 0-0 &e7 10 ❒e1 ♕c7 11 ❒f1 h6

The first new move, it seems, though clearly this is very logical, taking g5 under control both to prevent invasion by a white piece and, eventually (if he castles long), to play ...g5 himself.

12 ❒g3 0-0-0 13 &d2 ♔b8 14 h4 a6 15 &d3 b5

It might look strange that both sides are advancing pawns in front of their own kings, but there is some method in the madness. From White's perspective, he has a kingside space advantage and should make an effort to win the game on that side. Even moves like h4 are useful from a defensive standpoint in that they restrain Black's ...g5 break. Black's queenside advance seems less standard and correspondingly riskier, but if he stayed passive on that wing I could push my a- and b-pawns without too much trouble.

16 ❒h5

The immediate 16 a4 is also possible, with a likely transposition to the game.

16...cxd4

16...g6 is a slight concession in that it weakens the dark squares on the kingside, and the h6-pawn isn't too thrilled either. After 17 ❒g3 I think Black is struggling – amongst other ideas, something like ♕c1 would force him into an uncomfortable decision about what to do with his h-pawn.

17 cxd4 ♕b6

This seemed very provocative to me.

18 a4

Duly provoked.

18...b4

Houdini wants to get going with 18...g5. I must confess I'd missed that my knight journey to h5 facilitated this advance, which I thought I had under control. After 19 axb5 axb5 20 &e3 ❒hg8 (20...gxh4 is very natural but leaves the black kingside pawns rather weak; *Houdini* likes the stoic 21 &f1 &hg8 22 &d3 when Black has four weak pawns and a difficult defensive task) 21 hxg5 hxg5 22 &h2 is rather typical for this type of position, with White invading on the squares weakened by Black's kingside attacking aspirations.

19 a5

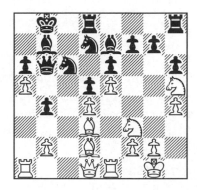

19...&xa5!

Brave. I think, from the psychological perspective at least, this is the correct decision – Black can now claim that he is better on the queenside (which should provide some insurance against getting mated there).

19...&a7 looks a bit grim, and I've won control of some useful dark squares on the queenside while artificially isolating the b4-pawn.

20 &xg7

Material parity has been restored and Black has some structural defects, but the knight on g7 is a bit out of it.

20...&c4 21 &c1

The engine suggests 21 b3, but after

21...&xd2 22 &xd2 &dg8 23 &h5 &g4 White has yet to establish a bind on the position.

21...h5

Kind of trapping the knight. It can get out, but the d4-pawn will drop, which has to count as some sort of moral victory for a French Defence player.

22 b3

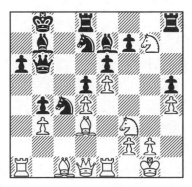

22...&a3

22...&dg8! was the more active approach. Part of the problem with not making notes to games on the same day they're played is that you forget everything you thought about. I don't know what my attitude was to this move, but looking at it now 23 &f5 (trying to dominate in the centre; 23 bxc4 dxc4 24 &xc4 &xg7 and White has no real trumps to speak of) 23...exf5 24 bxc4 dxc4 25 &xc4 leaves me with a strategically beautiful position, with my d-pawn ready to run, but rather too many black pieces pointing at g2 for my liking. This is serious counterplay.

23 &g5

23 ♗f4! improves. 24 ♘f5 exf5 25 e6+ is a real strategic threat so Black must move his king to the a-file, where it's worse placed. Then I put my bishop on g5. A nice idea, and one I'm rather annoyed to have missed.

23...♗xg5 24 ♘xg5 ♖hg8 25 ♘xh5 ♕xd4

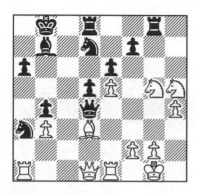

"Equal" says *Houdini*, which looks about right. I think I was celebrating my triumph on the kingside, but the elimination of my d-pawn and long-term strategic danger on the queenside should balance the chances.

26 g3

26 ♗h7? leads to our other material discussion, the exchange sacrifice: 26...♕xh4! 27 ♗xg8 ♖xg8 28 f4 (28 ♘xf7 ♘b5 followed by 29...♘c3 and Black's pieces completely dominate) 28...♖h8 and my position is collapsing – note that the attempt to support the knight and block the h-file with 29 g4 gets absolutely crushed by 29...d4 30 ♘e4 ♘c5!.

26...♘c5 27 ♗e2 ♕b2

Missing a peach of an exchange sac:

27...♕xd1 28 ♗xd1 ♖xg5!! 29 hxg5 d4 and the black pieces completely dominate.

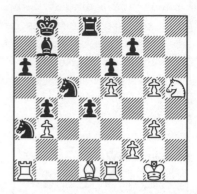

Houdini thinks it's equal but against a human with 10 moves to make in not-so-much time before the time control, Black will score much better than 50% in practice.

28 ♘xf7 ♖df8

28...♖c8 is good, adding to the queenside pressure.

29 ♘g5 ♗c8

29...♘xb3 is also possible: 30 ♘f6 ♗c8! (30...♘xa1 31 ♕xa1 ♕xa1 32 ♖xa1 ♗c8 33 ♘xg8 ♖xg8 34 f4 looks threatening – the h-pawn is ready to run, while none of the black pawns are similarly prepared).

30 ♘f6 ♖g7?

30...♘xb3 is better, with rough equality.

31 ♕c1?

Returning the favour. 31 ♗c4! is not a particularly difficult shot, which would have placed Black in grave difficulties. Again, it's annoying that I missed this, which would not be impossible to spot in a blitz game.

31...♕xc1 32 ♖axc1 ♘xb3

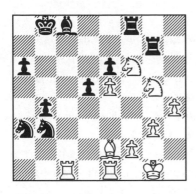

33 ♖xc8+!

Finally playing a good idea, even if it's rather obvious.

33...♖xc8 34 ♘xe6 ♖e7

34...♖a7 brings us back into the realm of exchange sacrifices. White has a nice game (four connected passed pawns!), for instance 35 ♗g4 a5 36 ♖d1 d4 37 h5 ♘c4 38 ♘xd4 ♘xd4 39 ♗xc8 ♔xc8 (knight checks don't help) 40 ♖xd4 ♘xe5 with a highly complicated position where Black obviously has compensation for the pawn with his two passers running down the board, but I don't know whether this is fully enough.

35 ♘xd5!?

This was my idea from several moves previously. 35 ♗g4 is also possible, with similar play to the last note.

35...♖xe6 36 ♗g4 ♖ce8

36...♖ee8 37 ♗xc8 ♔xc8 38 ♘xb4 is similar.

37 ♗xe6 ♖xe6 38 ♘xb4 a5 39 ♘d5 a4 40 f4 ♘c4 41 h5

Houdini gets excited around here, thinking White has a clear advantage. At least I share the machine's mistaken evaluations, if not its correct ones.

41...a3 42 ♘f6 a2 43 h6 ♘d6

This is all best play, by the way.

44 h7 ♘f7 45 f5 ♖e7 46 e6 ♘h8 47 g4 ♖g7

Now *Houdini* thinks I'm winning. But I'm not.

48 ♔h2

48 ♔f2 doesn't change much.

48...a1♕ 49 ♖xa1 ♘xa1

A rather unusual material balance. I took some comfort from the fact that Black has two knights, so if I manage to get his rook for knight and four pawns I'll be safe. Also, with my pawns so close to the edge, I was still hoping for some blunder or late chance, but it doesn't arise.

50 g5 ♘c2 51 g6 ♘d4 52 ♘h5 ♘xf5 ½-½

Two knights sometimes win against a blockaded pawn, but not one on h7!

Game 51
V.Anand-G.Kasparov
PCA World Championship,
New York 1995
Sicilian Defence

1 e4 c5 2 ♘f3 d6 3 d4 cxd4 4 ♘xd4 ♘f6 5 ♘c3 a6 6 ♗e2

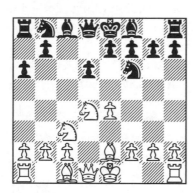

Following eight draws in the first eight games, this was the encounter which broke the deadlock in the Kasparov-Anand match in 1995. Vishy had done some excellent work on the Classical Scheveningen, which paid off handsomely after the match in wins against Topalov and other top players.

However, unfortunately for the challenger, the champion's preparation proved rather more effective during the match. After destroying Anand's Open Ruy Lopez, Kasparov started employing the Dragon Sicilian with Black, getting good positions and phenomenal results.

6...e6 7 0-0 ♗e7 8 a4 ♘c6 9 ♗e3 0-0 10 f4 ♕c7 11 ♔h1 ♖e8

Of course, this is an absolute opening tabiya, so I won't even pretend to attempt a superficial coverage. The system Anand employs was pioneered by GM Van der Wiel.

12 ♗f3 ♗d7 13 ♘b3 ♘a5 14 ♘xa5 ♕xa5 15 ♕d3 ♖ad8 16 ♖fd1 ♗c6 17 b4!?

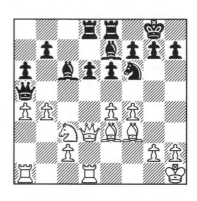

An interesting attempt to attack on the queenside, which is normally Black's domain in the Scheveningen.

17...♕c7

Of course not 17...♕xb4?? 18 ♖ab1 ♕a5 (18...♕a3 19 ♖b3) 19 ♗b6, winning even more than an exchange.

18 b5 ♗d7 19 ♖ab1 axb5 20 ♘xb5 ♗xb5 21 ♕xb5 ♖a8 22 c4 e5 23 ♗b6 ♕c8 24 fxe5 dxe5 25 a5 ♗f8 26 h3 ♕e6

White has definitely had the upper hand in the opening, emerging with two bishops and some long-term pressure against b7. However, Black is far from busted – that is, until the following couple of moves.

27 ℤd5!

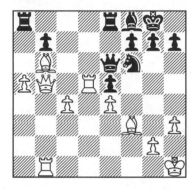

27...ᔡxd5??

Anand says that he was shocked by this move. White's 27th was cute, but did not really threaten anything, and White would still have had to show a way to break through.

By capturing on d5, however, Black creates a fantastic roller of white pawns on c4 and d5, which are all the more effective for being supported by the bishop pair.

It would be fascinating to know how Kasparov assessed the resulting position – was he optimistic, a whole exchange up? Or did he dislike his position to the extent that he felt he should "at least" grab some material to put some pressure on Anand, pressure which would be all the more intense given the competitive situation? In any

event, his position goes from playable to unplayable in the space of a move.

28 exd5 ♕g6 29 c5 e4

Of course the f3-bishop could not be allowed to operate down the h1-a8 diagonal after d6. However, this bishop has no difficulty finding a useful role elsewhere.

30 ♗e2 ℤe5

Playing to activate at least one piece besides the queen.

31 ♕d7 ℤg5 32 ℤg1

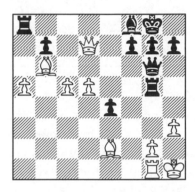

Black's "attack" has been summarily dealt with, while the pawns will march through. The weakness of b7 is fatal.

32...e3 33 d6 ℤg3 34 ♕xb7 ♕e6 35 ♔h2 1-0

Game 52
R.Ponomariov-M.Adams
Linares 2002
Ruy Lopez

This game is a remarkable example of the exchange sacrifice in that Ponomariov offers two such sacrifices in two different parts of the board.

1 e4 e5 2 ♘f3 ♘c6 3 ♗b5 a6 4 ♗a4 ♘f6 5 0-0 ♗e7 6 ♖e1 b5 7 ♗b3 0-0 8 c3 d5 9 exd5 ♘xd5 10 ♘xe5 ♘xe5 11 ♖xe5 c6 12 d4 ♗d6 13 ♖e1 ♕h4 14 g3 ♕h3 15 ♖e4 g5 16 ♕e2

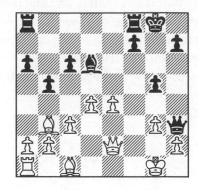

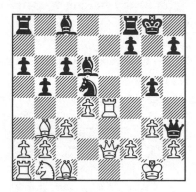

16...♘f6

By round 14 of the same event, a solution for Black had been found: 16...f5 17 ♗xd5+ (not 17 ♖e6?? ♗xe6 18 ♕xe6+ ♔h8 19 ♕xd6 – 19 ♗xd5 ♖ae8 – 19...♖ae8 20 ♗d2 f4 21 ♗xd5 cxd5 22 f3 g4 and White resigned in I.Smirin-A.Grischuk, Panormo 2001) 17...cxd5 18 ♖e6 f4 19 ♖xd6 ♗g4 20 ♕f1 ♕xf1+ 21 ♔xf1 ♖ae8 22 ♗d2 ♗h3+ 23 ♔g1 fxg3 24 hxg3 ♖e2 25 ♗e3 ♖xe3 26 fxe3 ♖f1+ 27 ♔h2 g4 28 ♖xd5 and a draw was agreed in R.Ponomariov-V.Anand, Linares 2002.

17 ♘d2 ♗f5 18 f3 c5

18...♘xe4 (a draw was agreed here in J.Polgar-A.Onischuk, European Team Ch., Batumi 1999) 19 ♘xe4 ♗xe4 20 fxe4 leaves White with a pawn, a perfect centre and the two bishops in return for the exchange.

It's inevitably risky to make definitive assessments of positions this close to theory, but certainly most top players have avoided this position with Black and one can see why. G.Sax-S.Atalik, Slovenian League 2000, continued 20...♗e7 21 ♗e3 ♔h8 22 ♖f1 f5 23 ♗e6 ♕g4 24 ♕xg4 fxg4 25 ♗d7 ♖xf1+ 26 ♔xf1 b4 27 ♗xc6 bxc3 28 bxc3 ♖b8 29 e5 ♖b2 30 d5 ♔g7 31 d6 and Black resigned. In Atalik's notes to the game, he criticized his 18th move.

19 ♕f2 c4 20 ♗c2 h6 21 b3 cxb3 22 axb3 ♖fc8 23 ♗b2 ♗b4

This doesn't turn out especially well. The position is extremely tense, with the capture on e4 having to be assessed at every move. This capture would lead to similar play to that seen in the note to Black's 18th.

24 ♖e5 ♗xc2 25 cxb4 ♗g6 26 ♖c5!

This is the point. White takes advantage of his odd pawn structure to get control of the c-file.

26...♖e8 27 ♘f1 ♖ad8 28 d5 ♘d7 29 ♘e3!

Exchange sacrifice number two.

This time, like Anand in his game against Kasparov, Ponomariov is willing to give up the exchange for a pair of dynamic passed pawns on c5 and d5.

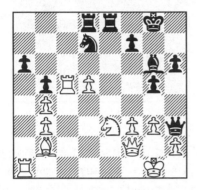

29...h5 30 f4 h4 31 f5 hxg3 32 hxg3 ♗h5 33 d6 ♖e4 34 ♖ac1

The threat of playing a rook to c8 and attacking the weakened black king meant that Adams was no longer able to resist the proffered exchange. However, the pawns march through rapidly. **34...♘xc5 35 bxc5 ♔h7 36 ♗f6 ♖g8 37 d7 ♖h4 38 ♕g2 ♗f3 39 ♕xh3 ♖xh3**

The f3-bishop, h3-rook and g5-pawn create a similar pattern to that in Ponomariov's game against Anand from the same tournament (see the note to Black's 16th), but in a much less effective form.

40 ♔f2 g4 41 ♘f1

There are no more threats and the d-pawn will collect a rook.

41...♖h5 42 d8♕ ♖xd8 43 ♗xd8 ♖xf5 44 ♘e3 ♖h5 45 ♗h4 1-0

Game 53
Z.Gyimesi-G.Sax
Hungarian Championship, Szekesfehervar 2006
Queen's Indian Defence

1 d4 ♘f6 2 c4 e6 3 ♘f3 b6 4 g3 ♗a6 5 ♕b3 ♘c6 6 ♘bd2 d5 7 ♕a4 ♗b7 8 ♗g2 ♕d7 9 cxd5 exd5 10 0-0 ♗d6 11 ♘b1 ♘e5 12 ♕xd7+ ♘exd7 13 ♘c3 c6 14 ♗f4 ♗xf4 15 gxf4 ♔e7 16 ♖ac1 ♖hd8 17 ♖c2 ♘e8 18 ♘e5 f6 19 ♘xd7 ♖xd7 20 ♖fc1 ♘d6 21 ♘d1 ♘b5 22 e3 ♖g8 23 ♘c3 ♘d6 24 ♘e2 ♘b5 25 a4 ♘d6 26 ♘g3 g6 27 h4 ♖b8 28 h5 g5 29 fxg5 fxg5 30 ♗f3 ♖f8 31 ♔g2 ♔d8 32 ♗g4 ♖df7 33 f3 ♖e7

Another example of the power of the exchange sacrifice. Intuitively, this looks to me like quite a reasonable Carlsbad/Tartakower-Makogonov-Bondarevsky system for Black. In particular, his knight on d6 seems excellently placed, controlling the key squares c4, e4 and f5. However, it's all an illusion:

34 ♖xc6! ♘c4

34...♗xc6 35 ♖xc6 ♖f6 36 e4 doesn't help. The pawn is immune in view of the mate threat on c8.

35 ♖6xc4 dxc4 36 e4

The black rooks don't have any open files on which to focus their efforts. In particular, they are blocked out by White's fantastic centre pawns.

36...♖c7 37 d5 a6 38 ♘f5 ♗c8 39 ♘d4 ♗xg4 40 fxg4 ♖e8 41 ♔f3

Unsurprisingly, having just reached the time control (I presume) White is reluctant to radically change the character of the position by playing his knight to e6. However, he eventually finds the idea irresistible.

41...♔d7

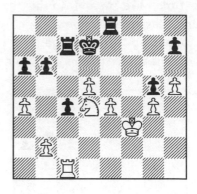

42 ♘f5

Playing the knight in to e6 is highly tempting but, unsurprisingly, allows Black to liquidate into a drawn rook and pawn endgame. Mihail Marin, himself a great exponent of the exchange sacrifice, has written of the psychological pressure which comes with being an exchange down, resulting often in players squandering their advantages by winning the exchange back prematurely.

Wells gives 42 ♔e3! ♔d6 43 ♘f3 (43 ♘c6 ♖xc6 44 dxc6 b5) 43...h6 (43...♖f8 44 ♘xg5) 44 ♔d4 with a clear advantage for White. He also notes 42 ♘c6?! b5 43 axb5 axb5 44 e5 ♖xc6 45 dxc6+ ♔xc6 46 ♔e4 ♖f8 "and again Black has become active".

42...♖c5 43 ♘g7 ♖e7 44 ♘e6 ♖xe6 45 dxe6+ ½-½

If anything, I'd feel slightly uncomfortable with White in this endgame – the black king can blockade on e5 and the queenside majority can prove highly annoying. However, either Sax doesn't share my optimism or (more likely) after suffering for so long he was unable to re-orient himself to playing for an advantage in a position which, admittedly, must be much closer to a draw than to a black win.

Game 54
D.Fitzsimons-S.Collins
Dublin 2011
Italian Game

---

1 e4 e5 2 ♘f3 ♘c6 3 ♗c4 ♗c5 4 c3 ♘f6 5 d3 a6 6 ♗b3 ♗a7 7 0-0 d6 8 ♖e1 0-0

I have happy memories of 8...♘g4 9 ♖e2 ♕f6 (J.Emms-S.Collins, British League 2010, 0-1 in 28), but I've already milked this game enough and think I will spare my publisher the tedium of editing it! In any event, I understand John included it in his book on the Italian Game, so interested readers are encouraged to go there.

9 h3 h6 10 ♘bd2 ♖e8 11 ♘f1 ♗e6

12 ♗c2

An ambitious approach from the diligent young Irish player. Rather than exchanging on e6, with a rather dry position, he retreats the bishop which is probably no better but leads to a much more complicated game.

12...d5 13 exd5

13 ♗d2 seems to be how Movsesian is handling it these days. It's easy to say this when one isn't facing a 2700 GM with the clock ticking, but this position doesn't strike me as overwhelmingly scary for Black.

13...♕xd5

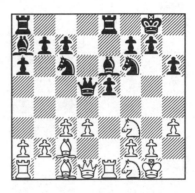

I think I have a reasonably good feel for how to play the black side of these Italian Game positions. Here, while not quite producing a novelty, I play a rare move (13...♗xd5 is what they normally do). This is a good example, I think, of theory getting something badly wrong. 13...♕xd5 is the most natural move in the world – if the queen is attacked, it can retreat to d7 or, as in the game, take up an aggressive position on the queenside.

14 ♘g3

14 ♕e2 was the scene of a real heavyweight battle: 14...♖ad8 15 ♘g3

♗c5 16 ♘h4 ♗f8 17 a4 ♘a5 18 ♗e3 c5 19 ♘f3 ♕d6 20 ♖ad1 ♕c7 21 ♘d2 c4 22 dxc4 ♘xc4 23 ♘xc4 ♗xc4 24 ♕f3 ♗d5 25 ♘e4 ♗xe4 26 ♗xe4 ♘xe4 27 ♕xe4 f6 28 a5 ♕xa5 29 ♖xd8 ♖xd8 30 ♕xb7 ♕b5 31 ♕c7 ♖d6 32 b4 ♕c6 33 ♕b8 ♕xc3 34 ♖c1 ♕xc1+ 35 ♗xc1 ♖d1+ 36 ♔h2 ♖xc1 37 ♕a8 ♖b1 38 ♕xa6 ♖xb4 39 ♕e6+ ♔h7 and by move 59 White had tired of trying to break down the black fortress and agreed a draw in T.Radjabov-L.Aronian, Dresden Olympiad 2008.

14...♖ad8 15 ♗e3

15...♗xe3 16 ♖xe3

16 fxe3 was played in A.Brkic-M.Klauser, Biel 2011 where Black opted for 16...♕d6 (1-0 in 47). During the game I was temped by 16...e4 (16...♕b5 17 ♕c1 e4 might be even better), when after 17 dxe4 Black will have nice play for the rest of the game against the white pawns on the e-file. I had won a blitz game with this idea (in a very similar position) about a week before the tournament, and was interested to see whether it worked in a real game.

16...♕b5 17 ♗a4 ♕xb2 18 ♖b1 ♕xa2

18...♕xc3!?, with a slight advantage for Black, was an alternative.

19 ♖xb7

19...♘d5!?

Dramatically changing the course of the game.

20 ♗xc6 ♘xe3 21 fxe3 ♗d5

I had missed that I could play 21...♖b8 22 d4 ♖xb7 23 ♗xb7 exd4 (23...♖b8 24 ♗e4!) 24 ♗c6 ♖b8 25 ♕xd4 ♕c4, when the position looks balanced.

22 ♖xc7 ♕a5

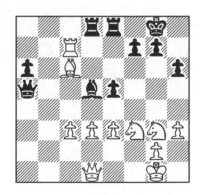

23 ♗xe8?

David should have gone for the unusual material balance of three pieces vs. two rooks: 23 ♗xd5! ♕xc7 24 c4. In fact my intention here was to sacrifice back before the three pieces whipped up an attack on my king: 24...♖xd5 25 cxd5 ♕c5 26 ♘f5 ♕xd5. I think this is roughly balanced.

23...♕xc7

Now Black is clearly on top.

24 e4 ♗e6

24...♗c4! is even better.

25 ♗a4 ♕xc3 26 ♘e2?!

26 ♗c2 is more tenacious, since after ...♖c8 the bishop can return to a4. However, White is passive, the d3-pawn is weak and the a-pawn is dangerous.

26...♕xd3 27 ♕xd3 ♖xd3 28 ♘xe5 ♖e3 29 ♘d4 ♖xe4 30 ♘ef3 ♗d5

I think Black should be winning in this endgame.

31 ♔f2 ♔f8 32 ♗c2 ♖e8 33 ♗a4 ♖b8 34 ♔e3 ♖b2 35 ♘e2 a5 36 ♘c3 ♗b7 37 g3 ♖b4 38 ♘d2 ♗c8 39 h4

39 ♘b3 ♗d7 40 ♗xd7 ♖xb3 keeps White under pressure on both wings.

39...♗e6 40 ♘de4 ♗b3 41 ♗c6

41 ♗xb3 was more tenacious.

41...a4

Now the blockade is broken and the a-pawn decides.

42 ♘d2 ♗c2 43 ♘d5 ♖g4 44 ♔f2 ♖d4 45 ♔e2 a3 46 ♘e3 ♗d3+ 47 ♔e1 a2 0-1

Game 55
A.Brkic-G.Jones
European Club Cup,
Fuegen 2006
Sicilian Defence

One of the early examples of Gawain's talent:

1 e4 c5 2 ♘f3 d6 3 d4 cxd4 4 ♘xd4 ♘f6 5 ♘c3 g6

The Dragon is, of course, an opening in which exchange sacrifices are common coin, both for White (a rook capturing a knight on h5 can prove highly effective) and, especially, for Black. We normally associate Black's counterplay with a structure-wrecking capture on c3. See, for instance, A.Karpov-V.Korchnoi, Game 2, Candidates Final 1974 (1-0 in 27), where Karpov prevailed due to his ability to prevent a double exchange sacrifice (!) on c3. However, Gawain demonstrates a different type of sacrifice here.

6 ♗e3 ♗g7 7 f3 ♘c6 8 ♕d2 0-0 9 ♗c4 ♗d7 10 h4 ♖c8 11 ♗b3 h5 12 0-0-0 ♘a5 13 ♔b1 ♘c4 14 ♗xc4 ♖xc4 15 ♘b3 ♕c7 16 ♗d4 ♖c8

Perhaps already contemplating the forthcoming transformation. As far as I can tell, this move is a novelty, with the majority of previous games (this being the Dragon, there are of course a few dozen games from this position) continuing with the sensible 16...♗e6 or 16...♗c6 to cover the d5-square.

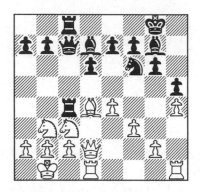

17 ♗xf6 ♗xf6!?

17...exf6 is possible. White can sink his knight into d5, but Black's dark-squared bishop is lurking in the background. If instead White goes for 18 ♕xd6, then 18...♖xc3 is a more traditional Dragon exchange sacrifice: 19 bxc3 (19 ♕xd7 ♖xc2 20 ♕xc7 ♖2xc7 is fine for Black) 19...♕xc3 20 ♕d3 ♕c7 with rich counterplay.

18 ♘d5 ♖xc2 19 ♘xc7 ♖xd2 20 ♖xd2 ♖xc7 21 g3

The immediate 21 ♖c2 looks better.

21...♗e5! 22 f4 ♗g7

Now Black has a weakness on g3 and a weak square on g4 to work with. With a pawn and a bishop (which, importantly, forms part of the bishop pair) for the exchange, Black has full compensation here. White didn't want to acknowledge this and soon declined a repetition.

23 ♖c2 ♖xc2

Placing all his faith in the bishops – indeed, Gawain manages to generate a lot of activity very quickly. It tends to be highly beneficial for a player who is the exchange down to hang on to his rook, so 23...♗c6 was a tempting alternative.

24 ♔xc2 f5!

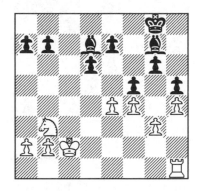

Opening the position for the bishops.

25 exf5 ♗xf5+ 26 ♔c1 e5!

Trying to get at the g3-pawn.

27 ♖d1 ♗h6 28 ♖f1 ♔f7 29 ♔d2 ♔f6 30 ♔e2 ♗g4+ 31 ♔d3 ♗f5+ 32 ♔e2 ♗g4+ 33 ♔d3 ♗f5+ 34 ♔c3

White declines a repetition here and gets duly punished.

34...exf4 35 gxf4 ♗h3 36 ♖f3 ♗g4 37 ♖f1 ♔f5!?

Now Gawain declines a repetition.

38 ♘d4+ ♔e4 39 ♖e1+ ♔d5 40 ♖e7 ♗xf4

41 ♖xb7??

A blunder on move 41, just as so often occurs. 41 ♘c2 keeps the balance.

41...♗e5 42 ♖b4 ♔e4 43 b3 ♗d7 44 ♖c4 d5 0-1

Game 56
V.Topalov-V.Anand
FIDE World Championship,
San Luis 2005
Sicilian Defence

---

1 d4 ♘f6 2 c4 e6 3 ♘f3 b6 4 g3 ♗a6 5 b3 ♗b4+

Black's fifth move used to be, as far as I can remember, almost obligatory, but recently the top players have been trying a slight twist: 5...♗b7 6 ♗g2 ♗b4+ 7 ♗d2 c5. In particular, Magnus Carlsen seems fond of this line for Black.

6 ♗d2 ♗e7

A sequence which is often seen in the Queen's Indian and the Catalan, but one which must appear odd to anyone who hasn't seen it before. Yusupov's explanation is authoritative: "What sense is there in Black's loss of tempo? The point is that after b2-b3, the natural square for White's bishop would have been b2. Later, perhaps, White will try to put his bishop on the long diagonal all the same, but on c3 it is less securely placed than on b2 and is also depriving the knight of its natural development square. On the other hand if White brings his knight out to c3, he will still have to remove his bishop from d2. So it turns out that Black's manoeuvre doesn't lose a tempo at all."

In other lines where this idea is used, the point is to restrict the opponent's possibilities. So, for instance, after 1 d4 ♘f6 2 c4 e6 3 g3 d5 4 ♘f3 ♗b4+ 5 ♗d2 ♗e7 (a favourite of Michael Adams) 6 ♗g2 0-0 7 0-0 c6 8 ♕c2 b6, White can try to get some benefit out of having his bishop on d2 but, being denied the normal b2-square, he more often plays 9 ♗f4, when each side has "lost" one tempo but White has been encouraged to play a system with his bishop on f4 which he might have preferred to avoid.

7 ♗g2 c6 8 ♗c3 d5 9 ♘e5 ♘fd7 10 ♘xd7 ♘xd7 11 ♘d2 0-0 12 0-0 ♖c8

This is an intensely theoretical position. In addition to the text move, Black has played 12...♘f6 on countless occasions.

13 e4 c5

By creating a situation of such tension between the white and black pawns, Black indicates his optimism that the tactics will resolve themselves in his favour or, at least, that he will be able to simplify the game. It may seem surprising that this idea can be used in the face of the dominant bishop on g2, but Black has his own trumps, not least the pin on the a6-f1 diagonal and the vulnerable position of the bishop on c3.

Black's principal alternative is 13...b5 attempting to pursue his main

thematic idea in the Queen's Indian, play on the light squares.

14 exd5 exd5 15 dxc5 dxc4

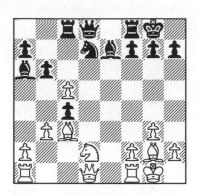

Yusupov: "The present position has arisen more or less by force from 13...c5. If you are unfamiliar with it, fathoming its nuances over-the-board is not so simple. In principle, positions so critical for the opening variation ought to be studied in the most thorough fashion, and subjected to detailed analysis in home preparation."

16 c6 cxb3 17 ♖e1

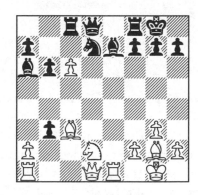

17...b2

17...♗b5 was the move played in the game in respect of which Yusupov made his remarks, A.Yusupov-G.Sax, Rotterdam World Cup 1989. After 18 ♘xb3 ♗xc6 19 ♗xg7 ♔xg7 20 ♘d4 ♗xg2 (20...♗f6 21 ♘xc6 ♖xc6 22 ♗xc6 ♗xa1 23 ♕xa1+ – Yusupov) 21 ♘f5+ ♔h8 22 ♖xe7 ♗h3 23 ♕d4+ ♘e5 (23...f6 24 ♖xd7 ♕e8 25 ♖xh7+ ♔xh7 26 ♕h4+ – Yusupov) 24 ♕xe5+ f6 25 ♕e2 ♗xf5 26 ♖d1 ♗g4 the players agreed a draw, but in a subsequent clash two top players continued the fight, albeit with the same result: 27 ♖xh7+ ♔xh7 28 ♕xg4 ♕e8 29 ♖d7+ ♖f7 30 ♖xf7+ ♕xf7 31 ♕xc8 ♕xa2 32 ♕f5+ ♔g7 33 ♕g4+ ♔h7 34 ♕h5+ ♔g7 35 ♕g4+ ♔h7 36 ♕h5+ ♔g7 ½-½, V.Kramnik-P.Leko, Moscow 2009.

However, as noted by Gershon and Nor, 17...♗b5 has fallen out of favour in view of the straightforward 18 axb3 with a good game for White. Yusupov already anticipated this development in his notes to his game with Sax: "How about taking on b3 with the pawn? Yes, this is not a bad rejoinder and may be best. I advise you to take a close look at 18 axb3 for yourself. The variations arising from it are very interesting."

18 ♗xb2 ♘c5 19 ♘c4 ♗xc4 20 ♕g4 ♗g5 21 ♕xc4 ♘d3 22 ♗a3 ♘xe1 23 ♖xe1 ♖e8 24 ♖xe8+

This was Topalov's improvement over a previous game where White played 24 ♗e4. In principle, the side the exchange down wants to keep all the rooks on the board, but it seems this is counterbalanced in the present position by the awkward pin on the e-file.

24...♕xe8 25 ♗d5

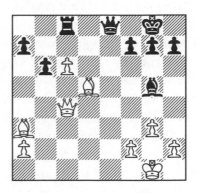

Gershon & Nor: "It is perhaps a good time to stop and look at the position. White's bishops are commanding the whole board, while Black's pieces are tied to defence – the queen is guarding f7, the rook is stopping the c6-pawn. Thus, despite being an exchange up, it is Black fighting for a draw. What he should do to achieve it is exchange the dark-squared bishops. As simple as that. But White's agreement would be required for that. Another plan might be to return the exchange, winning the c6-pawn in the process. Here too, White has a say. All in all, patience is the name of the game for Black – defending against White's threats. This is where Topalov's strategic plan can be fully understood: he does not threaten anything concrete, and lets the opponent boil."

25...h5

Gershon & Nor: "Anand's very first decision after the novelty raised many eyebrows. Black's king needs some air, but why the h-pawn, and why so far?

There is, of course, nothing wrong with criticizing the players, but Anand, who is not particularly known for spending 40 minutes of thought on one move, has been heavily criticized for playing the best move in the position. The point is that a superficial glance, coupled with the computer's 'help', will not reveal the key element of White's initiative, which happens to be the g4-square! It is an ideal square for the white queen where it works on both flanks. The game did not show it all, but only because Black did not allow it. The commentators were mostly influenced by him losing the pawn later on, but that is totally irrelevant to the move itself – Anand's famous intuition helped him to find the right solution."

Gershon and Nor go on to devote 15 pages of analysis to the remainder of the game, pointing out many beautiful variations which I recommend that the reader studies. For our purposes, I'll limit myself to a lighter analysis, but the most important point is to appreciate just how dangerous – and obviously dangerous – White's compensation is for the exchange after his 25th move, a compensation which a simple/traditional material count fails to appreciate. This is because material counts can't adjust to two highly significant factors – passed pawns (especially far-advanced passed pawns) and the two bishops. On a points count, White gets 7 points for his bishops on a3 and d5, and his pawn on c6, while

Black gets 8 for his bishop on g5 and his rook on c8.

26 ♔g2 ♗e7 27 ♗b2 ♗f6 28 ♗c1 ♕e7 29 ♗e3 ♖c7 30 h4 ♗e5 31 ♕d3 ♗d6 32 ♗g5 ♕e8 33 ♕f3 b5 34 ♗e3 ♕e5 35 ♕d1 ♕e8 36 ♕xh5 ♖xc6

37 ♗xa7

Gershon and Nor suggest that 37 ♕g6! would have led to a significant advantage. The threat to slowly build up kingside pressure with ♗d4 and h4-h5-h6 compels Black to return material: 37...♕f8 38 ♗d4 ♖c5!, but now after 39 ♗xc5 ♗xc5 40 ♕f5 followed by pushing the g-pawn, the f7-pawn is chronically weak. This simply looks lost for Black. There were many more adventures after the move played in the game, with both players missing chances, but the final result was a draw.

37...♖a6 38 ♗d4 ♗f8 39 ♗e5 b4 40 ♕f5 g6 41 ♕f4 ♕e7 42 ♗d4 ♖a5 43 ♕f3 ♗g7 44 ♗b6 ♖b5 45 ♗e3 ♗c3 46 ♗g5 ♕a7 47 ♕d3 ♖b6 48 ♗e3 ♕a6 49 ♗xf7+ ♔xf7 50 ♕d7+ ♔f8 51 ♕d8+ ♔f7 52 ♕c7+ ♔g8 53 ♕xb6 ♕xa2 54 ♕xg6+

♔h8 55 ♕c6 ♕f7 56 g4 ♙g7 57 h5 b3
58 ♕e4 b2 59 h6 ♙f6 60 ♙d4 ♔g8 61
♙xf6 ♕xf6 62 ♔g3 ♕b6 63 ♕c4+ ♔h7
64 g5 ♕g6 65 ♕c7+ ♔g8 66 ♕b8+ ♔f7
67 ♕b7+ ♔f8 68 ♕b8+ ♔f7 69 ♕b3+
♔f8 70 ♕f3+ ♔e7 71 ♕e3+ ♔d7 72
♕d4+ ♔e6 73 ♕xb2 ♕xg5+ 74 ♔f3
♕h5+ 75 ♔e4 ♕f5+ 76 ♔e3 ♕g5+ 77 f4
♕g3+ 78 ♔e4 ♕e1+ 79 ♔f3 ♕f1+ 80
♔g3 ♕g1+ 81 ♕g2 ♕b1 82 ♕c6+ ♔f7
83 ♕d7+ ♔f6 84 ♕g7+ ♔e6 85 ♕e5+
♔f7 86 ♕h5+ ♔f6 87 ♕g5+ ♔f7 88
♕h5+ ♔f6 89 ♕h4+ ♔f7 90 h7 ♕e1+ 91
♔g4 ♕d1+ 92 ♔g5 ♕d8+ 93 ♔h5 ♕d5+
94 ♕g5 ♕h1+ 95 ♕h4 ♕d5+ 96 ♔g4
♕d1+ 97 ♔g3 ♕e1+ ½-½

Game 57
V.Bologan-E.Rozentalis
Belfort 1998
Petroff Defence

1 e4 e5 2 ♘f3 ♘f6 3 ♘xe5 d6 4 ♘f3
♘xe4 5 d4 d5 6 ♙d3 ♙e7 7 0-0 ♘c6 8
c4 ♘f6 9 ♘c3 0-0 10 h3 ♘b4 11 ♙e2
dxc4 12 ♙xc4 c6

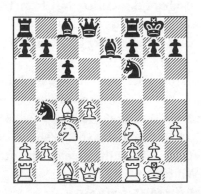

13 a3

Bologan notes that his exchange sacrifice in this game was inspired by a game between Anand and Yusupov. That game had continued 13 ♜e1 ♘bd5 14 ♕b3 ♘b6 15 ♙d3 ♙e6 16 ♕c2 h6 17 ♙d2 ♘bd5 18 a3 ♘xc3 19 bxc3 c5 20 ♜xe6! fxe6 21 ♜e1 ♕d6 22 ♙c4 ♘d5 23 ♕e4 with excellent compensation for White in V.Anand-A.Yusupov, Dortmund 1998 (½-½ in 64).

13...♘bd5 14 ♜e1 ♙e6 15 ♙d3 h6 16 ♙d2 ♜e8

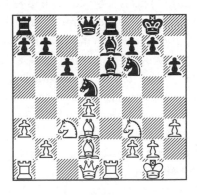

Bologan suggests 16...♕c8 to prevent White's next move.

17 ♜xe6!

Bologan, who cracked out this move having lost his previous three games, enthusiastically gives it two exclamation marks and comments: "Forward, into the abyss! In sacrificing a clear exchange, I knew full well that I might end up with a fourth straight goose-egg, but what is chess, in the end? It's a game!"

17...fxe6 18 ♙g6

An important tempo.

18...♖f8 19 ♕e2 ♘c7 20 ♖e1

Another wonderful annotation by Bologan: "This is a basic principle: first, complete your development, and then think about intensifying your initiative. Clearly, White is not going to be able to deliver mate on h7 immediately, but Black is also not going to find it easy to simplify his defense by exchanges."

20...♗d6 21 ♗b1 ♕e7?!

Creating an unpleasant line-up on the a3-f8 diagonal.

Bologan suggests 21...♖e8, but White retains excellent compensation in any case.

22 ♘e5! ♗xe5 23 dxe5 ♘fd5 24 ♘xd5

♘xd5

Taking with the c-pawn returns the exchange, while if 24...exd5? instead then 25 ♕d3 gives White a decisive attack.

25 ♕e4 g5 26 ♕g6+ ♕g7 27 ♕xe6+ ♔h8 28 h4!

White now has a pawn and the bishop pair, while his initiative is unabated.

28...♘f4 29 ♕c4 ♖ad8 30 ♗c3

The white bishop on the long diagonal pointing towards the exposed black king reminds me of A.Shirov-T.Radjabov, Linares 2004 (1-0 in 66), another model game on the theme of the exchange sacrifice, but I can't annotate everything...

30...♘d5 31 hxg5 hxg5 32 ♗d2 ♘f4 33 ♗b4 ♕f7?

Blatny gives 33...♖fe8 34 e6 ♖d4 as equal, but Bologan continues 35 ♕c2 ♖xb4 (or 35...♖xe6 36 ♖xe6 ♘xe6 37 ♗c3 c5 38 ♕e2) 36 axb4 ♖xe6 37 ♖xe6 ♘xe6 38 ♕f5 with a clear advantage for White.

34 e6 ♘xe6 35 ♗xf8 1-0

Game 58
S.Collins-A.Baburin
Nagoya Open 2009
Alekhine Defence

This game had a striking impact on my assessment of exchange sacrifices. Alex Baburin was my guest for a week in Japan, during which we shared first place in the Nagoya Open. Our game seemed uneventful, just another instance in the unfortunate series of games where I have failed to demonstrate any advantage against Alex's eternal Alekhine Defence. It was only when I returned to the hotel that my computer made a remarkable suggestion. I understand that this idea is actually well-known in Alekhine Defence theory, but I've never really looked at this body of knowledge (nor has Alex, as far as I'm aware).

1 e4 ♘f6 2 e5 ♘d5 3 d4 d6 4 ♘f3 dxe5 5 ♘xe5 c6

6 ♗e2

Black's tricky move order has one major trap, namely that after 6 c4? ♘b4! White can't meet the threat of ...♕xd4 and ...♘c2+ in a convenient way. No less a player than Michael Adams fell for this 6...♘b4 move (though he somehow managed to draw). I myself lost a bad game to Alex in this line, before using the trick myself to win an easy game in a rapidplay event in Japan.

6...♗f5 7 0-0

Kasparov essayed 7 g4 against Short in the Russia vs. the World rapid in 2002, but after 7...♗e6 Black quickly obtained the better position.

7...♘d7 8 ♘f3 e6 9 c4

I could have prepared this move with 9 a3, but I just didn't see/believe Black's idea. Besides, moving the rook's pawn looks a little slow, and 9...b5!? could be a complete solution.

9...♘b4!?

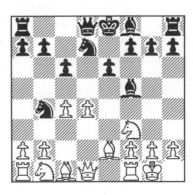

Were the knight to retreat, White would have a risk-free advantage. Going forward is the only attempt to complicate the play.

10 ♘c3

10 a3 ♘c2 11 ♖a2 allows 11...♘xd4. However, this looks like fantastic compensation for White after 12 ♕xd4 intending 12...♗xb1 13 ♗g5, as played by Carlsen amongst others.

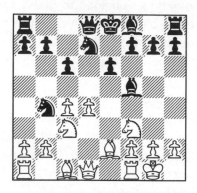

10...♘c2 11 ♖b1 ♘b4 12 ♖a1

Meekly agreeing to a draw. The move White wants to play is 12 ♗g5, but of course the "problem" is 12...f6 (12...♗e7 13 ♗xe7 ♕xe7 14 ♖c1 looks great for White).

However, White can play a fantastic exchange sacrifice: 13 ♗e3 ♗xb1 14 ♕xb1 after which, despite not even being a pawn down, Black's position is critical.

White has plans of opening the b-file (a3, b4, b5) and/or the d-file (d5) and seems to have an excellent attack everywhere. A couple of sample lines:

a) 14...♘b6 15 ♖e1 ♕d7 16 a3 ♘a6 17 b4 ♘c7 18 a4 continues to push Black around.

b) 14...♗e7 15 ♕e4 ♔f7 16 d5 exd5 17 cxd5 ♘b6 18 dxc6 when the opening of the a2-g8 diagonal spells danger for the black king. Note that the "extra" exchange (on a8 or h8) isn't really playing – the light-squared bishop, nominally an inferior piece, is very much for choice at the moment.

12...♘c2 13 ♖b1 ♘b4 ½-½

Chapter Four
Dynamic Factors

Time

Time is obviously a big subject, of which development is but one sub-topic. A great study is provided by the mini-match between Kasparov and Kramnik in the Berlin Defence. This was conducted, in the main, in their World Championship match, but in two subsequent games Kasparov showed a depth of understanding which substantially developed the variation.

On setting out to write this chapter, I had intended to include Game 16 from the Kasparov-Karpov match in 1986, which was the famous attack in the Zaitsev Ruy Lopez featuring the quiet 31 ♔h2!!. In fact this game is too complicated to analyse here, and I have nothing to add to the comments of previous writers. Interested readers are referred to Kasparov's books on his matches with Karpov, the latest of which covers this game in a tidy 25 pages.

Other useful examples of quiet moves can be found in Open Sicilians where White plays ♔h1 (after castling short) or ♔b1 (after castling long). Again, the rationale seems to be to make a useful prophylactic move which will ultimately be necessary, hence retaining maximum flexibility for one's own attacking plans. I should note that the jury is out in relation to these moves – for instance, John Nunn has discussed such moves in a section called "Laziness" (!), where he writes of the situation where one's opponent has an irritating possibility: "You have to consider this same possibility every move until you become fed up with it and spend a tempo ruling it out completely. The most common manifestation of this form of laziness is preventing a possible check by the opponent. You have to calculate the check in every single line, and in the end you just preempt the check by moving your king.

There are, of course, many situations in which such a move is perfectly reasonable, but there are also many in which the loss of time is important. Playing ♔h1 after 0-0 (or ♔b1 after 0-0-0) may be just such a waste of time. When such a move is justifiable, it is normally because of a concrete reason rather than because it is annoying to have to do a bit more calculation."

Game 59
G.Kasparov-V.Kramnik
World Championship
(Game 1), London 2000
Ruy Lopez

1 e4 e5 2 ♘f3 ♘c6 3 ♗b5 ♘f6 4 0-0 ♘xe4 5 d4 ♘d6 6 ♗xc6 dxc6 7 dxe5 ♘f5 8 ♕xd8+ ♔xd8 9 ♘c3

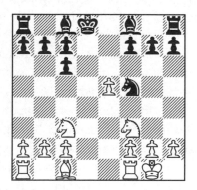

The question of time is centrally linked with the associated ideas of development and piece co-ordination. This is Kramnik's explanation of the current position in his ChessBase DVD: "Visually it looks pretty good for Black because Black has two bishops, he has definite control on white squares, and it looked like, well, after all, why should White be better at all in this position? But there is one little thing which is, unfortunately, a very important one: Black cannot castle anymore. And so it means that it's very, very difficult for Black to connect his rooks. I would say that if you take out all four rooks in this position, off the board, then Black would be simply better. But the main problem of Black in this line is how to get co-ordination of his pieces. There are simply not so many squares for his pieces, and the main problem is both rooks, a8 and h8, how to get them into the game."

9...♗d7

Kramnik understandably varied his setup in the latter half of the match. Kasparov had taken time-outs in Games 5 and 7 (in both of which he had opened with 1 c4), and his ability to work during matches is legendary. This ability is exemplified by two battles in the Ruy Lopez. First, in his 1995 match with Anand where, after Anand used the Open Variation to make a comfortable draw in Game 6 (Anand's notes state ruefully on the move 14 ♘f3 "As we all know now, Kasparov blew a hole into this variation in the 10th game with 14 ♗c2, but let's not jump ahead."), Kasparov used an old idea of Tal's to win a beautiful game in Game 10 which, combined with his successful and surprising use of the Dragon Sicilian with Black, enabled him to easily defeat a challenger who would develop into one of the great champions. Second, in their mini-match in the FIDE Grand Prix Rapid in Moscow in 2002, Khalifman opted for the Bird's Defence (3...♘d4 – not a bad move, by the way). Kasparov was surprised and drew Game 2 but by the time of Game 4 was fully prepared and won in 23 moves with a crushing attack.

As a side note to a side note, this propensity of Kasparov's to work during matches is one of the factors which cost him the title. Surprised by Kramnik's good (though hardly devastating) preparation in the Grünfeld which won Game 2, after a couple of draws with the Queen's Gambit Accepted he switched to the Nimzo. While he lost Game 10 (an appalling game by Kasparov's standards), the main drawback of this opening choice was that it seems it was learned and prepared during the match (at least this is Kramnik's view), leaving Kasparov exhausted during the games.

Game 9 continued 9...h6 10 ♖d1+ (This forces the king to e8, but as Game 13 shows, Kramnik was happy to play with his king on e8 in any event. By the time of Game 13, Kasparov already appeared despondent: 10 h3 ♔e8 11 ♘e4 c5 12 c3 b6 13 ♖e1 ♗e6 14 g4 and the draw was agreed here.) 10...♔e8 11 h3 a5 12 ♗f4 ♗e6 13 g4 ♘e7 14 ♘d4 ♘d5 15 ♘ce2!. White had a certain edge but Kramnik gradually brought the posi-

tion to safety in 33 moves.

10 b3 h6 11 ♗b2 ♔c8

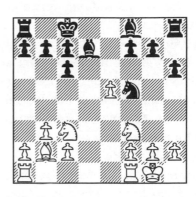

Again Kramnik's explanation cannot be improved upon: "Okay, Black's idea is very simple and difficult at the same time to realize. So his idea is to play ...b6, ...♔b7, and then to get at least one rook out of a8, so to get it to e8, and then to slowly maybe to play ...c5, ...♗e6 and so on."

12 h3

A near-universal move in the Berlin, covering g4 and ultimately supporting the idea of a kingside pawn advance with f4-f5 supported, if necessary, with g4. This is a plan which Kramnik beautifully defuses in this game – Kasparov's pawn will land on f4, but a draw will be agreed on the next move. Given the number of variations in the text where Black was just in time to stop e6, f4-f5 or ♘f4, it was natural for Kasparov to seek to save a tempo.

Game 3 saw:

12 ♖ad1 b6 13 ♘e2

Now there is no ...♘g6 to prevent ♘f4.

13...c5 14 c4

Kramnik notes that 14 ♘f4 ♗c6 15 ♖fe1 ♔b7 16 e6 is dangerous only for White: 16...♗xf3 17 gxf3 ♗d6 18 ♗e5 ♗xe5 19 ♖xe5 ♘d4 when the knight is dominant. Interestingly, *Houdini* gives 20 ♖xd4 as equal here: 20...f6 (20...cxd4 21 exf7 and White is not worse) 21 ♖xc5 bxc5 22 ♖c4 with full compensation for the exchange.

14...♗c6 15 ♘f4 ♔b7

Kramnik gives a fantastic explanation of why he waited for e6 before taking on f3, but it's not central to the time theme so we'll skip it.

16 ♘d5 ♘e7 17 ♖fe1 ♖g8!!

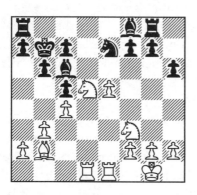

The product of 40 minutes thought. Black covers g7 and prepares ...g5.

18 ♘f4

Another very important aspect of the time theme is rushing. Kramnik gives some analysis of why direct approaches with 18 e6 or 18 ♘h4 don't work, and in support of his recommendation, 18 ♖d2!? (which he also suggests at move 17), he says as follows: "Maybe the best would be to play something like ♖d2, just to make a semi-waiting move, and to see what is Black's next. But again, this is an important point, that Kasparov likes more direct play, it's not really his style to play this kind of semi-waiting move, and to wait for the opponent to act. It's more in his style to act himself, to find something more concrete. I am absolutely convinced that if Karpov would play this position with White, he would play some move like ♖d2 without too much hesitation. This is really his style; 'Okay, I improve a little bit my position, and let you play. Make your move.' But Kasparov is always searching for a direct approach, and in this particular endgame, in this Berlin Defence, the most dangerous approach usually is not the most direct one. This kind of little useful moves are very annoying for Black usually. This is what my experience shows."

A quick check shows that Kramnik is spot on: in Karpov's best games collection, a game against Tony Miles from Biel 1990 is featured, where Karpov responded to the Berlin by quietly doubling his rooks on the d-file and won beautifully.

18...g5 19 ♘h5 ♖g6

Kramnik gives 19...♘g6! as better.

20 ♘f6 ♗g7 21 ♖d3

Now after the simplifying 21...♗xf3 22 ♖xf3 ♗xf6 23 exf6 ♘c6 Black had a comfortable game and went on to draw in 53 moves.

Returning to the main game:

12...b6 13 ⌶ad1 ♘e7

15 ♘e1

14 ♘e2

As Kramnik notes, 14 ⌶d2 became fashionable after the match: 14...c5 15 ⌶fd1 ♗e6 16 ♘e2 (Kramnik points out that 16 ⌶d8+ ♔b7 17 ⌶xa8 ♔xa8 18 ⌶d8+ is not dangerous in view of 18...♔b7 when ...♘c6 will expel the rook) 16...g5 17 h4 g4 18 ♘h2. This position (which can also arise with ⌶d8+ and ⌶xa8 thrown in at an earlier stage) is rather unclear and is still theoretically debated. When Anand tried it with White against Kramnik in Mainz 2001, he lost to a nice shot: 18...h5 19 ⌶d8+ ♔b7 20 ⌶xa8 ♔xa8 21 ⌶d8+ ♔b7 22 ♘f4 ♘g6 23 g3 c4! 24 bxc4? and now the tactical vulnerability of the d8-rook was demonstrated with 24...♘xf4 25 gxf4 g3! 26 ♘f1 (26 fxg3 ♗c5+) 26...gxf2+ 27 ♔h2 ♗xc4 and White resigned.

14...♘g6

Stopping ♘f4. Kramnik shows that 14...c5 15 ♘f4 ♘c6 16 e6! (16 ⌶fe1 ♘d8!) 16...♗xe6 17 ♘xe6 fxe6 18 ⌶fe1 ♘d8 19 ♘e5 is much better for White.

Now White aims for f4-f5, taking advantage of the knight on g6 (which doesn't cover f5, as it used to from e7, and will get hit by the advancing white pawns). Kramnik gives 15 ⌶d2 c5 16 ⌶fd1 ♗e6 17 ⌶d8+ ♔b7 18 ⌶xa8 ♔xa8 19 ⌶d8+ ♔b7 and Black can play ...♗e7 since the h8-rook is protected.

15...h5!

Masterful reaction from Kramnik, cutting out g4 ideas.

16 ♘d3

Kramnik: "White starts to manoeuvre. He probably wants to get ♘f4 still, followed by ⌶fe1 and e6, so he wants to execute the same plan, but I think, at least in this game, he's just one tempi (sic) not in time."

As Kramnik notes, while ...h5 would have been dangerous with a knight on f3 in view of ♘g5, here 16 ♘f3 can simply be met by 16...♗e7, when White has blocked his f4 plan.

16...c5 17 c4

Kramnik's comment about White being a tempo short is illustrated by 17

♘ef4 ♘xf4 18 ♘xf4 ♗f5, when the attack on the c2-pawn makes all the difference. 19 c4 ♔b7 20 ♖fe1 ♖e8 and Black stops e6.

17...a5! 18 a4 h4

19 ♘c3

Now after 19 ♘ef4 ♘xf4 20 ♘xf4 ♗f5, ...♗c2 is still a threat, with similar consequences to those outlined in the note to White's 17th, and if 21 ♖d2 then 21...♗e7 threatening ...♗g5 (Kramnik).

19 f4 can be blocked either with ...♗f5 or 19...♖h5!? (Kramnik).

19...♗e6

The more active 19...♗f5 was rejected by Kramnik on the grounds of 20 ♘d5 ♔b7 21 ♘e3 with an important hit on the bishop. Giving up the bishop with 21...♗xd3 or 21...♖h5 is clearly better for White, but after 21...♗e6 22 f4 Black's position starts to collapse.

20 ♘d5 ♔b7 21 ♘e3 ♖h5!

21...♘e7 allows 22 ♘f4 (Kramnik).

22 ♗c3

22 f4 ♘e7 and there is no f5 and no ♘f4.

22...♖e8 23 ♖d2 ♔c8 24 f4 ♘e7 25 ♘f2 ♘f5 ½-½

1 e4 e5 2 ♘f3 ♘c6 3 ♗b5 ♘f6 4 0-0 ♘xe4 5 d4 ♘d6 6 ♗xc6 dxc6 7 dxe5 ♘f5 8 ♕xd8+ ♔xd8

The role of time in this position is well summarized by my teammate John Cox in his definitive work on the Berlin: "White's assets are fairly clear. One, he is ahead in development (and also in space). Two, if all the pieces but the kings were magically removed from the board Black would have to resign. And three, Black's king is stuck in the centre of the board and will almost always block at least one of his rooks from entering the game along the back rank for some time to come. These considerations suggest that White will win games in this opening in two ways:

first by obtaining the initiative, perhaps by opening the centre with a pawn sacrifice, and exploiting his active pieces to force decisive gains, secondly by slowly and carefully exchanging pieces, advancing his majority, creating a passed pawn and winning the ending. This impression is more or less correct, and of the two, the former is the more common. It is a great mistake as White in this opening to imagine that exchanges will automatically lead the game towards victory. Just as often they serve the opposite purpose of dissipating White's initiative and converting the centralized Black king from a weakness into a strength. Moreover, when we consider Black's strengths we will see that the most fundamental of these is the possibility of blockade. More often than not, once Black manages to erect his fortifications White's chances of victory are negligible. White must strive if at all possible to strike before then."

9 ♘c3 h6

The two K's subsequent encounter at Wijk aan Zee continued the discussion. After 9...♚e8 10 h3 ♗e7 (this is a more usual way of playing with the king on e8 than the hybrid ...♗d7 and ...♚e8 adopted in Astana; ...♚e8 and ...♗e7 has been championed by Wang Yue, recommended by Shirov and well explained by Leonid Kritz) 11 ♗g5 ♗xg5 12 ♘xg5 h6 13 ♘ge4 b6 14 ♖fd1 ♘e7 15 f4 ♘g6 16 ♖f1 h5 17 ♖ae1 ♗f5 18 ♘g3 ♘e7 19 ♘xf5 ♘xf5 20 ♚f2 ♘d4

21 ♖c1 ♖d8 22 ♖fd1 ♚e7 23 ♘e4 h4 24 b4 ♖h5? (Black would have been fine after 24...f6) and now, instead of the 25 ♘g5? of G.Kasparov-V.Kramnik, Wijk aan Zee 2001 (½-½ in 46), Kasparov gives 25 g4! "and we go home" since taking on g3 and h3 loses a piece to ♖xd4 and ♘f5, and otherwise f5 is coming.

No dent was made during the rapid game in Zurich 2001 either: 9...♗d7 10 ♖d1 ♚c8 11 ♘g5 ♗e8 12 ♘ge4 b6 13 h3 ♚b7 14 g4 ♘e7 15 ♗f4 h5 16 f3 c5 17 ♚f2 ♘c6 18 ♘d5 ♘d4 19 c3 ♘e6 20 ♗g3 ♗c6 21 ♖d2 hxg4 22 hxg4 c4 23 ♚g2 ♖d8 24 ♖ad1 ♗a4 25 ♖e1 ♗c6 26 ♖ed1 ♗a4 27 ♖e1 ♗c6 and a draw was agreed.

10 h3 ♗d7 11 b3 ♚e8

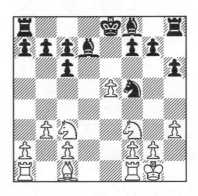

We can glean Kasparov's thoughts on the Berlin Wall from Dokhoian's notes in *New in Chess*: "It is Black's king (or more correctly its placing) that really determines the character of the subsequent play. With it at c8 the play is sharper, but the weakness of the kingside and the inactivity of the rook at a8 are felt. The position of the king at e8 is more passive and it usually involves different plans for moving the remaining pieces, than when it is at c8. The main idea of the move in the game is to exchange the usually inactive rook at a8 for the rook at d1. The drawback to the plan is that Black's king remains in the centre and prevents the other rook at h8 from coming into play."

12 ♗b2 ♖d8 13 ♖ad1 ♘e7 14 ♖fe1 ♘g6 15 ♘e4

As Dokhoian notes, this setup of the white pieces (♘e4 and ♖e1) is particularly effective when the king is on e8.

15...♘f4?

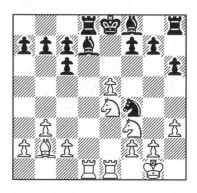

Allowing the following breakthrough.

16 e6!! ♘xe6 17 ♘d4

Playing to mate Black in the middle of the board. Have a look at the section on queenless middlegames for further examples. Dokhoian suggests that 17 ♗e5! would have been even stronger.

17...c5?

The product of one hour's thought and, it seems, a mistake in a difficult

position. 17...♖h7 has been suggested as the best defence but Black's position remains unattractive.

18 ♘f5 ♖h7 19 ♗f6 ♖c8

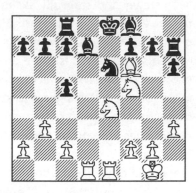

20 ♗xg7

Kasparov suggests 20 f4! as more dangerous.

20...♗xg7 21 ♘xg7+ ♔xg7 22 ♘f6+ ♔e7 23 ♘xd7 ♖d8

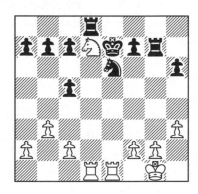

White is now only a bit better, but Kramnik was very low on time and probably exhausted having dealt with the earlier attacking effort. Kasparov goes on to win nicely.

24 ♘e5 ♖xd1 25 ♖xd1 ♘f4 26 ♔h1 ♖g5 27 ♘g4 ♖d5 28 ♖e1+ ♔f8 29 ♘xh6 ♖d2

30 ♖e5 ♖xf2?

Dokhoian gives 30...♖xc2 31 ♖f5 ♖xf2 32 ♘g4 ♖xg2 33 ♖xf4 ♖xa2 as the best defence, with drawing chances.

31 ♖f5 ♔g7 32 ♘g4 ♖xg2 33 ♖xf4 ♖xc2 34 ♖f2

Black has not taken enough pawns to have realistic drawing prospects.

34...♖c3 35 ♔g2 b5 36 h4 c4 37 h5 cxb3 38 axb3 ♖c5 39 h6+ ♔f8 40 ♘f6 ♖g5+ 41 ♔h1 1-0

As an addendum, the following game shows Kasparov handling the black side of the Berlin with something considerably short of mastery:

Game 61
J.Polgar-G.Kasparov
Russia vs. The World (rapid)
Moscow 2002
Ruy Lopez

1 e4 e5 2 ♘f3 ♘c6 3 ♗b5 ♘f6 4 0-0 ♘xe4 5 d4 ♘d6 6 ♗xc6 dxc6 7 dxe5 ♘f5 8 ♕xd8+ ♔xd8 9 ♘c3 h6

It would be remiss of me not to give my own pathetic effort with the white pieces here, just to show how easy it can be to completely mishandle these positions:

9...♔e8 10 h3 h6 11 b3 a5 12 ♗b2 h5 13 a4

I'm not a huge fan of this move. Bringing the queen's rook to d1 looks more active.

13...♗b4 14 ♘e4?

The knight does absolutely nothing on this square. The g5-outpost is not especially threatening. 14 ♘e2!, à la Polgar, was much stronger. The knight should go to f4, with g5 reserved for the other knight. Alternatively, the knight can come to d4 to trade off the black knight.

14...h4!

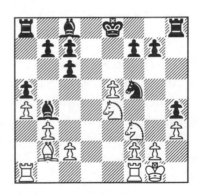

Of course! Black fixes the kingside structure, thus securing complete stability for his f5-knight and his position in general.

15 c4

This weakening of the b3-pawn and the d-file doesn't look especially inspired either, but by this stage it was clear I had completely lost the thread of the game.

15...♗d7 16 ♗c3 ♗xc3 17 ♘xc3 ♗e7

Normally Black's king in the centre is a problem in the Berlin, affecting his ability to connect his rooks. Here the king is superbly placed and the black rooks have excellent prospects.

18 ♘e4 ♖ad8 19 ♖fd1 ♗e6 20 ♔f1 b6 21 ♔e1 c5 22 ♖xd8 ♖xd8 23 ♖d1 ♘d4 24 ♘xd4 cxd4 25 ♘g5 c5

Black was clearly better and won easily in S.Collins-C.Balogh, Kallithea 2008. I had the misfortune not only to play this game during the European Club Cup, but also while playing on a team with two Berlin experts, GM Jon Parker and IM John Cox. If I'm not mistaken, they were playing on either side of me during this game, and kept looking at my position in disbelief. That evening they explained my mistakes over beers, while Parker ruefully remembered a time in the early 90's when everyone used to play this badly against the Berlin.

10 ♖d1+ ♔e8 11 h3 ♗e7

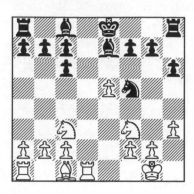

An idea which has been played as early as move nine in this line. Many Berlin specialists have gone in for this line, even after the Polgar-Kasparov game, but after Polgar's 12th move White scores a stunning 80%, which is generally a sign that Black should seek a different direction.

11...a5 was Kramnik's choice in Game 9 of his match with Kasparov, as discussed before.

12 ♘e2! ♘h4

This knight would have to go here after g4 anyway. Wedberg makes the good point that a disadvantage of the ...♗e7 setup is that Black no longer has ...♘e7 in response to g4.

13 ♘xh4 ♗xh4 14 ♗e3 ♗f5

Wedberg gives some analysis here: 14...♗d7 15 ♖d4 ♗e7 16 ♖ad1 ♖d8 17 ♘f4 a6 18 ♘h5 ♖g8 19 g4 with a slight advantage for White.

14...♔e7?? 15 g3 ♗g5 16 f4 wins the bishop.

15 ♘d4 ♗h7 16 g4 ♗e7 17 ♔g2 h5 18 ♘f5

18...♗f8

Taking on f5 would leave White with a threatening pawn roller.

19 ♔f3 ♗g6 20 ♖d2 hxg4+ 21 hxg4 ♖h3+

Exchanging a pair of rooks with 21...♖d8 still leaves White with all the play after 22 ♖ad1 ♖xd2 23 ♖xd2.

22 ♔g2 ♖h7 23 ♔g3 f6

Opening the game favours the developed side even more than the bishops, but it is hard to suggest alternatives.

24 ♗f4 ♗xf5 25 gxf5 fxe5 26 ♖e1 ♗d6 27 ♗xe5 ♔d7 28 c4 c5 29 ♗xd6 cxd6

30 ♖e6

The double rook endgame is a trivial win. White's initiative nets material.

30...♖ah8 31 ♖exd6+ ♔c8 32 ♖2d5 ♖h3+ 33 ♔g2 ♖h2+ 34 ♔f3 ♖2h3+ 35 ♔e4 b6 36 ♖c6+ ♔b8 37 ♖d7 ♖h2 38 ♔e3 ♖f8 39 ♖cc7 ♖xf5 40 ♖b7+ ♔c8 41 ♖dc7+ ♔d8 42 ♖xg7 ♔c8 1-0

Quiet!

The concept of quiet is especially surprising in two contexts.

The first is after a player has sacrificed material. There is a natural expectation that such sacrifices must be followed up quickly, but this is not always the case.

The second context arises during a sharp attack. The first four or five candidate moves will always be aggressive, but sometimes it is worth making a quiet prophylactic move.

> *Game 62*
> **G.Kasparov-M.Chiburdanidze**
> Baku 1980
> *King's Indian Defence*

1 d4 ♘f6 2 c4 g6 3 ♘c3 ♗g7 4 e4 d6 5 ♘f3 0-0 6 ♗e2 e5 7 ♗e3 ♕e7 8 d5 ♘g4 9 ♗g5 f6 10 ♗h4 h5 11 h3 ♘h6 12 ♘d2 c5 13 ♘f1 ♘f7 14 g4 hxg4 15 ♗xg4 g5 16 ♗xc8 ♖xc8

This position is often given with two exclamation marks after White's next move. In fact White's next move is extremely easy. It's Black's response which deserves punctuation.

17 ♘e3 gxh4??

An awful move. When your opponent gives you an extra option, and you take it, you have to make sure it is better than the option you would have been forced into. Here, with 17...♘h6, Black could have tested how badly White wants to sacrifice the bishop on h4. The fact that the f5-square is controlled is a critical improvement of Black's position.

That said, perhaps Chiburdanidze realized that her position was rather sketchy anyway, and decided to mix it up by grabbing a piece.

18 ♘f5 ♕d8 19 ♕g4 ♘g5 20 ♘xh4 ♖c7 21 ♘f5 a6 22 h4

This pawn is easily worth a piece. If it doesn't actually win something due to the pin on the g-file, it has excellent chances of reaching h8.

22...♘h7 23 ♖g1 ♕f8 24 ♔e2 ♖a7 25 a4 b6 26 ♕h5 ♔h8 27 ♖g6 ♖d7 28 ♖ag1

The position is reminiscent of move 50 of some Closed Lopez where White has sacrificed a piece to get his knight to f5. Looking at the knight on b8 as the

'extra' piece shows how completely Black has lost the strategic battle.

28...♖ab7 29 ♕g4 ♖bc7 30 ♖g2 ♖b7 31 ♔f1

This could be viewed as rubbing it in, but I don't really think so. In sharp positions, Kasparov is always sensitive to putting his king into safety before the fireworks start. In this position, such a manoeuvre is trivial since Black has absolutely no counterplay, but a much more complex example may be seen in Game 16 of his 1986 match with Karpov.

31...♖a7 32 ♔g1 ♖f7 33 ♘e2 ♕c8 34 f4 b5

False activity since the a7-rook is unable to leave the second rank. However, it is impossible to criticize someone's play in a dead lost position.

35 axb5 axb5 36 cxb5 ♖ab7 37 h5 ♘f8 38 ♕h3 ♘xg6 39 hxg6+ ♔g8 40 gxf7+ ♔f8 1-0

Game 63
A.Miles-A.Beliavsky
Tilburg 1986
Nimzo-Indian Defence

1 d4 ♘f6 2 c4 e6 3 ♘f3 b6 4 ♘c3 ♗b4 5 ♗g5 ♗b7 6 e3 h6 7 ♗h4 g5 8 ♗g3 ♘e4 9 ♕c2 d6 10 ♗d3 ♗xc3+ 11 bxc3 f5 12 d5

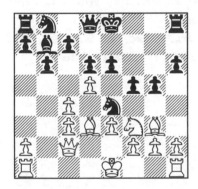

12...♘c5

White has played a topical pawn sacrifice. Accepting it seems too dangerous and structurally compromising, so Black's best established defensive method has been to offer one or two of his own with 12...♘d7. My 4NCL teammate Jonathan Parker once played a beautiful game here with Black, all the

more remarkable because he is a specialist in this "Kasparov Variation" (knights on c3 and f3 against the Nimzo) with White: 13 ♘d4 (similar play results from 13 ♗xe4 fxe4 14 ♕xe4 ♕f6) 13...♘dc5 14 dxe6 ♕f6 15 f3 f4! 16 exf4 gxf4 17 ♗f2 ♘xd3+ 18 ♕xd3 ♘c5 19 ♕e2 0-0-0 (Black had previously played 19...♖g8 and was assessed as clearly better in an old *Chess-Base Magazine*, but I prefer Jon's treatment) 20 0-0-0 ♖de8 21 ♖he1 ♖hg8 22 ♗g1 ♔b8 23 ♖d2 ♘xe6 and White, having no compensation for his mangled structure, went on to lose in A.Shneider-J.Parker, Port Erin 1999 (0-1 in 65).

Recent praxis seems to have focussed on 12...♘a6.

13 h4 g4 14 ♘d4 ♕f6 15 0-0 ♘xd3

15...♘ba6 was an attempt to improve but the current view seems to be that the 12th move alternatives are preferable.

16 ♕xd3 e5 17 ♘xf5 ♗c8

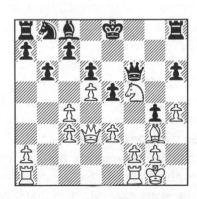

18 f4!!

A stunning idea and an important

novelty. Miles improves over one of his previous efforts: 18 e4 ♗xf5 19 exf5 (I initially thought that 19 f4 transposed to the note to Black's 18th move, but as John Emms pointed out to me, Black can play 19...gxf3 here; White is still doing reasonably well after 20 ♖xf3 but there is no point in giving Black an extra option) 19...♘d7 20 f4 gxf3 21 ♕xf3 0-0-0 22 a4 a5 23 ♖a2 ♖dg8 24 ♗f2 h5 25 ♖e2 ♖g4 26 ♖e4 ♖hg8 27 ♖xg4 ♖xg4 and I'm a big fan of Black's position, A.Miles-J.Timman, Cologne 1986 (0-1 in 53).

One of the benefits of having a Nimzo-Indian expert as an editor is that he keeps you correct on positions like this. John Emms reminds me that Kasparov had previously essayed 18 ♘d4!? (anticipating our next game, Anand-Wang Hao) 18...exd4 19 cxd4 ♕f5 (or 19...0-0 20 f3 ♕g7 21 ♔h2 ♘d7 22 e4, S.Gligoric-P.Popovic, Budva 1986 (½-½ in 29)) 20 e4 ♕g6 21 ♕c3 0-0 22 ♖fe1 ♘d7 23 e5 with a typical dynamic effort from the greatest player in history, G.Kasparov-J.Timman, Hilversum 1985 (1-0 in 41).

18...♕xf5

18...♗xf5 19 e4 and retreating the bishop will allow captures on e5 and d6 followed by a collapse in the middle.

19 e4 ♕h5 20 fxe5 dxe5 21 c5!

White has a pawn and an overwhelming initiative for the piece. As in the previous example, the inability of Black to use his extra pieces in any constructive fashion is key to his downfall.

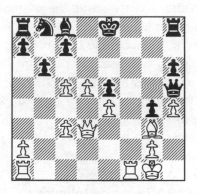

21...♔d8 22 d6 ♕e8

22...c6 keeps the position more closed but leads to a monster pawn on d6. White can retain compensation by bringing his queen's rook into play or force his way through with the sequence 23 d7 ♘xd7 (23...♗xd7 24 ♕d6 wins) 24 ♕d6 and White has a winning initiative.

23 dxc7+ ♔xc7 24 ♕d5 ♘c6 25 ♖f7+ ♗d7 26 ♖af1 ♖d8 27 ♖1f6

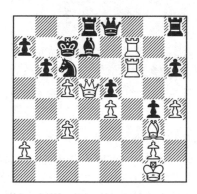

Nominally Black is a piece (for some pawns) up, but in reality he's an exchange down since the h8-rook isn't helping.

27...♔c8 28 cxb6 axb6 29 ♕b5 1-0

White's structural concerns remain, but getting his knight to b5 is a significant improvement over having it stuck on g3.

16...♘xb5 17 ♗xb5 ♕c7 18 ♔e2 ♗e6 19 ♗e3!

Mamedyarov does not jealously guard his bishop pair, but instead plays for maximum activity in the endgame.

19...♗c4+ 20 ♗xc4 ♘xc4 21 ♖b4 ♘xe3 22 ♔xe3 ♖d7 23 ♖hb1 ♔c6 24 ♖1b2 ♖hd8 25 ♔e2

There's no clear route to safety for Black. Mamedyarov has one of the best techniques of the top players and went on to win, S.Mamedyarov-A.Huzman, Warsaw 2005 (1-0 in 41).

Returning to the main game:

10 ♗e3 0-0 11 ♕b3 ♕c7 12 ♗b5 ♘ec6 13 ♘e2 ♘a5

A position which has been extensively tested at the top level.

14 ♕b4

Kramnik tried 14 ♕a4 in his draw with Wang Hao in Wijk aan Zee 2011.

14...e5 15 0-0 ♗e6?

Game 64
V.Anand-Wang Hao
Wijk aan Zee 2011
Nimzo-Indian Defence

1 d4 ♘f6 2 c4 e6 3 ♘c3 ♗b4 4 f3 d5 5 a3 ♗xc3+ 6 bxc3 c5 7 cxd5 ♘xd5 8 dxc5

The main line.

8...♕a5

Black has also tried 8...f5 but targeting the queenside pawns immediately is the most natural approach.

9 e4 ♘e7

And here all plausible knight retreats have been tested. An example:

9...♘c7 10 ♕d4 f6 11 ♕b4 ♘c6 12 ♕xa5 ♘xa5 13 ♖b1 ♗d7 14 ♘e2 e5

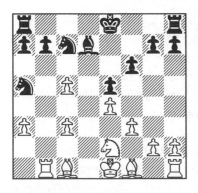

White has an extra pawn but a shattered structure. However, he has a stock sacrifice which turns the tables:

15 ♘d4! 0-0-0

A wise decision. 15...exd4 16 cxd4 leaves White with a dominating centre and two pawns for the piece. Furthermore, the a5-knight and b7-pawn are both targets.

Tempting White into the stock sacrifice in this variation. Alex Baburin in *Chess Today* comments: "The only game, in which 14 ♕b4 was tried, went 15...♘a6 16 ♗xa6 bxa6 17 ♖fd1 ♗e6 18 c6 ♘c4 19 ♗c5 ♖fc8 20 ♕b7± Moskalenko-Delchev, Benidorm rapid open 2007. Perhaps Black can improve on that game with 18...♖fd8 or 18...♖fc8. In any case, only practice will tell if White can get an edge in this line." There have since been a number of games with 15...♘a6, all ending in draws.

16 ♘d4!

The bishop on e6 means that Black doesn't have any real options other than taking.

16...exd4 17 cxd4 ♘bc6 18 ♕c3 ♘e7 19 ♖fd1 ♖ad8 20 ♗f2!

Black's pieces have no scope since the white pawns control all the key squares.

20...a6 21 ♗g3 ♕c8 22 ♗f1 b6

Baburin gives 22...♘ac6 23 ♗d6 ♖xd6 24 cxd6 ♘g6 25 d5 ♘ce5 26 ♕d4 ♗d7 27 f4 with a decisive advantage for White.

23 ♖ab1

23...♘b3

Black tries desperately to change the course of the game, but in the resulting position White will have a pawn for the exchange, coupled with an imposing centre and the bishop pair.

24 ♖xb3 ♗xb3 25 ♕xb3 bxc5 26 d5 ♘g6 27 ♕b6

Now a6 falls.

27...f5 28 ♗xa6 ♕d7 29 ♗b5 ♕f7 30 exf5 ♕xf5 31 ♕xc5 ♖c8 32 ♕d4 ♖fd8 33 a4 1-0

Initiative in Queenless Middlegames

One of the most effective strategies I have employed, especially when playing against weaker players, has involved dynamic treatments of queenless middlegames.

The very terminology of "queenless middlegames" is unfamiliar to many players until relatively late in their chess development, and this marks a very significant gap in their understanding. Basically, if the queens (and one or two pieces) have come off the board, it is often too early to treat the position as a "pure" endgame (for instance, by seeking to bring one's king into active play), since there are enough remaining pieces to create serious mating (and other) threats. The weakness of a king in the centre in such positions is often emphasized by the exchange of queens, since a queen covers a lot of important defensive squares (for instance, it is much easier to land a knight fork on c7 once the black queen has been exchanged).

Game 65
R.Shiyomi-S.Collins
Japanese Ch'ship 2009
Scotch Four Knights

These notes are based on my annotations for the Japan Chess Association magazine.

At first sight, there isn't much to this game (my shortest of the Championships). However, I think it is a nice illustration of one of the most important opening principles: in the Open Games (1 e4 e5), development is the most important concept until well into the middlegame. In this game, White forgot this principle, and so ended up losing without making any obvious blunders.

1 e4 e5 2 ♘f3 ♘c6 3 d4 exd4 4 ♘xd4 ♘f6 5 ♘c3 ♗b4 6 ♘xc6 bxc6 7 ♗d3 d5

8 exd5

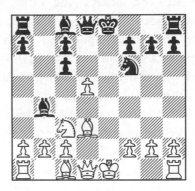

8...♕e7+!?

A slight twist on the main lines – I was happy to get my young opponent out of the theory books and into a complex queenless middlegame. I became aware of this line after struggling to get any advantage against it on ICC.

8...cxd5 is normal, when 9 0-0 0-0 10 ♗g5 c6 is a very well established line.

9 ♕e2 ♕xe2+ 10 ♔xe2 cxd5

Black can also take on d5 with the knight, and perhaps this is sounder.

11 ♘b5! ♗a5

12 c3?

This is not energetic enough. Both

sides need to rush to complete development and occupy the e-file, and White should have been more ambitious. His move is appealing in that he prepares a smooth ♖e1 and ♔f1(+), but Black can play too, and this plan is not too difficult to cut across.

Both 12 ♗f4 and 12 ♗d2 ♗b6 13 a4 offer White a normal opening edge.

12...a6 13 ♘d4 0-0 14 f3?

Now White gets into trouble on the e-file. 14 ♖e1 would have retained equality.

14...♖e8+

15 ♔d1?

My opponent was, quite rightly, worried that after 15 ♔f2 he is vulnerable to ideas with ...c5, ...♗b6 and ...c4+, but some precise calculation shows that White can hang on here: 15...c5 16 ♘b3 ♗b6 17 ♗c2 and Black has a great position after 17...a5 but White is still very much in the game.

15...c5

Now there is no hope for White, since he cannot prevent an opening of the centre files.

16 ♘f5

This allows me to execute my idea, but there was nothing better. 16 ♘e2 ♖a7!, followed by ...♖ae7, is extremely strong.

16...c4

This took me a while to see, but then I noticed that I could force the position at move 18, after which the position is clearly winning for Black.

16...♘e4 was my first intention, but after 17 fxe4 dxe4 18 ♘d6 ♖d8 (18...exd3!? 19 ♘xe8 ♗g4+ 20 ♔d2 ♖xe8 may give Black enough compensation, due to his enormous lead in development) 19 ♗xe4 ♖xd6+ 20 ♔c2 White is better.

17 ♗c2 ♗xf5 18 ♗xf5 d4

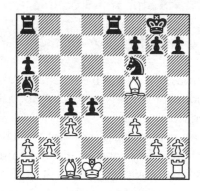

The attack plays itself.

19 ♗d2

19 cxd4 ♖ad8 20 ♗g5 is the other try, but after 20...♖xd4+ 21 ♔c1 ♘d5 Black has a decisive attack. It is worth emphasizing that the white king is in a lot of danger on the centre files – the queens are off, yes, but I am attacking with two extra rooks.

19...♖ad8 20 ♖c1

Not the most tenacious, but by this stage everything loses.

20...dxc3 21 bxc3 ♞d5 22 ♖e1

22...♞e3+

I can also take on c3, but I think my move is clearer.

23 ♖xe3 ♖xe3 24 ♔c2 ♖e2 25 ♖d1

I haven't attached unkind symbols to White's last moves since he is already lost, but they weren't the most tenacious.

25...♗b6 0-1

26 ♔c1 ♖exd2 27 ♖xd2 ♗e3 wins the rook.

Game 66
D.Smerdon-D.Johansen
Australian Championship,
Brisbane 2005
Sicilian Defence

1 e4 c5 2 c3 ♞f6 3 e5 ♞d5 4 d4 cxd4 5 ♞f3 ♞c6 6 cxd4 d6 7 ♗c4 ♞b6 8 ♗b3 dxe5 9 d5 ♞a5 10 ♞c3 ♞xb3 11 ♕xb3 e6 12 ♞xe5 exd5 13 ♗e3 ♗d6 14 ♕b5+

14...♗d7?

A rather serious opening mistake, since, as we shall soon see, the black king will be awfully placed in the centre in the ensuing queenless middlegame.

It is rather surprising (at least to me) that Black cannot use the time White will spend capturing the d5-pawn to mobilize his rooks to the centre of the board. However, while such positions are very concrete and each will turn on its own specifics, I think the explanation as to why the extra pawn doesn't matter here is that it is in the middle of the board (so White will be able to capture it without misplacing a piece) and that it will often fall either with check or with a threatened attack on the king.

14...♔f8 is the theoretical continuation, which is another story.

15 ♞xd7 ♕xd7 16 0-0-0 ♕xb5

Black is not sufficiently organized to get his king out of the centre. After 16...0-0-0 17 ♕a5 ♞c4 18 ♕xa7 ♞xe3 19 fxe3 ♕c6 20 ♖xd5 ♗b8 21 ♕d4

♖xd5 22 ♕xd5 ♕xd5 23 ♘xd5 White had an extra pawn and a dominant position in D.Sermek-J.Olivier, Cannes 1995 (1-0 in 37).

17 ♘xb5

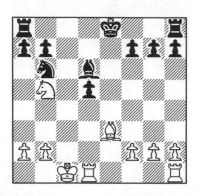

17...♖c8+

An even worse fate befell Black in the game D.Pavasovic-A.Panchenko, Pula 2001. After 17...♔d7 18 ♗xb6 axb6 19 ♖xd5 ♔c6 20 ♖hd1 ♗c5 21 ♘c3 ♖he8 22 a3 ♖e7 23 ♔c2 Black resigned due to inevitable loss of a piece or mate.

18 ♔b1 ♗b8

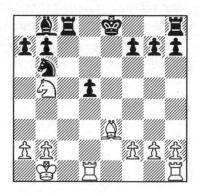

Black has managed to evacuate his bishop from the centre. However, his king remains in the middle and White will be able to use this factor to decisive advantage.

19 ♗xb6 axb6 20 ♖he1+ ♔d7 21 ♖xd5+

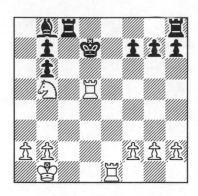

An illustration of the comment at move 14 – White takes a pawn while transferring his rook to an active position.

21...♔c6 22 ♖f5 ♖hf8

Nothing works. 22...♖cf8 23 ♘d4+ ♔d6 24 ♖fe5 g6 25 a4 and the black king is in serious danger of getting mated.

23 ♖h5 h6

23...♖cd8 is more tenacious, but after 24 ♖c1+ ♔d7 25 ♖xh7 White is a healthy pawn up with the better position.

24 ♘d4+ ♔d6 25 ♘f5+ ♔d7 26 ♘xg7

Winning a pawn and ruining Black's kingside structure.

26...♖c6 27 ♘f5 ♖e8 28 ♖xe8 ♔xe8 29 g3 ♖c5 30 b4 ♖c3 31 ♖xh6 ♗e5 32 f4 ♗c7 33 ♘d6+ 1-0

The arising rook and pawn endgame would be hopeless so Black drew the curtain here.

Game 67
V.Golod-R.Kasimdzhanov
Mainz (rapid) 2006
Nimzo-Indian Defence

1 d4 ♘f6 2 c4 e6 3 ♘c3 ♗b4 4 ♕c2 0-0 5 a3 ♗xc3+ 6 ♕xc3 b6 7 ♗g5 ♗b7 8 f3 h6 9 ♗h4 d5 10 e3 ♘bd7 11 cxd5 ♘xd5 12 ♗xd8 ♘xc3 13 ♗h4 ♘d5 14 ♗f2 c5

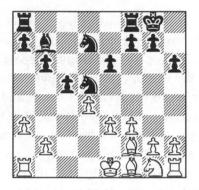

I've always been particularly impressed by the ability of certain top players to win the same theoretical position with both colours. Kasparov's successes in the Najdorf come to mind, demonstrating the strength of the white attack one day only to show the power of Black's counterplay the next. A particularly vivid example I saw live occurred in the European Team Championship 2003, where Ruslan Ponomariov won with both colours in consecutive rounds in the Keres Variation of the Chigorin Ruy Lopez (analysed elsewhere in this volume). Indeed, Ponomariov seemed in fantastic form during the event, his most notable loss occurring when his phone rang during play on his birthday!

The endgame currently under discussion is one of the theoretically hottest lines in the Nimzo-Indian with 4 ♕c2 (itself the most critical move). Certain deviations have gained prominence, notably White's 5 e4!? and Black's 6...d5!?, but the question as to the assessment of this endgame (more particularly, whether Black's lead in development provides sufficient compensation for White's two bishops) is still sharply contested.

15 ♘e2

As we will see, 15 e4 is the most popular move, with 15 ♗b5 also being tried quite frequently.

15...f5!

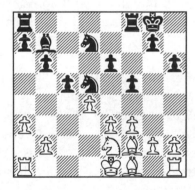

Enormously logical. Black, in addition to gaining kingside space, discourages the e4-advance since this would now result in the opening of the f-file (particularly significant given the vulnerable position of the bishop on f2 in the face of the black rook on f8, especially if White castles queenside) and the creation of a weak pawn on e4 which would rapidly be attacked by, amongst other pieces, the bishop on b7. Thus, the knight effectively maintains its position on d5, where it dominates the white pieces, attacks the e3-pawn, controls the b4-advance, and so on.

These considerations appear so compelling that I don't think 15 ♘e2 can be recommended, despite being tried by Golod (in this rapid game) and the theoretical giant, Sakaev. White just creates too many problems for his own development while not troubling Black's rapid activation of his own forces.

15...♖ac8 allows White to execute his idea with 16 e4 ♘e7 17 ♘c3. That said, after 17...cxd4 18 ♗xd4 ♖fd8 19 ♖d1 ♘c5 the players still agreed to a draw here in K.Sakaev-J.Lautier, Khanty Mansiysk 2005.

16 0-0-0

After this natural move, Black's initiative becomes too acute.

16 dxc5 ♘xc5 (or 16...bxc5 17 ♘f4 ½-½, R.Vera Gonzalez Quevedo-G.Meier, Merida 2008) 17 ♘d4 is a better treatment. However, Black has no problems here:

a) 17...♖ac8 18 b4 e5 19 ♘xf5 ♘b3 20 ♖b1 ♖xf5 21 ♖xb3 ♖ff8 22 e4 ♘f4 23 ♗e3 ♖fd8 24 g3 ♘e6 25 ♗h3 ♔f7 26 0-0 ♖c2.

This looks like it must be good for White, who has completed his development and has the two bishops and an extra pawn.

However, the active black pieces (in particular, his dominant rooks) prevent any active play – f4 would irreparably weaken the e4-pawn; bringing the rook from b3 to b1 to contest the c- and d-files would allow a penetration on the sixth rank; and trading on e6 would leave no real chances in the opposite-coloured bishop endgame, since after an exchange of all the rooks (surely the best White can hope for against such active black major pieces) the position is a trivial draw. In light of this, White decided to repeat with 27 ♖f2 ♖d1+ 28 ♔g2 ♖c7 29 ♖f1 ♖c2+ 30 ♖f2 ♖c7 31 ♖f1 ♖c2+ and a draw in R.Vera Gonzalez Quevedo-A.Onischuk, Montreal 2003.

b) 17...e5 18 ♘xf5 ♖xf5 19 e4 ♖f7 20 exd5 ♗xd5 21 ♗xc5 bxc5 and the active black pieces fully compensate for any structural deficit. After the continuation 22 0-0-0 ♗b3 23 ♖d3 c4 24 ♖c3 ♖f4 a draw was agreed in the game R.Markus-C.Balogh, Budapest 2002.

16...♖ac8

17 dxc5

This exchange doesn't help White. In light of the fact that his king hides on b1 anyway, it should have gone there immediately. However, Black could still have continued by bringing his rook to d8, with a substantial advantage.

17...♘xc5 18 ♔b1 ♖fd8!

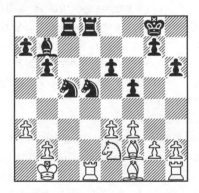

Completely paralysing the white army. The knight can't move in view of ...♘c3+, which means the light-squared bishop can't move at all. The dark-squared bishop has only one square which doesn't lose a pawn, and it's not a great square either.

19 ♖g1 e5

Bringing in the infantry. Golod now spots a tactical opportunity to liquidate, but it doesn't bring him any great relief.

20 ♘c1!? ♘c3+ 21 bxc3 ♖xd1 22 ♗c4+ ♗d5 23 ♖xd1 ♗xc4

The combination of a weak white structure and hugely more active black pieces (in particular, the knight on c1 is utterly dominated – any pretence at potential on a2 will be quickly quashed with ...a5) means this position is lost. Nonetheless, Kasim was very proud of his technique from here in light of the fact that this was a rapid game. I only wish I could play this well in normal chess!

24 ♗g3 ♖e8 25 h4 g5 26 hxg5 hxg5 27 ♔c2 ♔f7 28 ♖d6 ♗f1 29 ♖d2 e4 30 f4 ♗d3+ 31 ♔b2 g4 32 ♗h4 ♖c8 33 ♘a2 a5 34 g3 ♘a4+ 35 ♔a1 b5 36 ♖h2 ♗c4 37 ♖d2 ♔e6 38 ♗d8 ♗xa2 39 ♔xa2 ♘xc3+ 40 ♔b3 a4+ 41 ♔b2 ♘d5 42 ♗g5 ♘xe3 43 ♖h2 ♘c4+ 44 ♔c3 ♘xa3+ 45 ♔b4 ♘c2+ 46 ♔xb5 a3 47 ♖h6+ ♔d5 48 ♗e7 ♖b8+ 49 ♔a4 a2 50 ♖d6+ ♔c4 0-1

155

Game 68
**R.Kasimdzhanov-
E.Ghaem Maghami**
Asia Classical, Doha 2006
Nimzo-Indian Defence

1 d4 ♘f6 2 c4 e6 3 ♘c3 ♗b4 4 ♕c2 0-0 5 a3 ♗xc3+ 6 ♕xc3 b6 7 ♗g5 ♗b7 8 f3 h6 9 ♗h4 d5 10 e3 ♘bd7 11 cxd5 ♘xd5 12 ♗xd8 ♘xc3 13 ♗h4 ♘d5 14 ♗f2

So, the same endgame we saw in the last game.

14...f5

The Iranian grandmaster opts for the second-most popular continuation (the most popular being 14...c5 as in the previous game). The move has similar advantages as noted in that game in terms of safeguarding the d5-knight. However, without White's knight on e2, Kasim is able to complete his mobilization in a much smoother fashion:

15 ♗b5! c6 16 ♗d3 c5

16...e5 17 ♘e2 ♖ae8 has received the most high-level support, and appears more dynamic (in view of ideas

of taking on d4 and penetrating on e3). If anyone feels like trying 14...f5 I suspect this is where they should focus their efforts.

17 ♘e2

White has been in time to both get his bishop out and get his knight to e2 before Black isolated the d4-pawn. These are very significant accomplishments in an endgame where White's only problem is his lack of development. Indeed, over the next 3 or 4 moves we see Kasim complete his development, after which Black can only beg for a draw.

17...♖ad8

A clash between two giants some eight years previously had continued 17...♖ac8 18 0-0 cxd4 19 ♘xd4 ♘e5 20 ♗e2 ♘c4, which definitely fits the bill better since it creates more immediate threats. (Note, as John Watson has correctly identified, when playing against the bishop pair you have to create early threats and, to this end, it often makes sense to open the position early. Refusing to do this can result, as in the main game, in the opponent gradually opening the position on his own terms.) 21 ♖fc1 ♘cxe3 22 ♘xe6 ♖fe8 23 ♖xc8 ♗xc8 24 ♘d4 ♗d7 25 ♗xe3 ♘xe3 26 ♖c1 ♖d8 27 ♔f2 f4 28 g3 ♘f5 29 ♘xf5 ♗xf5 30 ♔e1 fxg3 31 hxg3 ♖d7 32 b4 and White somehow won this rather equal endgame in G.Kasparov-V.Kramnik, Moscow 1998 (1-0 in 62).

18 0-0 e5 19 ♖ad1

19...♘e7

Not a good direction for this piece – we can see from the note to Black's 17th that Kramnik managed to land it on e3.

Black's position is, in my view, technically lost, since White has two bishops on an open (or soon to be open) board with no compensation. This may seem like a radical assessment (perhaps it's wrong!), but if you gave this position to Kramnik with White against anyone over 10 games I can't see him scoring less than 8 or 9. Kasim is no technical slouch either, of course, and his play from here is excellent.

20 ♘c3 ♔h8 21 ♖fe1 a6 22 ♗c2 g5

Note that White has not hurried to take on c5, instead improving his pieces to the maximum. Black couldn't disrupt this plan since exchanging himself on d4 would have opened the position even more than in the game (the e-pawns would have been removed).

Black's last move is definitely ill-advised in that he weakens the long dark-squared diagonal, down which the white bishop will dominate without an opponent (surely the presence of the black king on h8 is also grist to White's mill). However, the defence of such a position is turgid and, as I opined in the note to Black's 19th, technically impossible against well-trained GM opposition.

23 dxc5 ♘xc5 24 b4 ♘e6 25 ♗b3

The importance of an open position in bishop vs. knight struggles is sometimes misunderstood. I always used to think bishops needed open positions because then they could operate down the full length of a diagonal. This is true, but is only part of the story. The more significant factor is that, in an open position, a knight cannot have a central outpost (i.e. it can't be supported by a pawn in the middle).

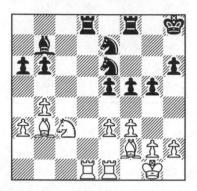

Thus the knights end up getting kicked to poor squares or, as in this game, divert their own army to run to their defence. Note the huge importance in this context of White having a pawn on e3 (covering the d4- and f4-squares) rather than on e4.

25...♗c8 26 ♘a4 b5 27 ♘b6 ♘g7 28 ♘xc8 ♘xc8 29 e4

Basically winning an exchange.

29...fxe4 30 ♗c5 exf3 31 ♗xf8 ♖xf8 32 gxf3 ♘e7 33 ♖xe5 ♘g6 34 ♖d6! 1-0

A sweet finish.

Game 69
R.Fischer-M.Euwe
Leipzig Olympiad 1960
Caro-Kann Defence

---

1 e4 c6 2 d4 d5 3 exd5 cxd5 4 c4 ♘f6 5 ♘c3 ♘c6 6 ♘f3 ♗g4 7 cxd5 ♘xd5 8 ♕b3

8 ♗e2!? is quite a decent alternative with which Normunds Miezis beat Rainer Buhmann in the Staufer Open 2011 (1-0 in 32).

8...♗xf3 9 gxf3

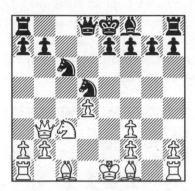

9...e6

Leading to the notorious endgame. 9...♘b6 is more ambitious but is generally believed to be quite dubious after either 10 ♗e3 or 10 d5.

10 ♕xb7 ♘xd4 11 ♗b5+ ♘xb5 12 ♕c6+ ♔e7 13 ♕xb5 ♘xc3

13...♕d7 has been the main line in this variation for years, with an endgame which is very close to equality after, for instance, 14 ♘xd5+ ♕xd5 15 ♗g5+ f6 16 ♕xd5 exd5 17 ♗e3 ♔e6 18 0-0-0. It is interesting that even in a position this simplified, the black king is sometimes a target (for instance, White can occupy the e-file with tempo) although, on balance, it is excellently placed, supporting the passed d-pawn and preparing to nestle on f5 from where it can menace the shattered white kingside pawns.

14 bxc3

14...♕d7?!

This line, seemingly buried by the text game, has had a second lease of life following the discovery of 14...♖b8!, a move advocated by Lars Schandorff in his book on the Caro-Kann. Black sacrifices a pawn but takes comfort in the horrible white pawn structure and the active black pieces. This move played a part in the event wherein Sam Shankland completed his GM title: after 15 ♕c5+ ♔e8 16 ♕xa7 ♗d6 17 ♗f4 ♗xf4 18 ♕a4+ ♔e7 19 ♕xf4 ♕a5 20 0-0 g5 21 ♕d4 ♖hd8 he achieved an effortless draw against the strong GM Robert Hess at Berkeley 2011. I saw this game live and watched Hess struggle for about an hour to find something in this endgame, while Sam walked around the room with the calm and confident air of someone whose prep had paid off.

15 ♖b1!

As Fischer notes, this wasn't his idea: "Months before the game I had showed this line to Benko and he suggested this innocent-looking move.

Upon looking deeper I found that, horrible as White's pawn structure may be, Black can't exploit it because he'll be unable to develop his kingside normally. It's the little quirks like this that could make life difficult for a chess machine."

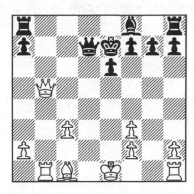

15...♖d8?

Black spends time bringing his rook to d7 but it can simply be exchanged. Fischer gives 15...♕xb5 16 ♖xb5 ♔d6 17 ♖b7 f6 18 ♔e2 ♔c6 19 ♖f7 a5 20 ♗e3 "with an enduring pull", though Kasparov notes that 20...♖b8! was still Black's best chance.

16 ♗e3 ♕xb5 17 ♖xb5 ♖d7

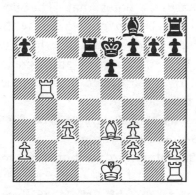

18 ♔e2!

Exchanging off the opponent's only good piece is clearly the best plan, but many players would have simply gone after the a-pawn instead.

18...f6 19 ♖d1 ♖xd1 20 ♔xd1

Black's development disadvantage is completely decisive, notwithstanding White's inferior structure.

20...♔d7 21 ♖b8!

The same concept as at move 18, but obviously very straightforward. White wins the a-pawn anyway since Black has to prevent ♗c5.

21...♔c6 22 ♗xa7 g5 23 a4 ♗g7

24 ♖b6+!

Kasparov notes that "Transposing into the bishop ending by 24 ♖xh8 ♗xh8 25 ♗d4 would also have won, but Fischer, by his own admission, was 'still trying to decide how to squeeze the most out of it.'"

24...♔d5 25 ♖b7 ♗f8 26 ♖b8 ♗g7 27 ♖b5+ ♔c6 28 ♖b6+ ♔d5

Repeating the position from move 24.

29 a5 f5 30 ♗b8 ♖c8 31 a6 ♖xc3 32

♖b5+?!

Kasparov notes that White missed an immediate win with 32 ♖d6+! ♔c5 33 ♖d7.

32...♔c4?

32...♔c6 33 ♖a5 ♗d4 would have set a trap after 34 ♗e5? ♖c5!, but either Kasparov's 34 a7 (with an extra piece) or Fischer's 34 ♔e2 lead to a win.

33 ♖b7 ♗d4 34 ♖c7+ ♔d3 35 ♖xc3+ ♔xc3 36 ♗e5! 1-0

Fischer's use of his rook on the b-file was absolutely magical.

> ### Game 70
> ### A.Grischuk-E.Bareev
> Russian Championship,
> Moscow 2004
> *Caro-Kann Defence*

1 e4 c6 2 d4 d5 3 exd5 cxd5 4 c4 ♘f6 5 ♘c3 ♘c6 6 ♗g5

This is White's sharper option on move six, which can lead to a range of positions depending on Black's response. The solid 6...e6 is respectable, and even 6...♗e6!? is quite playable. However, the critical response has to be going after the white d-pawn:

6...dxc4 7 ♗xc4 ♕xd4

Many specialists like Wang Yue and Shankland prefer to interpose 7...h6, when White has a number of options, but if he retreats to h4 then Black can take on d4 in greater safety.

8 ♕xd4 ♘xd4 9 0-0-0 e5 10 f4 ♗g4 11 ♘f3

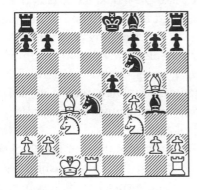

This type of play, which is not normally associated with an endgame, is highly characteristic because the black king is stuck in the middle. White's aim isn't so much a mating attack (although there are certainly some mating motifs in the position), but rather to bring all his pieces into play with tempo.

11...♘xf3

11...♗xf3 is another major option.

12 gxf3 ♗xf3 13 fxe5 ♗xh1 14 exf6

14...♖c8

I played this line myself in a local Irish league game. My opponent played 14...♗f3, which is dubious: 15 ♖d3! (instead of my inane 15 ♗b5+? ♗c6 16

♘d5 0-0-0 17 ♘b6+ axb6 18 ♖xd8+ ♔c7 19 fxg7 ♗xg7 and White struggled to draw in S.Collins-M.Schmidt, Armstrong Cup 2011/12) 15...♖c8 (15...♗c6 16 ♘b5! wins) 16 ♖e3+ ♔d7 17 ♖xf3 ♖xc4 18 fxg7 ♗xg7 19 ♖xf7+ ♔c6 20 ♖xg7 and White has good chances to convert his material advantage.

14...h6! was the big discovery after the text game, for instance 15 ♘b5 ♖c8 16 fxg7 ♗xg7 17 ♘d6+ ♔d7 and a draw was agreed in D.Andreikin-W.So, Lubbock 2009.

15 ♖e1+ ♔d7 16 ♖d1+

16...♗d6

16...♔e8 obviously gives White the option of a repetition. D.Jakovenko-E.L'Ami, Wijk aan Zee 2007, continued 17 ♗e2 (Dautov suggests 17 ♗d3!?, when in his main line of 17...♖xc3+ 18 bxc3 ♗c6 he misses 19 ♗b5!!, winning) 17...h6 18 ♗h4 g5 19 ♗g3 ♗e4 20 ♗g4 ♖xc3+ 21 bxc3 ♗a3+ 22 ♔d2 h5 23 ♔e3 ♗c2 24 ♗d7+ ♔f8 25 ♖e1 ♔g8 and White didn't manage to find full compensation, going on to lose in 45 moves.

17 ♗e2!

Threatening ♗g4+.

17...gxf6 18 ♗xf6 ♗g2 19 ♗e5 ♔e6 20 ♗xd6 ♖hd8 21 ♗g3 ♖xd1+ 22 ♔xd1

Everything has been pretty forced since move 17, leaving an endgame where White has reasonable winning chances. Grischuk goes on to demonstrate great technique.

22...a6 23 ♔d2 ♔f5 24 ♗d3+ ♔g4 25 ♘d1 ♔g5 26 ♗xh7 ♖f8 27 ♗d3 f5 28 h4+ ♔h5 29 ♗e2+ ♔g6 30 ♗f4 ♗e4 31 ♘c3 ♗c6 32 a3 ♖e8 33 h5+ ♔f6 34 h6 ♔g6 35 ♗d3 ♖e7 36 ♗c2 ♗f3 37 ♗d3 ♖e8 38 ♗c4 ♗c6 39 ♗e2 ♖e7 40 ♗d3 ♖e8 41 a4 ♖d8 42 ♔e3 ♖e8+ 43 ♔d2 ♖d8 44 ♔e3 ♖e8+ 45 ♔f2 ♖d8 46 ♗c2 ♖e8 47 ♗e3 ♖e7 48 ♘e2 ♗e4 49 ♗b3 ♖e8 50 ♘d4 ♔h7 51 ♗f4 ♖c8 52 ♘f3 ♗b1 53 ♘e5 ♖d8 54 ♗f7 ♖d6 55 ♗e8 1-0

Game 71
A.Kosten-S.Collins
British League 2002
English Opening

This game was, for a long time, the best I had played, since it was the first time I had beaten a good grandmaster by just improving my position move by move. It also provides an example of how a very slight initiative in a queenless middlegame can develop into something quite problematic.

1 c4 e5 2 g3

This interpretation of the English – fianchettoing the king's bishop before committing either knight – was popularised by Kosten in his book *The Dynamic English* and, more recently, by Mihail Marin in his 3-volume series.

2...♘f6 3 ♗g2 c6

This system, pioneered by Keres, is one of the most logical responses to 2 g3. Black prepares to occupy the centre since White has refused to do so himself.

4 d4

4 ♘c3 d5 5 cxd5 cxd5 6 ♕b3 ♘c6! is a crucial tactical idea which makes the whole line work. After 7 ♘xd5 ♘d4 8 ♘xf6+ gxf6 9 ♕d1 ♕c7 10 ♔f1 ♘c2 11 ♖b1 ♗e6 12 b3 ♖c8 Black has a fantastic bind and has scored extremely well

from this position over several games. J.Hodgson-M.Illescas Cordoba, Wijk aan Zee 1993 (0-1 in 45) is one of the better examples.

4...exd4

Recently the solid 4...♗b4+ 5 ♗d2 ♗xd2+ 6 ♕xd2 d6 has gained popularity.

5 ♕xd4 ♘a6!?

A relatively fresh approach, preparing to develop the pieces. The traditional main line starts with 5...d5, where Black accepts a structural weakness in exchange for easy development.

6 ♘f3 ♗c5 7 ♕e5+ ♕e7

7...♗e7 has also done fine in practice.

8 ♕xe7+ ♗xe7 9 0-0

9 ♘c3 seems more precise, inhibiting the d5-break. After 9...d5 10 cxd5 ♘b4 11 0-0 ♘bxd5 12 ♘xd5 ♘xd5 13 e4 ♘b4 the position is the same as in the main game but with the b1- and a6-knights off the board. This means that White is much better placed to mobilize his queenside and connect his rooks. After 14 ♗d2 0-0 15 a3 ♘d3 16

♗c3 ♘c5 17 ♖fe1 ♘a4 the position was balanced in M.Gurevich-V.Bologan, Corsica 2005 (1-0 in 75).

9...d5 10 cxd5 ♘xd5

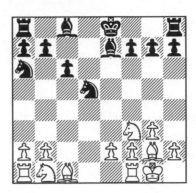

11 e4?!

Too ambitious. 11 ♘d4 0-0 12 ♗xd5 cxd5 leads to a balanced endgame.

11...♘db4 12 ♘e1

Otherwise the knight comes to d3, gaining the bishop pair. However, hanging on to the bishops comes at a price – Black's queenside initiative rapidly develops.

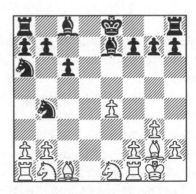

12...♘c5 13 ♗d2 a5 14 ♗c3

14 ♘c3 completes development of the minor pieces, but after 14...♗e6 15

a3 ♘bd3 16 ♘xd3 ♘xd3 Black is comfortably on top.

14...♗e6?

Imprecise. 14...0-0 maintains a big advantage.

15 b3

15 ♗xg7 ♖g8 16 ♗e5 mixes things up. Black maintains some advantage after either taking on a2 with the knight or playing the bishop to c4, but the position would be less clear than in the game.

15...0-0 16 ♘d2 ♖fd8 17 ♘ef3 ♗g4 18 a3

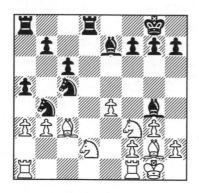

18...♗xf3

18...♘bd3 maintains all the advantages of Black's position.

19 ♗xf3

19 ♘xf3 is a better attempt, but Black retains some advantage: 19...♘c2 20 ♖a2 ♘xa3 21 ♖xa3 ♘xe4 22 b4 and White's position is too loose, for example 22...♖d3 (22...♘xc3 23 ♖xc3 axb4 24 ♖e3 ♗c5 25 ♖e5 ♗f8 and the three black pawns are more dangerous than the white knight) 23 ♖e1 ♘xc3 24 ♖xe7 ♘e2+ 25 ♖xe2 ♖xa3 26 bxa5 ♔f8 27

♖b2 ♖a7 and Black will pick up the a5-pawn, leaving him with a clear advantage.

19...♘c2 20 ♖a2 ♘d4 21 ♗d1

21 ♗xd4 ♖xd4 is excellent for Black.

21...♘b5 22 ♗a1

22...♘xa3

An amusing knight tour has netted a pawn. Soon more material falls.

23 ♖xa3?

23 e5 was the best attempt.

23...♖xd2 24 b4 ♘d3 25 ♖xa5 ♖xa5 26 bxa5 ♗c5 27 ♗b3 ♘xf2 28 ♔g2 h5 29 g4 ♘xg4+ 30 ♔g3 ♖d3+ 31 ♖f3 ♖xf3+ 32 ♔xf3 ♘xh2+ 33 ♔g2 ♘g4 34 ♗c3 ♔f8 35 e5 ♔e7 36 ♔f3 g6 37 ♔f4 ♘e3 38 ♗d2 ♘d5+ 39 ♔f3 ♗d4 40 ♔e4 ♗c3 41 ♗g5+ ♔e6 42 ♗c4 ♗xe5 43 a6 bxa6 44 ♗xa6 f5+ 45 ♔f3 ♗f6 46 ♗c1 c5 0-1

Attack

Attack is a topic which has been very well covered by other authors. In particular, I can warmly recommend Jacob Aagaard's award-winning two-volume manual.

Here I have not tried to set out

comprehensively the basic principles of attack, but rather just to show a few nice games, many of which were featured in *Chess Today*.

1 d4 e6 2 ♘f3 f5 3 g3 ♘f6 4 ♗g2 ♗e7 5 0-0 0-0 6 c4 d6

This is a line in which Simon is probably the world's leading expert. While he has suffered his fair share of reversals, he also has some remarkable scalps, including Ivan Sokolov.

The present game must have also been pleasant enough – beating a 2700+ player with Black in 20 moves doesn't happen every day.

7 ♕c2 a5 8 ♘c3 ♘c6 9 b3 e5 10 dxe5 dxe5 11 ♖d1 ♕e8 12 ♘b5

12 ♘d5 has scored well (3/3 in my database) and just looks like a more sensible move because it hits more im-

portant pieces and squares, and taking on d5 will always be unfavourable for Black.

12...♕h5!!

The passive 12...♗d8 was played in the preceding game to reach this position, but Simon needs no second invitation to sacrifice his queenside in order to get at the white king.

13 ♘xc7 f4 14 ♘xa8 ♗c5

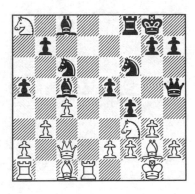

Simon is a natural attacking player. Over the course of several games against him, and playing at a number of tournaments where he competes, it really seems like the material balance just doesn't register with him – or, at least, is a distant second to king safety. Most players would feel the need, having given up a rook, to play a forcing continuation, but Simon just improves the bishop and puts pressure on the g1-a7 diagonal.

15 ♖d5?

In *Chess Today*, Mikhail Golubev recommended instead 15 gxf4 intending 15...♗f5 16 e4 ♗xe4 17 ♕e2 ♖xa8 18 ♗b2. I can't fault this. I also haven't found a clear way for Black to demonstrate full compensation, though no doubt Simon would have found something unpleasant. However, I suspect very few human players would find such a counter-intuitive move, opening up the white king – the rationale is that, by taking the pressure off the g3-pawn, White gets a little room to breathe.

15...♘b4

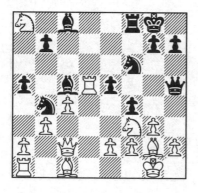

Now Black is better in all lines.

16 ♖xe5

Or 16 ♕b2 ♘bxd5 17 cxd5 ♘g4 with an overwhelming attack.

16...♘xc2 17 ♖xh5 ♘xh5 18 ♖b1 fxg3 19 hxg3

19 ♘c7 was more tenacious, though 19...♗f5 keeps Black well on top.

19...♘xg3 20 ♖b2 ♗f5 0-1

> ## Game 73
> **L.Fressinet-N.Brunner**
> French League 2011
> *Semi-Slav Defence*

1 d4 d5 2 c4 c6 3 ♘c3 ♘f6 4 e3 e6 5 ♘f3

♘bd7 6 ♗d3 dxc4 7 ♗xc4 b5 8 ♗d3 ♗d6 9 ♗d2 ♗b7 10 ♖c1 ♖c8 11 ♘g5 a5 12 ♕f3 ♗a8 13 0-0 ♗e7 14 ♕h3 b4 15 ♘a4 c5

Black has executed the standard freeing advance in Semi-Slav structures, with one small problem... he loses on the spot.

16 ♗g6! 0-0

16...fxg6 17 ♘xe6 wins the queen. 16...♖f8 also doesn't help: 17 ♘xe6.

17 ♗xh7+ ♔h8 18 dxc5 ♘xc5 19 ♘xc5 ♖xc5 20 ♖xc5 ♗xc5 21 ♗g6+ ♔g8 22 ♗xf7+! ♖xf7

And now for an echo of T.Petrosian-B.Spassky, World Championship 1966, 10th game:

23 ♕h8+! 1-0

Game 74 **V.Chuchelov-A.Shirov** German League 2011 *Semi-Slav Defence*	

Alexei Shirov is one of my favourite players. I have been particularly impressed by his ability to champion aggressive, attacking chess at the highest level over a period of a couple of decades. While there are other very strong GMs of a highly aggressive bent (one thinks of Sutovsky, Volokitin, Fedorov at his peak), only Shirov has managed to consistently achieve excellent results amongst the very elite, as shown by his various performances in Linares and his remarkable match victory over Vladimir Kramnik.

This game is particularly interesting because it showcases Shirov's ability to set the board alight even in a very quiet-looking, strategic position.

1 ♘f3 d5 2 d4 ♘f6 3 c4 c6 4 ♘c3 e6

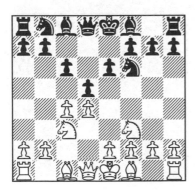

5 e3

Shirov has had many magical games with both colours after 5 ♗g5, meriting a specially devoted chapter in his first collection of best games, *Fire on Board*, where he covers the Botvinnik Variation, 5...dxc4 6 e4 b5 7 e5 h6 8 ♗h4 g5 9 ♘xg5 hxg5 10 ♗xg5 ♘bd7. This line has been largely displaced at top level by the Moscow Variation, 5...h6, and the equally interesting gambit line after 6 ♗h4!? dxc4 7 e4 g5 (7...b5 transposes to the Botvinnik) 8 ♗g3 b5. However, I am not aware of any actual refutation of the Botvinnik Variation.

5...♘bd7 6 ♕c2 ♗d6 7 b3

Probably the most quiet continuation available here. 7 ♗e2 and 7 ♗d3 also lead to relatively tranquil play. Shirov's own patent, 7 g4, would have been a foolhardy choice in this game.

7...0-0 8 ♗e2 b6

8...dxc4 is clearly not indicated when White can recapture with the b-pawn, so Shirov develops calmly.

9 0-0 ♗b7 10 ♗b2 ♖c8 11 ♖ad1

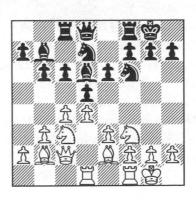

11...c5

11...♕e7 is much more popular, but there is nothing wrong with the immediate strike in the centre.

12 dxc5 ♘xc5 13 ♕b1 ♕e7 14 ♘g5 ♘fe4 15 ♘gxe4 dxe4 16 ♖d2 f5

In their blitz game in Moscow 2010, Caruana played the alternative try 16...♗b8 against Kramnik, ultimately losing in 28 moves. Shirov has different ideas for this bishop.

17 ♖fd1

17...♗xh2+!

A move which I can't get my various engines to suggest, though as soon as it's executed on the board they all give an assessment of equality.

18 ♔xh2 ♕h4+ 19 ♔g1 f4 20 ♘b5 ♘d3

Golubev notes the immediate draw with 20...fxe3 21 fxe3 ♕f2+ 22 ♔h2 ♕h4+, but Shirov plays for more.

21 ♗xd3 exd3 22 e4?

As Golubev notes, 22 exf4! would leave Black with nothing better than perpetual after 22...♗xg2 23 ♔xg2 ♕g4+ 24 ♔f1 ♕h3+ 25 ♔g1 ♕g4+.

22...f3

It was Kasparov who pointed out that a pawn in the attack is frequently worth a piece (as demonstrated in his game against none other than Shirov in Linares 1997). Here the f3-pawn is a monster.

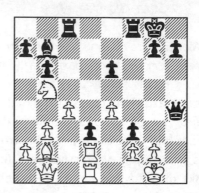

23 ♗e5

The computer's first line is 23 ♕xd3 fxg2 24 f3 ♕h1+ 25 ♔f2 ♖cd8 26 ♘d4 e5 with a continuing attack.

23...♗xe4!

Simple and good. Black also had a couple of other ways to increase his attacking firepower, including 23...fxg2 and 23...♖c5.

24 ♗g3 ♕h6 25 ♘d4

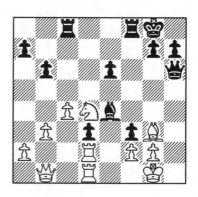

25...♖c5!

Child's play for an attacker of Shirov's class – the rook swings into the attack. White is totally busted and no further commentary is required.

26 gxf3 ♖xf3 27 ♖xd3 ♖xd3 28 f3 ♕e3+ 29 ♗f2 ♖g5+ 30 ♔f1 ♖xd1+ 0-1

> ### Game 75
> **V.Kramnik-E.L'Ami**
> Wijk aan Zee 2011
> *English Opening*

Kramnik has a remarkable ability to generate vicious attacks from the quietest of openings. This game strongly reminds me of V.Kramnik-N.Short, Dortmund 1995 (1-0 in 25), where Kramnik unceremoniously checkmated Nigel in a turgid QGD.

1 ♘f3 ♘f6 2 c4 g6 3 ♘c3 d5 4 cxd5 ♘xd5 5 d3

I don't think Grünfeld exponents will be losing sleep over this although, as with all of Kramnik's opening choices with White, it is more poisonous than it looks.

5...♘xc3

A concession, of course, opening the b-file, strengthening White's centre and exchanging the well-placed knight on d5. However, it must be said that L'Ami eventually manages to win the pawn on c3, so perhaps there's something to be said for his idea after all.

5...♗g7 would be my choice in this little-explored position.

6 bxc3 ♗g7 7 ♕c2 0-0

I'm also not entirely wild about this one. In these positions I prefer to do useful stuff on the queenside (...c5 and ...♘c6) and wait with castling until after the white king has committed himself.

8 g3 c5 9 ♗g2 ♘c6 10 h4!

Using the target created by Black's 7th move. White's play looks easier since he has a clear plan.

10...♘b4

Golubev suggests 10...♗g4 as an interesting alternative, though L'Ami's play looks logical.

11 ♕d2 ♘d5 12 ♗b2 ♕a5 13 h5 ♘b6?

Inconsistent. Golubev indicates that after 13...♗xc3 14 ♗xc3 ♕xc3 15 ♕xc3 ♘xc3 16 hxg6 hxg6 17 ♖c1 ♘xa2 18 ♖xc5 White has enough for a pawn, though I think his winning chances can't be that serious considering that he no longer has a queenside.

14 hxg6 hxg6 15 a4!

Now when the knight takes on a4, it will be subject to an unpleasant pin.

15...♗d7

16 ♔f1!

Such positions are meat and drink to Kramnik, who is one of the best calculators in the game. The white king steps off the dangerous a5-e1 diagonal so that White can focus completely on the attack.

16...♘xa4 17 ♕g5

Just like in the Chuchelov-Shirov game, simply counting the pieces on the kingside suggests that Black can't defend here.

17...♕b6

Houdini initially thinks 17...♖fe8 is okay, but I don't believe it and I'm right not to. After 18 ♕h4 ♔f8 (trying to in-

clude the queen in the defence via h5 after 18...c4 fails to 19 ♕h7+ ♔f8 20 d4) White has the tremendous shot 19 c4!!

19...e5 (19...♗xb2 20 d4! is the point, breaking through on the dark squares) 20 ♘g5 and *Houdini* can't defend: 20...♕b6 21 ♗c1 e4 22 ♖a3 exd3 23 ♖xd3 ♗f5 24 e4 ♗e6 25 ♘h7+ ♔g8 26 ♘f6+ ♔f8 27 ♗h6 ♕b1+ 28 ♔e2 ♕b2+ (28...♕c2+ 29 ♔e3! wins) 29 ♔f3 ♗xh6 30 ♕xh6+ ♔e7 31 ♘xe8 with an attack sufficient to win decisive material.

18 ♕h4 ♖fe8 19 ♗c1!

Exchanging the dark-squared bishops will decisively compromise Black's position.

19...e5 20 ♕h7+ ♔f8 21 ♗h6 ♗xh6 22 ♕xh6+ ♔e7 23 ♘xe5 1-0

Game 76
A.Shirov-V.Kramnik
Wijk aan Zee 2011
Scotch Game

Finally, a battle between two heroes of the attacking section.

1 e4 e5 2 ♘f3 ♘c6 3 d4 exd4 4 ♘xd4 ♘f6 5 ♘xc6 bxc6 6 e5 ♕e7 7 ♕e2 ♘d5 8 c4 ♘b6 9 ♘c3 ♗b7!?

Kramnik's special preparation.

10 ♗d2

Kramnik had essayed the same line in round one: 10 ♗f4 g6 11 h4 ♗g7 12 0-0-0 0-0 13 h5 ♖ae8 14 ♖e1 ♗a6 15 ♕e4 ♕c5 16 ♗g3 ♗xc4 17 hxg6 fxg6 18 ♘a4 ♘xa4 19 ♕xc4+ ♔h8 20 ♖h4 d5 21 ♕c2 ♕xc2+ 22 ♔xc2 ♘c5 with sufficient compensation for the pawn in I.Nepomniachtchi-V.Kramnik, Wijk aan Zee 2011 (½-½ in 36).

10...g6 11 ♘e4 0-0-0 12 a4!?

We'll skip a detailed analysis of the opening phase. After this move, a pitched battle arises.

12...♗a6 13 ♕e3

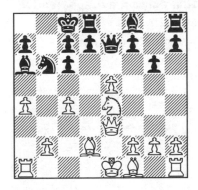

13...♕xe5!!

Committing Black to serious material sacrifices. The computer initially hates it but then gives an assessment of equal. The thematic 13...d5 also looks quite playable but is nowhere near as incisive.

14 ♗c3 ♗b4!

Development!

15 ♗xb4 ♖he8 16 f3 d5

The e4-knight is falling (although, as will be seen, ultimately it earns an enemy rook in exchange), but Black also has loose pieces on the queenside.

17 a5?!

17 cxd5 looks counter-intuitive, opening the position, but it was the best move at White's disposal here. 17...♗xf1 18 ♔xf1 cxd5 (or 18...f5!? – Golubev) 19 a5 dxe4 20 axb6 ♕b5+ 21 ♕e2 ♕xb4 22 ♕a6+ ♔d7 23 bxa7 (23 bxc7 ♔xc7 24 ♕xa7+ ♔d6 25 ♕xf7 is also a perpetual, this time delivered by the black queen: 25...♕b5+ 26 ♔g1 ♕c5+ 27 ♔f1 ♕b5+) 23...♕xb2 24 h4 e3 25 ♕d3+ ♔c6 26 ♕a6+ ♔d5 27 ♕d3+ ♔c6 and White is constrained to deliver perpetual since 28 ♖a6+?? loses to 28...♔b7.

17...♘xc4 18 ♕xa7 ♕xb2 19 ♕xa6+ ♔d7 20 ♖d1 ♕xb4+ 21 ♔f2

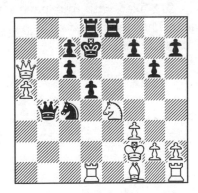

21...♖xe4!

Perhaps this is too obvious to merit an exclamation point, but I'm giving it one anyway.

22 fxe4 ♕c5+ 23 ♔e1 ♕b4+ 24 ♔f2 ♕c5+ 25 ♔e1 ♘b2!

Repeating once, then deviating – classic chess psychology. Shirov errs on the very next move.

26 exd5?

Unsurprisingly, opening the e-file doesn't help. However, White had no completely satisfactory continuation: 26 ♕e2 ♘xd1 27 ♕xd1 (27 ♔xd1? loses to 27...♖b8) 27...♖e8 28 ♕d2 ♖xe4+ 29 ♗e2 ♖a4 30 ♖f1 f5 31 a6 ♖a1+ 32 ♗d1 h5 33 ♖f2 ♖xa6 with four pawns and some residual initiative for the piece.

26...♕c3+ 27 ♖d2

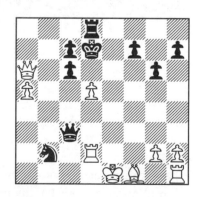

27...♕c1+?

Winning a rook for free, but not the best. 27...♖e8+ 28 ♗e2 ♕c1+ 29 ♔f2 ♕xd2 (Golubev) and White has a major tactical weakness on e2.

28 ♔e2 ♖e8+ 29 ♔f3 ♕xd2 30 ♕xc6+ ♔d8 31 ♕f6+ ♖e7 32 ♔g4?

Losing. White had a couple of more tenacious alternatives:

a) 32 ♔g3 ♘d3 33 ♗xd3 ♕xd3+ 34 ♔h4 ♔e8! with a continuing attack.

b) 32 ♗a6!? seems at first to reach the promised land, but ultimately falls short: 32...♘d3 33 ♔g3 (or 33 ♕h8+? ♖e8 34 ♕f6+ ♔d7 35 ♕xf7+ ♔d6 36 ♕f6+ ♔xd5 37 ♗b7+ ♔c5 38 ♕c6+ ♔b4 39 ♖b1+ ♔a3 with no more checks – an easy variation to see in time trouble!) 33...♕e3+ 34 ♔h4 and now 34...♘c5!! is great for Black in all lines (34...♘e1 35 ♖g1!! is only a draw, apparently).

32...♘d1!

Accurately calculated – the black king escape the checks.

33 ♕h8+ ♔d7 34 ♗b5+ c6! 35 ♗xc6+ ♔c7 36 d6+ ♕xd6 37 ♖xd1 ♕xd1+ 38 ♗f3 h5+ 39 ♔g3 ♕e1+ 40 ♔h3 ♕e6+ 41 ♔h4 g5+ 42 ♔xg5 ♕g6+ 43 ♔f4 f6! 0-1

Index of Openings

Figures refer to page numbers.

Index of Complete Games